United Nations peace operations and International Relations theory

Manchester University Press

United Nations peace operations and International Relations theory

Edited by
Kseniya Oksamytna and John Karlsrud

Manchester University Press

Published by Manchester University Press
Oxford Road, Manchester M13 9PL
www.manchesteruniversitypress.co.uk

British Library Cataloguing-in-Publication Data is available

ISBN 978 1 5261 4887 2 hardback
ISBN 978 1 5261 7448 2 paperback

First published by Manchester University Press in hardback 2020

This edition first published 2023

Typeset by New Best-set Typesetters Ltd

Contents

List of tables

Preface and acknowledgements

This volume emerged from our workshop on *Norms and Practices of Peace Operations: Evolution and Contestation* at the European Workshops in International Studies (EWIS) organised in Cardiff, 7–10 June 2017. The workshop intended to study changes in norms and practices of UN peace operations since the end of the Cold War. We are very grateful to the organisers of EWIS 2017, Christian Bueger and Benjamin Tallis, for accepting our workshop proposal, and to the participants who presented their papers, providing distinct thematic as well as theoretical perspectives, forming the basis for this volume. Although for various reasons not all papers became chapters in this volume, all participants enriched the workshop by sharing their insights and commenting on colleagues' work.

During our discussions, we agreed that there indeed had been many changes in the practices of, and the literature on, UN peace operations. This literature is one of the fastest-growing sub-fields of International Relations. However, there was no book that provided a one-stop-shop for students and scholars who wanted to get an overview of different perspectives of International Relations theory applied to UN peace operations.

While the workshop provided a first big step towards realising such a volume, there were numerous smaller steps taken over the following three years. One year after our first meeting, some of the

Preface and acknowledgements

authors met again in San Francisco at the ISA Annual Convention, at the panel *Norms and Practices of Peacekeeping Operations*. We are very grateful for the feedback from Lise Howard (Chair) and Katia Coleman (Discussant), as well as comments from the audience.

We would also like to use the opportunity to express our deep gratitude to Anthony R. Mason and Jonathan de Peyer, Senior Commissioning Editors at Manchester University Press, for wanting to publish our book. Tony, later replaced by Jon, both took a strong interest in the project. We would like to thank them, as well as the peer reviewers for very helpful inputs and suggestions. We are also very grateful to John Banks for attentive and constructive copy editing.

We are of course particularly indebted to the contributing authors. Without their active participation and engaged discussion over the last three years, resulting in their excellent chapters, this book would not have come to fruition. We are grateful to all of them for their patience during the years that the volume was in preparation. We also thank those of them who joined at later stages on short notice for their flexibility. Finally, Mats Berdal deserves a special thanks for excellently weaving together the empirical and theoretical dimensions of the book in the concluding chapter.

London and Oslo, March 2020

Notes on contributors

Mats Berdal is Professor of Security and Development in the Department of War Studies at King's College London. His recent publications include 'United Nations peacekeeping and the responsibility to protect', which appeared in *Theorising the Responsibility to Protect*, edited by Ramesh Thakur and William Maley (Cambridge University Press, 2015), and 'The state of UN peacekeeping: Lessons from Congo' (*Journal for Strategic Studies*, 2016). In 2015–16, he served as a Member of the Commission of Inquiry on Afghanistan set up by the Norwegian government to evaluate Norway's civilian and military involvement in Afghanistan from 2001 to 2014. His latest publication is 'NATO's landscape of the mind: Stabilisation and statebuilding in Afghanistan' (*Ethnopolitics*, 2019, online first).

Sarah von Billerbeck is Lecturer in Politics and International Relations and co-Director of the UN and Global Order Programme at the University of Reading. She is the author of *Whose Peace? Local Ownership and United Nations Peacekeeping* (Oxford University Press, 2017) and has published numerous articles on the UN, peace operations, international organisations, and legitimacy. She has been a Visiting Research Fellow of the University of Oxford and served as Reviews Editor for *International Peacekeeping*. She previously served as a Political Affairs Officer for the UN peacekeeping operation in Congo (MONUC). Her latest publications are '"Mirror, mirror on the wall": Self-legitimation by international organizations' (*International Studies Quarterly*, 2020) and 'No action without talk? UN peacekeeping, discourse, and institutional self-legitimation' (*Review of International Studies*, 2020).

Ingvild Bode is Senior Lecturer in International Relations at the University of Kent. She is the author of *Individual Agency and Policy Change at the United Nations* (Routledge, 2015) and the co-author of *Governing the Use-of-Force: The Post-9/11 US Challenge on International Law* (Palgrave, 2014, with Aiden Warren). She has published in journals such as the *European Journal of International Relations, Global Governance*, and *Review of International Studies*. Ingvild is Associate Editor of *Global Society: Journal of Interdisciplinary International Relations* and a member of the Board of Directors, Academic Council on the United Nations System (ACUNS).

Philip Cunliffe is Senior Lecturer in International Conflict at the University of Kent. He is the author of *Legions of Peace: UN Peacekeepers from the Global South* (Hurst, 2013) and *Cosmopolitan Dystopia: International Intervention and the Failure of the West* (Manchester University Press, 2020). He is the Editor-in-Chief of *International Peacekeeping*. He is also a founding member and co-chair of the British International Studies Association Peacekeeping and Peacebuilding Working Group. His latest publication is 'Framing intervention in a multipolar world' (*Conflict, Security and Development*, 2019).

Georgina Holmes is a Leverhulme Early Career Research Fellow in the Department of Politics and International Relations, University of Reading. She is a founding member and co-convener of the BISA Peacekeeping and Peacebuilding Working Group and Visiting Research Fellow at the National University of Rwanda. Her research examines how women are integrated into peacekeeping operations; norms and practices in peacekeeping, peacekeeping training, and gender and security sector reform in African and European militaries. Georgina has published articles in several peer-reviewed journals including *Millennium: Journal of International Studies, International Peacekeeping, Journal of Intervention and Statebuilding, Journal of Genocide Studies and Prevention,* and *Security Dialogue.* She is the author of *Women and War in Rwanda: Gender, Media and the Representation of Genocide* (I.B. Tauris, 2013).

Charles T. Hunt is Vice-Chancellor's Senior Research Fellow and ARC DECRA Fellow at the Social & Global Studies Centre in the School of Global, Urban and Social Studies at RMIT University, Melbourne, and a non-resident Research Fellow at the UN University Centre for Policy Research (UNU-CPR), New York. He is Editor-in-Chief of *Global Responsibility to Protect* and on the editorial board of the *Journal of International Peacekeeping.* He is author or editor of six books on issues of peace, conflict and human protection, including *UN Peace Operations and International Policing* (Routledge, 2015). His latest articles include 'UN stabilisation operations and the problem of non-linear change' (*Stability,* 2020, with Adam Day) and 'Stabilization at the expense of peacebuilding in UN peacekeeping operations: More than just a phase?' (*Global Governance,* 2020, with David Curran).

John Karlsrud is Research Professor at the Norwegian Institute of International Affairs. He is a member of the Editorial Boards of, inter alia, the journals *International Peacekeeping* and *Contemporary Security Policy.* Karlsrud has been a Visiting Fulbright Fellow at the Center on International Cooperation at New York University and visiting Research Fellow at the International Peace Institute. He has recently published *Multinational Rapid Response Mechanisms: From Institutional Proliferation to Institutional Exploitation* (Routledge, 2019, with Yf Reykers). His latest article is 'From liberal peacebuilding to stabilization and counterterrorism' (*International Peacekeeping,* 2019). His latest book is *The UN at War* (Palgrave, 2018).

Notes on contributors

Marion Laurence is Research Fellow at the Centre for International Policy Studies and the Graduate School of Public and International Affairs at the University of Ottawa. She holds a PhD from the University of Toronto. Her research has been supported by the Social Sciences and Humanities Research Council (SSHRC), the Ontario government, the University of Toronto, and Global Affairs Canada. Her latest publication is 'An "impartial" force? Normative ambiguity and practice change in UN peace operations' (*International Peacekeeping*, 2019).

Lucile Maertens is Lecturer in Political Science and International Relations at the University of Lausanne and Associate Faculty at the Center for International Studies at Sciences Po Paris. She is currently director of the Centre of International History and Political Studies of Globalization at the University of Lausanne. She was a visiting fellow at the Montreal Centre for International Studies at the University of Montreal, the Center for International Earth Science Information Network at the Columbia University, and the Department of War Studies at King's College London. Her latest publication is 'From blue to green? Environmentalization and securitization in UN peacekeeping practices' (*International Peacekeeping*, 2019).

Carla Monteleone is Professor of Political Science and International Relations at the University of Palermo. She has been a visiting scholar at Columbia University and Georgetown University, and she was awarded a Fulbright Schuman scholarship. She has contributed to several national and international research projects, including on Italian foreign policy, on the impact of the Eurozone crisis on the Europeanisation of the foreign policy of southern EU member states, on the role of the United States in the contemporary spatially fragmented international system, and on American military bases in Europe. She is currently on the editorial board of the *Journal of Transatlantic Studies*. Her latest book is *Italy in Uncertain*

Times: Europeanizing Foreign Policy in the Declining Process of the American Hegemony (Lexington Books, 2019).

Kseniya Oksamytna is Research Associate on an ESRC-funded project 'Democratization and UN Peacebuilding' in the Department of War Studies at King's College London. She has published on the UN Security Council's engagement with human rights NGOs, Ukraine's participation in peacekeeping, and the EU's military training mission in Somalia. She has recently co-edited a special section 'Norms and practices in UN peacekeeping: Evolution and contestation' (*International Peacekeeping*, 2019, with John Karlsrud). Her latest articles are 'Leadership selection in United Nations Peacekeeping' (*International Studies Quarterly*, 2020, with Vincenzo Bove and Magnus Lundgren) and 'Decorating the "Christmas Tree": The UN Security Council and the Secretariat's recommendations on peacekeeping operations' (*Global Governance*, 2020, with Magnus Lundgren).

Yf Reykers is Assistant Professor in International Relations at the Faculty of Arts and Social Sciences at Maastricht University. He was a Research Fellow at KU Leuven and a visiting scholar at the Center on International Cooperation (CIC) at New York University and at the Department of Political Science at Aarhus University. His work has been published in, amongst others, *Contemporary Security Policy, Cooperation and Conflict, European Security, International Peacekeeping*, and *Parliamentary Affairs*. He is co-editor of the volume *Multinational Rapid Response Mechanisms: From Institutional Proliferation to Institutional Exploitation* (Routledge, 2019, with John Karlsrud).

Emily Paddon Rhoads is Assistant Professor of Political Science at Swarthmore College. She has been a visiting scholar at Columbia University, the International Peace Institute, and the Sauve Foundation. She is the author of *Taking Sides in Peacekeeping: Impartiality and* *the Future of the United Nations* (Oxford University Press, 2016) and several articles on civilian protection, humanitarianism, and peacekeeping. Her latest articles are 'Putting human rights up front: Implications for impartiality and the politics of UN peacekeeping' (*International Peacekeeping*, 2019) and 'Close cousins in protection: The evolution of two norms' (*International Affairs*, 2019, with Jennifer Welsh).

United Nations peace operations and International Relations theory: An introduction

Kseniya Oksamytna and John Karlsrud

International Relations (IR) theories may seem abstract and arcane. With this book, we want to dispel this stereotype. The contributors to this volume demonstrate how IR theories can be applied to a very practical problem: UN peace operations,[1] one of the main instruments of international conflict management. Besides peace operations, the chapters shed light on many other aspects of international affairs, such as multilateral co-operation, the role of international bureaucracies, and evolution and contestation of norms. At the same time, the reader whose interest in the volume has been sparked by its thematic focus will find state-of-the-art research on the main issues affecting UN peace operations, ranging from the impact of rising powers to a widening space for individual initiative.

UN peace operations have undergone multiple transformations over more than seventy years of their existence. They have developed from small-scale observation missions to multidimensional operations with military, police, and civilian personnel in charge of a wide range of tasks. UN peacekeepers have organised elections, helped deliver humanitarian assistance, protected civilians, advised on security sector reform, facilitated community reconciliation, and fought rebel groups. This evolution has been gradual, although the end of the Cold War was a powerful impetus for change. The question of why UN peacekeeping operations take the shape that they do has become a major concern in the IR literature only recently, despite the fact that these operations are multi-billion-dollar undertakings fundamentally reshaping lives of people around the world.

In the past, UN peacekeeping scholarship and IR literature have been criticised for the lack of mutual engagement. Two decades ago, Paris (2000: 30) called UN peacekeeping scholarship 'a secluded outpost within IR' for its distance from the major political science debates and emphasis on policy relevance. Two years later, Jakobsen (2002: 267–8) criticised 'the preoccupation with practical issues and case studies that has always characterised the study of peace operations'. Yet the IR scholarship could also be blamed for the lack of rapprochement: there was 'limited attention paid to the role and purpose of peace operations from within the intellectual context of International Relations theory' (Pugh 2003: 104). Even in the second half of the 2000s, Bures (2007: 407) observed that the literature on peacekeeping was 'idiosyncratic and atheoretical', while Lindley (2007: 3) characterised it as 'a surprisingly theory-free zone'. As late as 2015, peacekeeping research was described as 'largely a-theoretical' and 'focused on the practical concern' (Diehl and Druckman 2015: 94).

In fact, the peacekeeping literature has frequently used IR theories, but the application has often been implicit rather than explicit. The situation has begun to change recently as a result of two trends: first, peacekeeping scholars have emphasised the connection between their work and the broader IR literature; second, the interest in peacekeeping as a subject for developing and testing IR theories has surged among political scientists. As a result, major IR concepts – power, sovereignty, collective action, delegation, and gender – have found new applications in the peacekeeping scholarship, while peacekeeping has become a source of conceptual development and empirical innovation in the IR literature. This is an overdue development, considering the political and material resources that member states, international organisations, and civil society actors have invested in peacekeeping.

This volume analyses UN peacekeeping as an *international institution* in the broad meaning of the term. International institutions have been defined as 'persistent and connected sets of rules (formal and informal) that prescribe behavioral roles, constrain activity, and shape expectations' (Keohane 1989: 3). We look not only at formal rules that shape peacekeeping (such as the UN Charter or the Security Council voting procedures) but also at norms (such as gender equality or environmentalism), principles (such as host states' consent and impartiality), and practices (such as consultations with non-state actors or penholdership).

There are two main uses of this volume. First, it allows the reader to understand UN peacekeeping through different theoretical lenses. Second, it is a practical example of how IR theories – such as realism, liberal institutionalism, rational choice institutionalism, sociological institutionalism, constructivism, practice theory, critical security studies, feminist institutionalism, and complexity theory – can be applied to a specific policy issue. Applying these theories helps us understand why UN peacekeeping, as an international institution, has evolved in the direction that it has and functions in the way that it does.

Most analyses of peacekeeping, as well as of other issues in IR, often draw on several theoretical traditions, rather than one theory. We are grateful to our contributors for agreeing to this experiment which entailed thinking about peacekeeping through a single theoretical lens – even though it might not be the tradition on which they primarily draw in most of their work. We hope that by bringing various theoretical perspectives together, this volume will encourage theoretical eclecticism and not reify boundaries between different schools of thought.

The remainder of this chapter is structured as follows. First, we familiarise the reader with a (necessarily brief) history of UN peacekeeping. Second, we discuss the changing character of peacekeeping and the emergence of new concerns, ideas, and tasks. Third, we survey the main actors involved in peacekeeping governance. Fourth, we provide an overview of the main themes in the peacekeeping literature. Fifth, we survey the main methodologies and sources of data in peacekeeping research. Sixth, we acknowledge the volume's limitations by discussing a theory which is not covered in this edition: historical institutionalism. Finally, we provide an outline of the volume.

Peacekeeping: From interposition to stabilisation

Peacekeeping has not been provided for in the UN Charter. Instead, it has been 'invented', and its principles have been gradually codified – and subsequently redefined. The creators of peacekeeping, Canadian Prime Minister Lester Pearson and UN Secretary-General Dag Hammarskjöld, would have struggled to recognise the practice today. The first UN peacekeeping force was deployed in response to the 1956 Suez Crisis.[2] Whilst earlier precedents of multinational observer groups existed both in UN and non-UN contexts (Mac-Queen 2006), the UN Emergency Force (UNEF) was the first example of military peacekeeping. UNEF supervised the withdrawal of French, British, and Israeli forces from the Egyptian territory and, following its completion, observed the ceasefire and served as a buffer between Israeli and Egyptian forces. Two years into UNEF's deployment, Hammarskjöld presented a study of mission's experience to the General Assembly, in which he proposed 'certain basic principles and rules which would provide an adaptable framework for later operations' (as cited in MacQueen 2006: 75). The three main principles of peacekeeping were the consent of the parties, neutrality, and non-use of force except in self-defence.

Despite being the 'holy trinity' of peacekeeping, these principles have been broadened and reinterpreted over time, indeed providing 'an adaptable framework'. Deployed just four years after UNEF, the 1960 mission in Congo, facing a civil war and state collapse,

4

used controversial tactics to protect civilians from violence and to preserve Congo's territorial integrity. These tactics were at the time unacceptable to the major powers, triggering a crisis of peacekeeping (Fröhlich and Williams 2018). In 1973, in the context of the second UN Emergency Force, the self-defence rule was relaxed to include the 'defence of the mission' (Findlay 2002: 19), which would subsequently provide the basis for the use of force to protect civilians.

The model of peacekeeping pioneered by UNEF remained dominant throughout the Cold War, with a few notable exceptions. Military observers and lightly armed soldiers monitored ceasefires and separation lines, thus promoting confidence between the parties and allowing negotiations to proceed. These operations are called traditional or 'first-generation' peacekeeping. The end of the Cold War gave rise to several trends. With the demise of bipolarity, the Security Council was no longer blocked by the East–West rivalries and could use peacekeeping more actively. As the notion of human security gained traction, 'soft security' concerns – human rights, child soldiers, and wartime sexual violence – became more prominent. The UN's willingness to assist with post-independence or democratic transitions necessitated taking up such unfamiliar tasks as 'running elections, creating new police forces, repatriating refugees, and overseeing the demobilization of armies and the reintegration of deeply divided societies' (Barnett 2009: 567). These operations were referred to as 'second-generation' peacekeeping. Various other definitions were offered, such as 'extended' or 'wider' peacekeeping (Findlay 2002: 6). The concept that gained the most currency is 'multidimensional' peacekeeping, reflecting the fact that instead of a single central task – confidence-building – missions had multiple responsibilities.

The term 'third-generation' peacekeeping was used for 'peace enforcement' missions, or operations that employed or threatened force to impose a settlement (Doyle and Sambanis 2006: 11). The experiments with peace enforcement in Somalia and Bosnia were followed by a debate about the utility of force (Tharoor 1995; Berdal 2000). Despite doubts and apprehensions, neutrality was recast as impartiality in the early 2000s: the influential Brahimi Report argued that impartiality meant adhering to the principles of the UN Charter, not passivity in the face of violence perpetrated by one of the parties. Transitional administrations in Kosovo and East Timor have been sometimes described as the 'fourth generation' of peacekeeping (Katayanagi 2014: 127). Others have reserved the term 'fourth-generation' for non-UN operations, like those by the EU, the African Union, or NATO (Bercovitch and Jackson 2009: 75).[3]

Recasting neutrality as impartiality in the 2000s opened the door to a possibility of using force against a faction that reneges on the peace process or grossly violates human rights. In response, the UN stressed the difference between strategic and tactical consent: the former is granted by a legitimate host government and remains indispensable, while consent of the so-called 'spoilers' attempting to disrupt the peace process is treated differently (Johnstone 2011). This is especially true in contemporary stabilisation missions that support the extension of state authority, which sometimes entails assisting with the restoration of government's control over territory where rebel groups, and even terrorist groups, continue to operate (Karlsrud 2017). Yet it created a new set of problems: for example, after inconclusive elections, it might be difficult to determine who speaks for the legitimate host government (Karlsrud 2016: chapter 3). As we see, neither the foundational principles of peacekeeping nor peacekeepers' day-to-day activities are immune to change and contestation.

Another way of thinking about the post-Cold War evolution of peacekeeping is by looking at the expansion and contraction in the numbers of deployed peacekeepers. For example, during the first 'surge', between 1989 and 1994, 20 new operations were deployed, raising the number of peacekeepers from 11,000 to 75,000. These numbers fell dramatically after the failures in Somalia, Rwanda, and Bosnia. For a while, the very survival of peacekeeping was in question. Yet after a period of soul-searching, the Security Council started authorising even more ambitious missions in what became the second 'surge'. Large operations were established in Kosovo, East Timor, Sierra Leone, and the Democratic Republic of Congo in 1999. The numbers of peacekeepers kept rising throughout the first decade of the twenty-first century, reaching a 'plateau' at the beginning of the second decade, and exhibiting a downward trend since 2016 (International Peace Institute 2018). This plateauing has allowed for the development of a more consistent and professional approach to the management of peacekeeping.

The changing character of peacekeeping

The changes have been not only quantitative but also qualitative. Unlike UNEF, which focused on a short list of clearly defined tasks, contemporary peacekeeping missions fulfil more than a dozen functions and can consist of over twenty thousand troops supported by a large civilian component. The first UN multidimensional operation supervised Namibia's transition to independence in 1989–90 by assisting in the organisation of the first election. Electoral assistance became one of the central activities in the early post-Cold War operations, although this focus has attracted academic criticism (Paris 2004). The second large multidimensional mission, the 1992 mission in Cambodia, was the first operation with a dedicated human rights component (Månsson 2006). It also ran a voter education campaign using its own radio station (Oksamytna 2018). The missions in Namibia and Cambodia broke new ground in several other respects. In Namibia, efforts to have gender-balanced staff were undertaken, and UN civilian police monitored the local police (Howard 2008). In Cambodia, new responsibilities included refugee assistance and help with disarmament; the latter would become a typical element of peacekeeping mandates from the 1990s onward (MacQueen 2006: 147).

Disarmament expanded to encompass not only demobilisation but also reintegration of former combatants, sometimes accompanied by repatriation or resettlement of foreign combatants. Restructuring and training of militaries, police forces, and other law enforcement authorities became known as security sector reform (Benner et al. 2011). Some missions monitored arms embargoes, helped bring war criminals to justice, or assisted the host government with the management of natural resources. In addition, many missions empowered various segments of the local population, such as women, youth, or civil society. In the late 2010s, local-level reconciliation received attention, in contrast with the past neglect of this area (Autesserre 2010). Finally, and quite controversially, some missions assisted the host government in combating insurgencies and stabilising key areas (Karlsrud 2015).

The expansion of tasks generated fears about conflicting mandates, the mismatch between ambition and resources, and the lack of doctrine. As the UN peacekeeping bureaucracy grew in size, it elaborated policy, guidance, and training materials for various peacekeeping functions. Efforts are under way to develop tools for measuring performance and ensuring accountability in peacekeeping (Lottholz and von Billerbeck 2019; Lundgren et al. 2020b). Perhaps the most important debate focuses on the 'primacy of politics' in peacekeeping, as called for by experts inside and outside the UN (UN 2015; see also Berdal and Ucko 2015). It remains to be seen if it leads to significant changes in peacekeeping policy and practice. Ensuring that peacekeeping missions receive clear strategic direction is complicated by the sheer number of actors involved in the governance and management of UN peacekeeping.

UN peacekeeping governance

National diplomats and military experts, UN officials in New York and in missions, other organisations in the UN family, NGOs, and experts are engaged in the conversation on peacekeeping. The

Security Council bears the primary responsibility for the maintenance of international peace and security. The UN Charter outlines
several mechanisms that the Council can use to fulfil this role.
They fall under Chapter VI, Pacific Settlement of Disputes, or
Chapter VII, Action with Respect to Threats to the Peace and
Acts of Aggression. Since peacekeeping was not explicitly envisaged
in the Charter, the Cold War practice was characterised by Secretary-
General Dag Hammarskjöld as falling under 'Chapter VI and a
half'. Most missions in the twenty-first century, especially those
with a mandate for protection of civilians, have been authorised
under Chapter VII, the 'enforcement' chapter. The Council's five
permanent veto-holding members (China, France, Russia, the UK,
and the US) are referred to as the P5. France, the UK, and the
US, the three 'Western' members, are called the P3. The Council
has ten non-permanent members elected for two-year terms. Elections take place every year to replace five of the ten non-permanent
members.

The General Assembly has several committees where peacekeeping is discussed: the Special Political and Decolonisation Committee
(the Fourth Committee) for the substantive aspects and the Administrative and Budgetary Committee (the Fifth Committee) for the
financial aspects. Of relevance is also the Special Committee on
Peacekeeping Operations known as C-34 because it had initially
consisted of 34 members contributing troops to peacekeeping
operations. Today it has almost 150 members. Developing countries
are the main contributors of troops and police to UN peacekeeping:
in late 2018, the top ten contributors of uniformed personnel were
Ethiopia, Rwanda, Bangladesh, India, Nepal, Pakistan, Egypt,
Ghana, Indonesia, and Tanzania.

Developing countries seek to use the General Assembly committees to influence the evolution of peacekeeping (Cunliffe 2013:
225; Sharland 2018: 25). Since the Fifth Committee approves
peacekeeping budgets, its willingness to finance civilian peacekeeping
functions can affect the institutionalisation and implementation of

new agendas. Peacekeeping operations and peacekeeping-related posts in New York are financed mostly from the peacekeeping support account (and a small portion of the expenses are financed from the regular UN budget). The payments into the peacekeeping support account, unlike voluntary contributions to the budgets of UN agencies like the UN Development Programme, are obligatory (and thus called 'assessed contributions'), and the P5 contribute at a higher rate to reflect their special responsibilities. The UN regular budget for 2018–19 was $5.4 billion, of which $106 million was spent on peacekeeping.[4] The peacekeeping support account was $6.7 billion, bringing the overall peacekeeping spending to $6.8 billion, which was almost 29 per cent more than the allocation for all other Secretariat's activities combined.

After the Security Council authorises peacekeeping operations and the General Assembly approves their budgets, the UN Secretariat assumes the responsibility for their management. The UN peacekeeping bureaucracy is a 'fragile, extremely decentralized, and highly politicized organization' (Benner et al. 2011: 35), which consists of officials at New York headquarters spread across several departments and staff deployed to more than a dozen field missions. Like officials of any other international organisation, UN staff transform broad directions of intergovernmental bodies 'into workable doctrines, procedures, and ways of acting in the world' (Barnett and Finnemore 2004: 5). The Secretariat prepares budget proposals and guidance documents for peacekeeping missions, such as command directives, rules of engagement, concepts of operation, force requirements, and initial operational plans. The Secretariat also reports to the Security Council on both thematic and country-specific issues related to peacekeeping. Country-specific reports not only transmit information about the developments on the ground, which can influence Council's decision-making,[5] but also outline options for the way forward (Oksamytna and Lundgren 2021). The Department of Peacekeeping Operations (DPKO) was created in 1992 and the Department of Field Support (DFS) was created in 2007. In 2019, the DPKO was renamed the Department of Peace Operations and the DFS was renamed the Department of Operational Support. Political missions and peacebuilding offices, which lack a military component, are managed by the Department of Political and Peacebuilding Affairs.

The UN Secretariat appoints the leadership of peacekeeping operations: the civilian head of the mission, the Special Representative of the Secretary-General (SRSG), and senior uniformed staff (the Force Commander and Police Commissioner), albeit not without member states' interference (Oksamytna et al. 2020). Mission leadership plays an important role in determining how the operation implements its mandate. Peacekeeping missions have a considerable degree of discretion in interpreting Security Council resolutions. SRSGs enjoy 'significant delegated authority to set the direction of the mission and to lead its engagement with the political process on the ground' (UN DPKO 2008: 68; see also Karlsrud 2013). Force Commanders devise military strategies. Troops and police officers voluntarily supplied by member states carry out military and police duties. While the Secretariat develops training materials, it is the responsibility of troop-contributing countries to ensure that their personnel receives appropriate pre-deployment training. Civilian specialists, who are recruited by the Secretariat internationally and locally, are in charge of a variety of political, peacebuilding, and support tasks.

External actors also take an active part in debates on UN peacekeeping. NGOs stepped up advocacy aimed at the Security Council or specific missions during the humanitarian crises of the early and mid-1990s (Labonte 2013; Oksamytna 2017). Karlsrud (2016) has suggested the term 'linked ecologies' to describe informal policy alliances between diplomats, bureaucrats, activists, and researchers in international organisations and at the UN in particular. Such alliances have been referred to as the 'third' or 'outside-insider' UN, while the 'first UN' is an arena for intergovernmental negotiations and the 'second UN' is the bureaucracy (Weiss et al. 2009).

For example, actors from across the 'three UNs' have promoted the agendas on women and on children in conflict and post-conflict situations. In the former case, the coalition included the UN's Office of the Special Adviser on Gender Issues; the NGO Working Group on Women, Peace and Security; and elected Council members Namibia, Bangladesh, and Canada (Tryggestad 2008). In the latter case, the coalition included the SRSG for Children and Armed Conflict; Human Rights Watch and other NGOs; France; and many elected members (Bode 2018).

Peacekeeping governance is characterised by 'shifting attention and participation' (Lipson 2010: 253), linked to the rotation of non-permanent Security Council members; changing priorities of, and relations among, the P5; Secretariat reforms; turnover of mission personnel; and ebbs and flows in NGO funding cycles. This complexity makes UN peacekeeping a fertile ground for developing and testing theories of international co-operation, institutional evolution, and normative change.

Main themes in the peacekeeping literature

Before the recent advances in peacekeeping theorising, the field had been dominated by historical accounts of peacekeeping's evolution, including memoirs of former UN officials and diplomats; in-depth case studies of specific missions; and investigations of individual countries' peacekeeping policies. Many of these studies are excellent resources for deepening the understanding of peace-keeping. However, as the literature on UN peacekeeping grew more diverse and sophisticated, three main theory-driven strands of scholarship emerged: first, the supply and demand, or reasons why states contribute personnel to peacekeeping operations or send missions to certain conflicts; second, the effects of peacekeeping, or positive and negative consequences of peacekeeping operations; and third, the relations between the 'global' and the 'local' in peacekeeping. While a detailed survey is impossible here, and overviews exist already (Fortna and Howard 2008; Gizelis et al. 2016), we discuss illustrative examples from each of the strands of scholarship, as well as how these strands draw on IR theories.

In terms of the *supply and demand*, scholars have established that peacekeepers are sent to more difficult and severe conflicts (Fortna 2008; Beardsley and Schmidt 2012), which are characterised by a higher number of civilian casualties (Gilligan and Stedman 2003). Within the country, peacekeepers are sent to more violent areas (Ruggeri et al. 2018). Nevertheless, both globally (Lundgren et al. 2020a; Coleman et al. 2020) and locally (Fjelde et al. 2019), peace-keepers often deploy to crisis areas with a delay, and many missions fail to reach the authorised strength (Passmore et al. 2018). Still, considering that troops, police, and most equipment are provided voluntarily by the member states, the UN's ability to deploy more than one hundred thousand uniformed personnel is impressive. Member states have different motivations for contributing personnel to peacekeeping missions, which may include financial benefits (governments are currently reimbursed at a rate of $1,428 per soldier per month, which might exceed deployment costs in some, but definitely not all, countries, as Coleman and Nyblade (2018) argue), experience, prestige, voice, and a desire to contribute to international conflict resolution for altruistic or strategic reasons.[6]

In terms of the *consequences of peacekeeping*, scholars have wondered whether peacekeeping 'works': whether it is a successful tool for resolving or, at a minimum, containing conflict (for an overview, see Di Salvatore and Ruggeri 2017). Most studies tend to reach the cautious conclusion that, under the right circumstances, at least some missions succeed. Doyle and Sambanis (2006: 335) argue that 'UN missions that are properly matched to the ecology of the conflict (and especially multidimensional PKOs [peacekeeping operations]) help foster positive peace and prevent the recurrence of war'. Fortna (2008) demonstrates that the chances of hostilities resuming are reduced by up to a staggering 85 per cent if peace-keepers are present. Missions with a large number of uniformed personnel are associated with reduced battlefield deaths (Hultman et al. 2014). Peacekeepers even have an impact on local conflict resolution (Ruggeri et al. 2017; Smidt 2020). Howard (2008) shows that operations that are flexible and adaptive can be effective.

Besides assessing peacekeeping operations' contribution to the mitigation or resolution of conflict, their ability to fulfil key mandated tasks has also been analysed. The presence of a UN mission with a large uniformed component correlates with a decrease in civilian killings (Hultman et al. 2013). Peacekeeping missions which are diverse in terms of national composition are more effective in fulfilling this task (Bove and Ruggeri 2016). Peacekeepers' presence goes hand in hand with a decrease in sexual violence (Hultman and Johansson 2017). UN peacekeeping missions with a humanitarian focus have been linked with better human rights performance in post-conflict countries (Murdie 2017).

Yet, sometimes, peacekeepers cause intentional or unintentional harm. Sexual exploitation and abuse of the local population have been linked with the spread of HIV/AIDS (Kent 2007). Environmental mismanagement has led to the introduction of cholera in Haiti (Lemay-Hébert 2014). While sexual exploitation and abuse are an intentional action by troops disobeying the UN's conduct and discipline regulations, the cholera outbreak in Haiti is an example of an unintended consequence of peacekeeping. Whilst the effects of peacekeeping missions on the local economy can be positive overall, unintended negative consequences include higher rents and unfair competition by well-resourced missions for local talent (Ammitzboell 2007). In terms of the effects on domestic politics in troop-contributing countries, there is a debate whether peacekeeping participation improves or weakens regime stability, democracy, or civil–military relations (Sotomayor 2014; Cunliffe 2018; Lundgren 2018).

In terms of *local–global relations*, statebuilding and peacebuilding activities of contemporary UN operations are 'extensive intrusions into the domestic affairs of other legally sovereign states' (Doyle and

Sambanis 2006: 22). Peacekeepers' tendency to promote Western values, like democracy and market liberalism, has been criticised for being inappropriate in some circumstances (Paris 2004; Richmond and Franks 2009). Peacebuilders have been accused of acting in a paternalistic fashion (Autesserre 2016). The most radical stream within this scholarship is the so-called 'hyper-critical' (the term is from Paris 2010: 338) school that believes that contemporary peacekeeping and peacebuilding are fundamentally destructive and illegitimate. For example, Western states have been suspected of shifting the costs of maintaining the world order (and their privileged position in this order) on to troops from developing countries that now provide the bulk of UN peacekeeping forces (Cunliffe 2013).[7] However, the UN and other international institutions have increasingly turned to the language of 'local ownership', yet scholars have questioned whether it can be reconciled with the overarching logic and priorities of foreign peacekeepers and peacebuilders (Caplan 2004; Lemay-Hébert 2012; Schia and Karlsrud 2013; von Billerbeck 2017).

Theory-informed peacekeeping research has been published in dedicated journals (such as *International Peacekeeping*), peace and security journals (such as *Journal of Peace Research*), and general IR journals (such as *International Organization*). The number of articles on peacekeeping in general IR journals has increased in recent years, pointing to an interest in the issue among political scientists and a willingness on the part of peacekeeping researchers to connect with the broader IR scholarship more explicitly.

Methods and data in the study of peacekeeping

Each of the three themes outlined above has featured a different mix of research methodologies. The literature on the supply and demand has often used quantitative analyses to investigate whether UN peacekeeping operations are sent to more difficult conflicts or whether their deployment is affected by trade ties (Stojek and

Tir 2015) or military alliances (Mullenbach 2005). Using a method which bridges quantitative and qualitative methods, Binder (2017) employed qualitative comparative analysis to investigate reasons behind international interventions in conflicts, peacekeeping operations being a subset of all interventions. Qualitative studies that analyse decision-making surrounding deployment of peacekeeping operations have looked at the policies of specific member states (an overview of P5's positions can be found in de Coning et al. 2017), although these studies are situated at the intersection of foreign policy analysis and IR and not always explicitly theoretical.

The study of reasons why countries provide peacekeepers has also used quantitative analyses or single, sometimes comparative, case studies. The quantitative literature has investigated whether democracies are more likely to contribute to peacekeeping operations (Lebovic 2004) and how mission composition influences the decision to contribute (Ward and Dorussen 2016). The qualitative literature has focused on the policies of specific troop-contributing countries; a useful overview of their positions can be found on the website of the *Providing for Peacekeeping* project (International Peace Institute et al. 2019).

The analysis of peacekeeping effectiveness has been dominated by quantitative studies of UN missions' effects on conflict or civilian victimisation, as described above, or specific outcomes, like democratisation (Steinert and Grimm 2015) or reduction in sexual violence (Johansson and Hultman 2019). On the other hand, studies of how, as opposed to whether, peacekeeping works have been mostly qualitative and used such concepts as local legitimacy (Whalan 2013) and transparency (Lindley 2007). Scholarship on the unintended consequences of peacekeeping tends to be descriptive, although systematic quantitative (Hultman 2010) and qualitative studies have started to appear (von Billerbeck and Tansey 2019 is the foundation of a comparative project on inadvertent enabling of authoritarianism).

An interesting development is the use of survey methodology to assess the effects of exposure to peacekeeping on state–society relations (Blair 2019). Surveys, focus groups, and participant observation have been employed to understand the role of peacekeepers' gender and their ability to contribute to mission's success (Karim and Beardsley 2017). Surveys have also been used in the literature on local–global relations to investigate the attitudes of the targets of peacekeeping – the so-called peacekept – towards the mission (Gordon and Young 2017). Among the three stands of scholarship, however, the analysis of local–global relations has gravitated the most towards qualitative methodologies.

The sources of data for peacekeeping scholarship have predominantly been archives, interviews, and various datasets (on the latter, see Clayton 2017 for an overview). Datasets are available on the number of troops and police contributed to peacekeeping operations by different member states (Kathman 2013); the gender of peacekeeping troops, police, and civilian staff (Smit and Tidblad-Lundholm 2018); nationalities and tenures of peacekeeping leaders (Bove et al. 2016); attacks on peacekeeping missions and peacekeepers' fatalities (Henke 2019); and tasks assigned to new and revised mandates (Di Salvatore et al. 2020). New sources of data might be made available by missions themselves, like data from Joint Mission Analysis Centres, which is so far available only for the joint African Union–UN mission in Darfur (Duursma 2019). This overview shows that the literature on peacekeeping is diverse not only thematically but also methodologically and characterised by increasing innovativeness and sophistication.

Limitations

Before proceeding to an overview of the volume's chapters, we acknowledge that there is a major IR theory that we do not cover: historical institutionalism. The applications of this theory in the peacekeeping literature have been few and far between, as compared with the scholarship on international organisations more broadly, although the notion of unintended consequences can be attributed to this brand of new institutionalism. In terms of peacekeeping's evolution, Daase (1999) conceptualises peacekeeping as a spontaneous institution, where precedent, institutional reform, or deviating practice (what historical institutionalists would call incremental adjustments) drive change. Mullenbach (2005) applies the historical institutionalist notion of sunk costs to the analysis of peacekeeping deployments, arguing that previous involvement in a crisis by a regional or international organisation increases the probability of a UN peacekeeping mission. Similarly, Binder (2017) argues that sunk costs – together with the interests of Security Council members, the moral pressure to assist people in need, and the host state's ability to resist international involvement – collectively explain the decision to authorise interventions, including peacekeeping operations. Howard and Dayal (2018) build on the notion of precedent and complemented it with a psychological explanation to account for the persistence of Chapter VII peacekeeping mandates. While few peacekeeping researchers would self-identify as historical institutionalists, many ideas and concepts from this theoretical tradition are present in the peacekeeping literature.

Outline of the book

All chapters in this volume seek to answer the same question using a specific theory of IR: Why does UN peacekeeping take the shape that it does? Following a brief overview of the main theoretical assumptions of a certain school of thought about the nature of international relations, the main actors, their motivations, and sources of change, chapters review how the theory has been applied in the field of peacekeeping. If the application has been limited, the authors offer their thoughts as to why this has been the case. The authors also offer a case study based on their own research to demonstrate the usefulness of the theory for peacekeeping research. The chapters usually round off with a discussion of the theory's potential for explaining or understanding UN peacekeeping.

Introduction

Starting with the classical IR theory, realism, Philip Cunliffe (Chapter 1) examines the effects of the distribution of power in the international system on peacekeeping. As peacekeeping is a major tool of peace and security in international relations, Cunliffe argues that realism offers a theoretical lens to examine and compare peacekeeping with other types of state behaviour in the peace and security domain. States compete for power through and over peacekeeping, he argues. By examining this, we can better understand great power competition for power, status, and prestige through international organisations. He concludes that peacekeeping, as we know it today, is a product of a unique post-Cold War unipolar moment – and thus should not be taken for granted as the international system continues to evolve.

In their chapter on liberal institutionalism, Carla Monteleone and Kseniya Oksamytna (Chapter 2) examine how insights from liberal institutionalism have been applied to UN peacekeeping, in particular to Security Council negotiations on peacekeeping deployments, domestic sources of member states' peacekeeping policy, and troop contributions. Focusing on Security Council negotiations, the chapter argues that the Council voting record provides only a part of the picture. To provide a more comprehensive picture, the chapter uses data on the sponsorship of peacekeeping resolutions to detect the existence of a dominant coalition which drives peacekeeping decision-making. This coalition has consisted of the US and European states in the recent period but can be challenged or replaced by a different coalition, depending on member states' preferences and strategies in the Council.

Similarly, rational choice institutionalism stresses the national interest of member states of international organisations but analyses the role of their secretariats as well. Member states might choose to delegate the execution of certain tasks to secretariats if it helps them advance their interest, creating a degree of autonomy for international bureaucracies. Since bureaucracies are assumed to be interested in expansion, states need to maintain overall control.

At the same time, as Yf Reykers argues in Chapter 3, it is not only the UN Security Council that delegates to the UN Secretariat in peacekeeping: the Secretariat, in turn, delegates to peacekeeping missions on the ground, which complicates oversight. In addition, the UN Security Council can authorise regional and sub-regional organisations to undertake peacekeeping missions, which poses unique problems in terms of delegation. Applying rational choice institutionalism can help scholars better understand the complex politics of mandating and control of UN peacekeeping and the relationships between the principals and many levels of agents of UN peacekeeping – member states, New York headquarters, and operations in the field.

Unlike rational choice institutionalism, which focuses on the interests of international organisations' member states and officials, sociological institutionalism argues that norms, rules, and cultures shape behaviour as well as constitute identities and self-images of actors. Through an examination of the preferences, interests, and behaviours of UN peacekeepers, sociological institutionalism can explain actions that may appear as inefficient or outright contradictory. Through a case study of local perceptions of local ownership among peacekeeping staff, von Billerbeck shows in Chapter 4 how staff are socialised to explain, legitimise, and accept actions, even when these actions do not align with the declared ideals of the organisation, and may lead to suboptimal outcomes.

Constructivism also attaches great importance to the role of international organisations' officials in shaping and interpreting the normative framework in which they operate. As Marion Laurence and Emily Paddon Rhoads observe in Chapter 5, the core norms guiding peacekeeping – consent, impartiality, and the non-use of force except in self-defence – have been contested and reinterpreted throughout the institution's history, allowing new approaches and areas of action to emerge. The most recent generation of constructivist research, including by the authors in the current volume, pays attention not only to the emergence and contestation of norms but also their practical implementation. In their case study of the UN mission in the Democratic Republic of Congo (MONUSCO), Laurence and Paddon Rhoads shows how constructivism can help explain the interpretation and (non-)implementation of norms in practice; how peacekeepers can have an impact on local norms, identities, and cultures; and how a rebalance between the norms of impartiality and stability in MONUSCO may reflect shifting norms at the global level.

Critical constructivism has some parallels with the reflexive strand of practice theory, which argues that agents perform socially meaningful practices guided by their background knowledge but remain capable of making choices based on their contextualised understanding of the situation. Ingvild Bode (Chapter 6) shows how practice theories, although often requiring significant efforts in gathering primary data, can help us access and understand change as well as continuity in peacekeeping. In her case study, she examines how the concept of competent practice helps understand continuous divergences over the protection-of-civilians norm in UN peacekeeping. Based on in-depth interviews with UN military advisers for a study conducted with John Karlsrud, the chapter demonstrates that different ways of conceptualising and performing protection of civilians are likely to persist regardless of the progressive strengthening of the norm.

Critical theory asks us to be reflective of the fact that no theories are neutral: all theories help us frame our understanding and select what we want to study and what is seen as less important. Lucile Maertens in Chapter 7 looks at the discursive construction and framing of new agendas in UN peacekeeping. The idea that security and insecurity are discursively constructed belongs to the critical security studies school. After reviewing the contribution of critical security studies to problematising the liberal orientation of the contemporary peacebuilding enterprise, Maertens investigates how the environment has been promoted to become an appropriate concern for UN peacekeepers, and how peacekeeping has been promoted to become relevant for environmental policies. Maertens then shows how this reciprocal engagement has contributed to two broader processes of environmentalisation of peacekeeping, and, more worryingly, the securitisation of the environment.

Like critical security studies, feminist institutionalism pays attention to gendered, racialised, and classed power relations. Georgina Holmes (Chapter 8) brings examples of structural inequalities in UN peacekeeping missions, such as the UN mission in Mali where peacekeepers from the developed and developing world perform different tasks, some of them more dangerous than others. Gender also creates inequalities. Seeking to achieve women's meaningful participation and end other forms of discrimination, feminist institutionalism seeks to uncover and disrupt existing formal and informal power structures, management practices, and institutional barriers that are gendered and produce gendered effects. Holmes analyses gender mainstreaming during the training and deployment of Ghanaian peacekeepers, especially how superficial changes made in response to the UN's demand for female peacekeepers were layered on top of well-entrenched ideas about male and female social roles.

The chapters discussed above point to the multiplicity of actors, interactions, and locations involved in the evolution of UN peacekeeping: the UN Security Council, UN officials at New York headquarters and in the field, troop-contributing countries, and regional organisations co-operating with the UN. Charles T. Hunt (Chapter 9) shows how UN peace operations can be studied as a complex social system with idiosyncratic behaviours in highly dynamic and nonlinear environments applying complexity theory. Hunt shows that, drawing on the insights of complexity theory, we are better able to understand the production of UN peacekeeping through global politics as well as their operations in practice. In conclusion, he also points to how UN peace operations can become part of the conflict systems they seek to manage and transform on systemic as well as individual levels.

Introduction

In the concluding chapter, Mats Berdal offers reflections about the state of the theory-driven UN peacekeeping literature and the IR discipline more broadly. He challenges the perception that the literature on UN peace operation has been largely atheoretical until recently. During the Cold War and in the 1990s, scholars studied peacekeeping and its connections to global politics on the basis of different theoretical perspectives, such as the English School. Professor Berdal also reminds us that when we talk about the 'UN', we should keep in mind that it is ultimately an intergovernmental organisation shaped by member states who design peace operations and also implement them by providing troops, which carry out the mandate in the field but often seek guidance from national capitals. UN peace operations involve a multiplicity of actors, levels, and locations. We hope that this volume will help our readers understand the complex world of UN peace operations through well-established and cutting-edge theoretical perspectives.

Notes

1　Contemporary peace operations are more multidimensional than traditional peacekeeping and often include elements of peacebuilding (and occasionally enforcement). In this book, the terms 'peace operations' and 'peacekeeping' are used interchangeably to refer to operations authorised by the UN Security Council and led by the UN Department of Peace Operations.
2　A distinction is made between groups of military observers deployed to oversee ceasefires in the Middle East in 1948 and Kashmir in 1949, on the one hand, and peacekeeping forces involving infantry battalions, such as UN Emergency Force, on the other hand (Diehl 2015).
3　Thakur and Schnabel (2001: 9–14) offer a different classification, arguing that the first generation was traditional peacekeeping; the second generation was non-UN peacekeeping (including both multinational observer groups and intervention forces); the third generation was multidimensional peacekeeping; the fourth generation was peace enforcement; the fifth generation was partnership peacekeeping (including partnerships with member states and regional organisations); and the sixth generation was transitional administrations.
4　Some peacekeeping posts in the Secretariat are long-term and funded from the regular budget; others fluctuate according to the number of deployed

peacekeepers and are funded from the Peacekeeping Support Account (Dijkstra 2016: chapter 3).

5 For example, the Secretariat might have under-reported important information on the Rwandan genocide to the Council (Barnett and Finnemore 2004: chapter 5).

6 For illustrative examples of qualitative and quantitative studies see, respectively, Bellamy and Williams (2013) and Sandler (2017). This literature is reviewed by Monteleone and Oksamytna (Chapter 2, this volume).

7 More scholarship that falls under the broad label of 'critical security studies' is reviewed by Maertens (Chapter 7, this volume).

References

Ammitzboell, Katarina (2007), 'Unintended consequences of peace operations on the host economy from a people's perspective', in Chiyuki Aoi, Cedric de Coning, and Ramesh Thakur (eds), *Unintended Consequences of Peacekeeping Operations* (Tokyo: UN University Press), 69–89.

Autesserre, Séverine (2010), *The Trouble with the Congo: Local Violence and the Failure of International Peacebuilding* (Cambridge: Cambridge University Press).

Autesserre, Séverine (2016), 'Paternalism and peacebuilding: Capacity, knowledge, and resistance in international intervention', in Michael N. Barnett (ed.), *Paternalism Beyond Borders* (Cambridge: Cambridge University Press), 161–84.

Barnett, Michael N. (2009), *The International Humanitarian Order* (Abingdon: Routledge).

Barnett, Michael N., and Martha Finnemore (2004), *Rules for the World: International Organizations in Global Politics* (Ithaca, NY: Cornell University Press).

Beardsley, Kyle, and Holger Schmidt (2012), 'Following the flag or following the charter? Examining the determinants of UN involvement in international crises, 1945–2002', *International Studies Quarterly*, 56:1, 33–49.

Bellamy, Alex J., and Paul D. Williams (eds) (2013), *Providing Peacekeepers: The Politics, Challenges and Future of United Nations Peacekeeping Contributions* (Oxford: Oxford University Press).

Benner, Thorsten, Stephan Mergenthaler, and Philipp Rotmann (2011), *The New World of UN Peace Operations: Learning to Build Peace?* (New York: Oxford University Press).

Bercovitch, Jacob, and Richard Jackson (2009), *Conflict Resolution in the Twenty-first Century: Principles, Methods, and Approaches* (Ann Arbor, MI: University of Michigan Press).

Berdal, Mats (2000), 'Lessons not learned: The use of force in "peace operations" in the 1990s', *International Peacekeeping*, 7:4, 55–74.

Berdal, Mats, and David H. Ucko (2015), 'The use of force in UN peacekeeping operations', *The RUSI Journal*, 160:1, 6–12.

von Billerbeck, Sarah B.K. (2017), *Whose Peace?: Local Ownership and United Nations Peacekeeping* (Oxford: Oxford University Press).

von Billerbeck, Sarah B.K., and Oisín Tansey (2019), 'Enabling autocracy? Peacebuilding and post-conflict authoritarianism in the Democratic Republic of Congo', *European Journal of International Relations*, 25:3, 698–722.

Binder, Martin (2017), *The United Nations and the Politics of Selective Humanitarian Intervention* (Cham: Palgrave Macmillan).

Blair, Robert A. (2019), 'International intervention and the rule of law after civil war: Evidence from Liberia', *International Organization*, 73:2, 365–98.

Bode, Ingvild (2018), 'Reflective practices at the Security Council: Children and armed conflict and the three United Nations', *European Journal of International Relations*, 24:2, 293–318.

Bove, Vincenzo, and Andrea Ruggeri (2016), 'Kinds of blue. Diversity in UN peacekeeping missions and civilian protection', *British Journal of Political Science*, 46:3, 681–700.

Bove, Vincenzo, Andrea Ruggeri, and Remco Zwetsloot (2016), 'What do we know about UN peacekeeping leadership?', *International Peacekeeping*, 24:1: 17–23.

Bures, Oldrich (2007), 'A mid-range theory of international peacekeeping', *International Studies Review*, 9:3, 407–36.

Caplan, Richard (2004), 'Partner or patron? International civil administration and local capacity-building', *International Peacekeeping*, 11:2, 229–47.

Clayton, Govinda (ed.) (2017), 'The known knowns and known unknowns of peacekeeping data', *International Peacekeeping*, 24:1, 1–62.

Coleman, Katharina, and Benjamin Nyblade (2018), 'Peacekeeping for profit? The scope and limits of "mercenary" UN peacekeeping', *Journal of Peace Research*, 55:6, 726–41.

Coleman, Katharina, Magnus Lundgren, and Kseniya Oksamytna (2020), 'Slow progress on UN rapid deployment: The potential perils of policy paradigms in international organizations', *International Studies Review*, https://doi.org/10.1093/isr/viaa030.

de Coning, Cedric, Chiyuki Aoi, and John Karlsrud (eds) (2017), *UN Peacekeeping Doctrine in a New Era: Adapting to Stabilization, Protection and New Threats* (Abingdon: Routledge).

Cunliffe, Philip (2013), *Legions of Peace: UN Peacekeepers from the Global South* (London: Hurst).

Cunliffe, Philip (2018), 'From peacekeepers to praetorians – how participating in peacekeeping operations may subvert democracy', *International Relations*, 32:2, 218–39.

Daase, Christopher (1999), 'Spontaneous institutions: Peacekeeping as an international convention', in Helga Haftendorn, Robert O. Keohane, and Celeste A. Wallander (eds), *Imperfect Unions: Security Institutions over Time and Space* (New York: Oxford University Press), 223–58.

Di Salvatore, Jessica, and Andrea Ruggeri (2017), 'Effectiveness of peacekeeping operations', in William R. Thompson (ed.), *Oxford Research Encyclopedia of Politics*, available at: http://politics.oxfordre.com/view/10.1093/acrefore/9780190228637.001.0001/acrefore-9780190228637-e-586 (accessed 31 July 2019).

Di Salvatore, Jessica, Magnus Lundgren, Kseniya Oksamytna, and Hannah M. Smidt (2020), 'Introducing the peacekeeping mandates (PEMA) dataset', working paper.

Diehl, Paul F. (2015), 'First United Nations Emergency Force (UNEF I)', in Joachim Koops, Norrie MacQueen, Thierry Tardy, and Paul D. Williams (eds), *The Oxford Handbook of United Nations Peacekeeping Operations* (Oxford: Oxford University Press), 144–52.

Diehl, Paul F., and Daniel Druckman (2015), 'Evaluating peace operations', in Joachim Koops, Norrie MacQueen, Thierry Tardy, and Paul D. Williams (eds), *The Oxford Handbook of United Nations Peacekeeping Operations* (Oxford: Oxford University Press), 93–108.

Dijkstra, Hylke (2016), *International Organizations and Military Affairs* (London: Routledge).

Doyle, Michael W., and Nicholas Sambanis (2006), *Making War and Building Peace: United Nations Peace Operations* (Princeton, NJ: Princeton University Press,).

Duursma, Allard (2019), 'Obstruction and intimidation of peacekeepers: How armed actors undermine civilian protection efforts', *Journal of Peace Research*, 56:2, 234–48.

Findlay, Trevor (2002), *The Use of Force in UN Peace Operations* (New York: Oxford University Press).

Fjelde, Hanne, Lisa Hultman, and Desirée Nilsson (2019), 'Protection through presence: UN peacekeeping and the costs of targeting civilians', *International Organization*, 73:1, 103–31.

Fortna, Virginia Page (2008), *Does Peacekeeping Work? Shaping Belligerents' Choices after Civil War* (Princeton, NJ: Princeton University Press).

Fortna, Virginia Page, and Lise Morjé Howard (2008), 'Pitfalls and prospects in the peacekeeping literature', *Annual Review of Political Science*, 11, 283–301.

Fröhlich, Manuel, and Abiodun Williams (2018), 'Conclusion', in Manuel Fröhlich and Abiodun Williams (eds), *The UN Secretary-General and the Security Council: A Dynamic Relationship* (Oxford: Oxford University Press), 211–24.

Gilligan, Michael, and Stephen J. Stedman (2003), 'Where do peacekeepers go?', *International Studies Review*, 5:4, 37–54.

Gizelis, Theodora-Ismene, Han Dorussen, and Marina Petrova (2016), 'Research findings on the evolution of peacekeeping', in William R. Thompson (ed.), *Oxford Research Encyclopedia of Politics*, available at: http://oxfordre.com/politics/view/10.1093/acrefore/9780190228637.001.0001/acrefore-9780190228637-e-25 (accessed 31 July 2019).

Gordon, Grant M., and Lauren E. Young (2017), 'Cooperation, information, and keeping the peace', *Journal of Peace Research*, 54:1: 64–79.

Henke, Marina E. (2019), 'UN fatalities 1948–2015: A new dataset', *Conflict Management and Peace Science*, 36:4, 425–42.

Howard, Lise Morjé (2008), *UN Peacekeeping in Civil Wars* (Cambridge: Cambridge University Press).

Howard, Lise Morjé, and Anjali Kaushlesh Dayal (2018), 'The use of force in UN peacekeeping', *International Organization*, 72:1, 71–103.

Hultman, Lisa (2010), 'Keeping peace or spurring violence? Unintended effects of peace operations on violence against civilians', *Civil Wars*, 12:1–2, 29–46.

Hultman, Lisa, Jacob Kathman, and Megan Shannon (2013), 'United Nations peacekeeping and civilian protection in civil war', *American Journal of Political Science*, 57:4, 875–91.

Hultman, Lisa, Jacob Kathman, and Megan Shannon (2014), 'Beyond keeping peace: United Nations effectiveness in the midst of fighting', *American Political Science Review*, 108:4, 737–53.

Hultman, Lisa, and Karin Johansson (2017), 'Responding to sexual violence: UN Peacekeeping and the protection agenda', *Global Responsibility to Protect*, 9:2, 129–46.

International Peace Institute (2018), 'Total number of uniformed peacekeepers deployed by type (January 1990 – December 2017)', available at: www.providingforpeacekeeping.org/peacekeeping-data-graphs (accessed 3 November 2018).

International Peace Institute, the Elliott School, and the Asia Pacific Centre for the Responsibility to Protect (2019), 'Providing for peacekeeping: Country profiles', available at: www.providingforpeacekeeping.org/profiles (accessed 31 July 2019).

Jakobsen, Peter Viggo (2002), 'The transformation of United Nations peace operations in the 1990s: Adding globalization to the conventional "end of the Cold War explanation"', *Cooperation and Conflict*, 37:3, 267–82.

Johansson, Karin, and Lisa Hultman (2019), 'UN peacekeeping and protection from sexual violence', *Journal of Conflict Resolution*, 63:7, 1656–81.

Johnstone, Ian (2011), 'Managing consent in contemporary peacekeeping operations', *International Peacekeeping*, 18:2, 168–82.

Karim, Sabrina, and Kyle Beardsley (2017), *Equal Opportunity Peacekeeping: Women, Peace, and Security in Post-conflict States* (New York: Oxford University Press).

Karlsrud, John (2013), 'Special Representatives of the Secretary-General as norm arbitrators? Understanding bottom-up authority in UN peacekeeping', *Global Governance*, 19:4, 525–44.

Karlsrud, John (2015), 'The UN at war: Examining the consequences of peace-enforcement mandates for the UN peacekeeping operations in the CAR, the DRC and Mali', *Third World Quarterly*, 36:1, 40–54.

Karlsrud, John (2016), *Norm Change in International Relations: Linked Ecologies in UN Peacekeeping Operations* (Abingdon: Routledge).

Karlsrud, John (2017), 'Towards UN counter-terrorism operations?', *Third World Quarterly*, 38:6, 1215–31.

Katayanagi, Mari (2014), 'UN peacekeeping and human rights', in Jared Genser and Bruno Stagno Ugarte (eds), *The United Nations Security Council in the Age of Human Rights* (Cambridge: Cambridge University Press), 123–53.

Kathman, Jacob D. (2013), 'United Nations peacekeeping personnel commitments, 1990–2011', *Conflict Management and Peace Science*, 30:5: 532–49.

Kent, Vanessa (2007), 'Protecting civilians from UN peacekeepers and humanitarian workers: Sexual exploitation and abuse', in Chiyuki Aoi, Cedric de Coning, and Ramesh Thakur (eds), *Unintended Consequences of Peacekeeping Operations* (Tokyo: UN University Press), 44–67.

Keohane, Robert O. (1989), 'Neoliberal institutionalism: A perspective on world politics', in Robert O. Keohane (ed.), *International Institutions and State Power: Essays in International Relations Theory* (Boulder, CO: Westview).

Labonte, Melissa (2013), *Human Rights and Humanitarian Norms, Strategic Framing, and Intervention: Lessons for the Responsibility to Protect* (Abingdon: Routledge).

Lebovic, James H. (2004), 'Uniting for peace? Democracies and United Nations peace operations after the Cold War', *Journal of Conflict Resolution*, 48:6, 910–36.

Lemay-Hébert, Nicolas (2012), 'Coerced transitions in Timor-Leste and Kosovo: Managing competing objectives of institution-building and local empowerment', *Democratization*, 19:3, 465-85.

Lemay-Hébert, Nicolas (2014), 'Resistance in the time of cholera: The limits of stabilization through securitization in Haiti', *International Peacekeeping*, 21:2, 198–213.

Lindley, Dan (2007), *Promoting Peace with Information: Transparency as a Tool of Security Regimes* (Princeton: Princeton University Press).

Lipson, Michael (2010), 'Performance under ambiguity: International organization performance in UN peacekeeping', *Review of International Organizations*, 5:3, 249–84.

Lottholz, Philipp, and Sarah B.K. von Billerbeck (2019), *Senior Leadership Performance Management in International Organizations* (Reading: University of Reading).

Lundgren, Magnus (2018), 'Backdoor peacekeeping: Does participation in UN peacekeeping reduce coups at home?', *Journal of Peace Research*, 55:4, 508–23.

Lundgren, Magnus, Kseniya Oksamytna, and Katharina P. Coleman (2020a, forthcoming), 'Only as fast as its troop contributors: Incentives, capabilities, and constraints in the UN's peacekeeping response', *Journal of Peace Research*.

Lundgren, Magnus, Kseniya Oksamytna, and Vincenzo Bove (2020b), 'Politics or performance? Leadership accountability in UN peacekeeping', working paper.

MacQueen, Norrie (2006), *Peacekeeping and the International System* (Abingdon: Routledge).

Månsson, Katarina (2006), 'Integration of human rights in peace operations: Is there an ideal model?', *International Peacekeeping*, 13:4, 547–63.

Mullenbach, Mark J. (2005), 'Deciding to keep peace: An analysis of international influences on the establishment of third-party peacekeeping missions', *International Studies Quarterly*, 49:3, 529–55.

Murdie, Amanda (2017), 'R2P, human rights, and the perils of a bad human rights intervention', *Global Responsibility to Protect*, 9:3, 267–93.

Oksamytna, Kseniya (2017), 'Civil society and the UN Security Council: Advocacy on the Rwandan Genocide', in Raffaele Marchetti (ed.), *Partnerships in International Policy-making: Civil Society and Public Institutions in European and Global Affairs* (London: Palgrave Macmillan), 131–45.

Oksamytna, Kseniya (2018), 'Policy entrepreneurship by international bureaucracies: The evolution of public information in UN peacekeeping', *International Peacekeeping*, 25:1, 79–104.

Oksamytna, Kseniya, Vincenzo Bove, and Magnus Lundgren (2020), 'Leadership selection in United Nations peacekeeping', *International Studies Quarterly*, https://doi.org/10.1093/isq/sqaa023.

Oksamytna, Kseniya, and Magnus Lundgren (2021), 'Decorating the "Christmas Tree": The UN Security Council and the Secretariat's recommendations on peacekeeping operations', *Global Governance*, 27:2.

Paris, Roland (2000), 'Broadening the study of peace operations', *International Studies Review*, 2:3, 27–44.

Paris, Roland (2004), *At War's End: Building Peace after Civil Conflict* (New York: Cambridge University Press).

Paris, Roland (2010), 'Saving liberal peacebuilding', *Review of International Studies*, 36:2, 337–65.

Passmore, Timothy J.A., Megan Shannon, and Andrew F. Hart (2018) 'Rallying the troops: Collective action and self-interest in UN peacekeeping contributions', *Journal of Peace Research*, 55:3, 366–79.

Pugh, Michael (2003), 'Peacekeeping and IR theory: Phantom of the opera?', *International Peacekeeping*, 10:4, 104–12.

Richmond, Oliver P., and Jason Franks (2009), *Liberal Peace Transitions: Between Statebuilding and Peacebuilding* (Edinburgh: Edinburgh University Press).

Ruggeri, Andrea, Han Dorussen, and Theodora-Ismene Gizelis (2017), 'Winning the peace locally: UN peacekeeping and local conflict', *International Organization*, 71:1, 163–85.

Ruggeri, Andrea, Han Dorussen, and Theodora-Ismene Gizelis (2018), 'On the frontline every day? Subnational deployment of United Nations peacekeepers', *British Journal of Political Science*, 48:4, 1005–25.

Sandler, Todd (2017), 'International peacekeeping operations: Burden sharing and effectiveness', *Journal of Conflict Resolution*, 61:9, 1875–97.

Schia, Niels Nagelhus, and John Karlsrud (2013), '"Where the rubber meets the road": Friction sites and local-level peacebuilding in Haiti, Liberia and South Sudan', *International Peacekeeping*, 20:2, 233–48.

Sharland, Lisa (2018), *How Peacekeeping Policy Gets Made: Navigating Intergovernmental Processes at the UN* (New York: International Peace Institute).

Smidt, Hannah M. (2020), 'United Nations peacekeeping locally: Enabling conflict resolution, reducing communal violence', *Journal of Conflict Resolution*, 64:2–3, 344–72.

Smit, Timo, and Kajsa Tidblad-Lundholm (2018), *Trends in Women's Participation in UN, EU and OSCE Peace Operations* (Stockholm: Stockholm International Peace Research Institute).

Sotomayor, Arturo C. (2014), *The Myth of the Democratic Peacekeeper: Civil-military Relations and the United Nations* (Baltimore: Johns Hopkins University Press).

Steinert, Janina Isabel, and Sonja Grimm (2015), 'Too good to be true? United Nations peacebuilding and the democratization of war-torn states', *Conflict Management and Peace Science*, 32:5, 513–35.

Stojek, Szymon M., and Jaroslav Tir (2015), 'The supply side of United Nations peacekeeping operations: Trade ties and United Nations-led deployments to civil war states', *European Journal of International Relations*, 21:2, 352–76.

Thakur, Ramesh, and Albrecht Schnabel (2001), 'Cascading generations of peacekeeping: Across the Mogadishu line to Kosovo and Timor', in Ramesh Thakur and Albrecht Schnabel (eds), *United Nations Peacekeeping Operations: Ad Hoc Missions, Permanent Engagement* (New York: UN University Press), 3–25.

Tharoor, Shashi (1995), 'Should UN peacekeeping go "back to basics"?', *Survival*, 37:4, 52–64.

Tryggestad, Torunn L. (2008), 'Trick or treat? The UN and implementation of Security Council resolution 1325 on women, peace, and security', *Global Governance*, 15:4, 539–57.

United Nations (2015), 'Report of the High-Level Independent Panel on Peace Operations (HIPPO) on Uniting Our Strengths for Peace: Politics, Partnership and People', A/70/95 – S/2015/446.

United Nations Department of Peacekeeping Operations (UN DPKO) (2008), *United Nations Peacekeeping Operations: Principles and Guidelines* ('Capstone Doctrine') (New York: United Nations).

Ward, Hugh, and Han Dorussen (2016), 'Standing alongside your friends: Network centrality and providing troops to UN peacekeeping operations', *Journal of Peace Research*, 53:3, 392–408.

Weiss, Thomas G., Tatiana Carayannis, and Richard Jolly (2009), 'The "third" United Nations', *Global Governance*, 15:1, 123–42.

Whalan, Jenni (2013), *How Peace Operations Work: Power, Legitimacy, and Effectiveness* (Oxford: Oxford University Press).

1

Realism

Philip Cunliffe

The International Relations (IR) theory of realism and the practice of peacekeeping would seem to be at odds with each other. Realist theorising in IR is traditionally focused on, for example, grand questions of geopolitical rivalry between major powers, on arms races between industrialised states with sophisticated weapons systems, on the dynamics of military and nuclear strategy. For realists, international peace is only ever a temporary reprieve and one produced by shifting alliances of mutual convenience and interest calibrated by the balance of power. The most important political actors in this framework are states. By contrast, the study and practice of peacekeeping is vested in solidifying peace through co-operation, which is structured by international organisations and agreements. In its more ambitious incarnations such as conflict transformation and peacebuilding, peacekeepers aim even to transform the context of conflict through crafting peace settlements. They might also engage in extensive social and political reforms that aim to suppress violent conflict through fostering economic growth, overseeing new judicial systems, protecting individual human rights, disarming militias, and even establishing systems of multi-party political competition. All of this is to be sustained through the moral authority and expertise provided by the supranational political authority of regional organisations or, in its most august incarnation, the UN.

The actors involved in peacekeeping are not only states but also international and regional organisations. That these actors may intensively intervene in other states as part of peacekeeping has important conceptual implications, as this effectively turns the units of conventional realist theorising – states – inside-out.

Yet on the other hand, the study of peacekeeping and the realist analysis of world politics clearly share basic and important affinities. Realist analysis and the study of peacekeeping are both concerned with the fundamental questions of war, peace, and order in the international arena. The study of peacekeeping is a sub-field of the wider discipline of international relations whereas realism is a major school of thought about international politics as a whole. Thus, given that peacekeeping concerns war and conflict, one might expect realist analyses to be strongly manifest in the field of peacekeeping studies. Yet, despite the fact that peacekeeping concerns the most fundamental questions of international order – peace and war, the legitimate use of force by the state, the question of state authority and power – this conceptual closeness of subject matter has not provoked any sustained interest from realist thinkers or those open to realist approaches. What is it then that keeps realist analysis and the study of peacekeeping so far apart?

Part of the reason for this continuing intellectual separateness might be the growth of middle-range theories in IR which have tended to crowd out studies directly inspired by realism (Mearsheimer and Walt 2013). It is also partly a question of scale. Whereas realism is focused on questions of peace and war in the competition between great powers in which the very shape of the international order itself may be at stake, peacekeeping is focused on smaller-scale wars and conflicts. While these 'small wars' may be terribly violent and destructive in terms of the overall levels of bloodshed (e.g. the conflicts that have persistently plagued Zaïre, now called the Democratic Republic of Congo, since the 1990s), they do not fundamentally alter or affect relations between great powers – and therefore never reach the realm of 'high politics' that tends to concern realists. Peacekeeping has traditionally been seen as an answer to the domestic anarchy of state collapse, ethnic conflict, and warlordism in poor and marginal areas of the international order. Peacekeeping was never intended to provide an answer to the systemic anarchy of the international order itself. Indeed, those peacekeeping operations that aim at extending the authority of the state, such as the UN missions in Mali and Lebanon, are precisely intended to restore functioning government to conflict zones within the country. By contrast, the predicate of modern-day realism is, of course, the permanent absence of a global government able to suppress conflict.

Unsurprisingly then, the theoretical underpinnings of the study and practice of peacekeeping have been broadly liberal. The study of peacekeeping has also drawn in what are effectively functionalist analyses of international public goods and radical variants of conflict transformation theories (e.g. Gaibulloev et al. 2009, and Richmond and Mac Ginty 2015, respectively). Yet I want to argue in this chapter that there are plenty of reasons why the study of peacekeeping would be improved by drawing on realist theorising. Equally I want to assert that peacekeeping might provide some useful opportunities for empirical testing, consolidation and extension of realist theorising. Part of the conceptual problem here is the changing character of international politics and questions of classification. Given the extensive overlap between low-intensity or counter-insurgency-style military operations and peacekeeping, and given the sheer numbers of military personnel that, in global terms, now routinely deploy in peacekeeping operations, the question arises: how should we classify peacekeeping?

Definitions are generated from theories in interaction with empirical observation, and perhaps the strong association of peacekeeping with liberal internationalism due to its historical association with the UN is overblown. For example, the range of French military operations across the Sahel and former French West Africa since the end of the Cold War – Operation Licorne, Operation Serval,

Operation Barkhane, Operation Sangaris – have been tightly bound to UN deployments (UNOCI, MINUSMA, MINURCAT, respectively) and with UN authorisation. French interventions could plausibly be classified as traditional military interventions to secure uranium deposits, to support allied and client states in the region, and/or to maintain order within a 'backyard' or neocolonial sphere of French influence. If this is true, then how should we consider the UN operations that co-deploy with French military operations? Should we see them as appendages of French military operations, or should we see peacekeeping operations as primary in conceptual terms, that is, French military operations deploying in support of supranational efforts? The answer goes beyond the scope of this chapter, but underlying this definitional issue is the larger question of changes in international order – changes by which traditional military interventions have had to be garbed as altruistic and co-operative, and legitimated by invoking supranational authority in a way that would have been far less common in even the recent past (Zolo 1997). In what follows, I first consider the status of realist theorising in peacekeeping, before considering what realism has to offer, with specific reference to three broad realist schools – classical, structural, and neoclassical.

Realism in peacekeeping

The limited influence of theoretical realism in peacekeeping not only reflects the role and purpose of peacekeeping being at odds with the concerns of realist theorising but also reflects the internal intellectual development of peacekeeping studies – which, as Roland Paris argued some time ago, was conducive to microtheorising, with the result that generalisation in peacekeeping studies failed to connect with larger questions of world order and major debates within IR theory (Paris 2000). This trend has continued, despite the fact that peacekeeping operations have grown and proliferated to such a scale that they no longer need to be studied on a case-by-case basis, as if they were an exotic sub-species of international politics. Yet within the field generalisation continues to be largely internally oriented, considering peacekeeping within its own terms and dynamics rather than connecting it to larger questions of world order. Critical theoretical approaches to 'hybrid peace', for example, consider peacekeeping practice largely on its own terms, whilst quantitative studies of peacekeeping too rarely compare peacekeeping to other kinds of similar activities, such as counter-insurgency campaigns and other forms of military intervention. The original danger identified by Paris remains – that of a conceptual collapse into self-referentiality. Peacekeeping thus still tends to be studied as a *sui generis* phenomenon, even if on a larger scale and depicted on a larger canvas. Unsurprisingly then, there seem to be few conceptual bridges that would connect the study and practice of peacekeeping to realism, understood as a quintessential IR theory oriented towards basic questions of world order and power-political competition.

At most, realism has existed as a foil in studies of peacekeeping, in which realism was to be exposed as failing to account in a satisfactory manner for the global development of peacekeeping since the end of the Cold War. The degree of sustained international co-operation needed to mount and sustain post-Cold War peacekeeping seems to make irrelevant conventional realist assumptions about narrowly egotistical states chary of co-operating. Thus realism in peacekeeping mostly stood as a synonym for crude self-interest, at best perhaps a corrective to the grandiloquent and classically idealist rhetoric that attached itself to peacekeeping at different periods.

Where realism has been applied to the study of peacekeeping, it has been done in a limited manner. In the latter case, Alan James's detailed empirical examination of peacekeeping was a nominally realist study in that James kept a firm grasp on questions of state interest and power in examining the formation and conduct of a wide variety of peacekeeping and para-peacekeeping operations (James 1990). Norrie MacQueen's study declared itself to be realist, yet it hinged part of the analysis around concepts such as failed states and globalisation, neither of which is easily assimilated into consistently neorealist theoretical frameworks (MacQueen 2006). Similarly Laura Neack used realism as a synonym for 'egoism' as opposed to 'altruism' in theorising middle-power participation in peacekeeping (Neack 1995). Nor was there any particular effort in these studies consistently to unpack and clearly differentiate distinct levels of analysis – such as unit-level (state behaviour) versus system-level (international order effects).

Nonetheless, the fact that applications of realism have been limited or patchy does not mean that they have been without insight. Neack, for instance, drew attention to the fact that Scandinavian peacekeeping states were also prolific arms exporters. Thus, counterintuitively Norway and Sweden were exporting both blue berets *and* military hardware to the same conflict-prone region: at the time of writing, the Middle East (Neack 1995: 188). This apparent paradox could be at once contained and made interesting within the context of a realist analysis, which could contextualise peacekeeping as one policy among others pursued by power-seeking and self-interested states. Such a contradiction would be difficult meaningfully to accommodate within large-n studies of peacekeeping that may nominally account for 'self-interest' in explaining peacekeeping behaviour, but fail to contextualise it among other kinds of state activities (e.g. Bove and Elia 2011). Similarly, MacQueen had the important insight that the growth of peacekeeping was driven by the collapse of geopolitical spheres of influence and contested battle zones stemming from the Cold War. Peacekeeping thus became possible in areas from which it would have been hitherto excluded such as Afghanistan, Central America, South-East Asia and southern Africa (MacQueen 2006: 14, *passim*). Such insight could come only from the macropolitical perspective offered by a global view on international order and peacekeeping. Alan James was also alert to the question of how spheres of influence shaped the outcomes and practices of peacekeeping (James 1990: *passim*).

Peacekeeping in realism

Considering things from the other end, what have realists said about peacekeeping? The answer is very little. John Mearsheimer notoriously disparaged peacekeeping in his renowned paper on post-Cold War international security, at precisely the point when tremendous new hopes had been vested in peacekeeping efforts in Africa and the Balkans (Mearsheimer 1994). It is important to note the precise character of Mearsheimer's claim. He did not offer any particular views on the effectiveness of peacekeeping with respect to conflicts within or between small powers, but rather said that peacekeeping was incapable of suppressing great-power conflict, and therefore could not be seen as an effective variant of or substitute for collective security. Thus, according to Mearsheimer, the existence of peacekeeping did not push into abeyance the continuing relevance of realist theorising. Whilst Mearsheimer's claims confronted rejoinders (e.g. Kupchan and Kupchan 1995), few saw fit to dispute his verdict on the limitations of peacekeeping and thus the lack of any hope for realising collective security.

Mearsheimer was obviously right – blue helmets patrolling a buffer zone would not be able to halt, deter, or reverse war between say, India and Pakistan or the two Koreas, or to halt another Russian advance on the Georgian capital, Tbilisi. Indeed, not only are blue helmets incapable of halting war between industrialised countries, they cannot meaningfully intercede in conflicts where great-power interests are significant, such as Georgia, Syria, or Ukraine. Here, we have a return to peacekeeping limited by spheres of influence. Where peacekeeping has interceded in such large-scale conflicts, it has been effective only when conducted with the assent of the belligerents, as with the UN mission that deployed at the end of the 1980–88 Iran–Iraq War. If realists never devoted particular attention to peacekeeping, as we have already seen, peacekeeping scholars returned the compliment by rarely considering realism. In this, however, peacekeeping scholars were also simply being carried by the tide of counter-realist scholarship that swept over the discipline at the end of the Cold War.

Yet Mearsheimer's evaluation was also off-kilter, as the clear implication of his reasoning was that peacekeeping would remain insignificant, effectively 'crowded out' by great-power competition within the international system, squeezed to the margins of international politics, in places like Lebanon and Angola. Yet, despite the fact that peacekeeping cannot prevent great power conflict or suppress the condition of structural anarchy in the international order, it has also clearly grown to a significance and scale that is still striking, to the point where peacekeepers exceed the global military deployments of all states – individually and collectively – except for the US. Mearsheimer's verdict on peacekeeping thus exemplifies the limits of realist theorising with respect to peacekeeping. That is to say, it is cast at such a high level of generality that it simply fails to capture much of the content of global political activity, even at the same time as it can be indubitably true.

Peacekeeping is not going to stop the Third World War, but that does not mean it is insignificant either. Mearsheimer's overall judgement was right and yet, even within that constraint, peacekeeping has very clearly expanded to become a keystone of international security – not only in the global scale and country-level intensity of peacekeeping operations but also as seen in its integration into both war-fighting and post-conflict stabilisation efforts in places such as Mali (e.g., see Karlsrud 2015). Given Mearsheimer's failure to give peacekeeping its due – even by his own standard of a hard-nosed focus on international security – what might we expect from realism to inform our analysis of peacekeeping? In what follows, we can divide realism into three broad types to organise the possible implications for the analysis of peacekeeping.[1]

Classical realism

Classical realism has enjoyed a revival in IR theorising over the last thirty years, going beyond the caricature of realism as little more than a stock of fables about human nature and idealist folly. The range and sophistication of international political theory associated with classical realism is perhaps better appreciated than ever (e.g. Scheuerman 2011, 2013). Yet much of this theorising still remains contained within purely theoretical outlooks rather than being applied to analysis of world politics. The new classical realism shows us that the intellectual range of thinkers such as E.H. Carr, Hans J. Morgenthau and others was wide, stretching far beyond merely analysing war or even being focused purely on states. E.H. Carr for instance believed that sustained forms of supranational co-operation in international security might emerge from the Second World War, while Morgenthau thought that the nuclear weapons made nothing less than world government necessary (Scheuerman 2013). Both Carr and Morgenthau wrote penetrating analyses of international law and organisation, stretching across both the interwar and Cold War period (Morgenthau 1983).

To give one example of the range of insight available in classical realism, consider Morgenthau's paper on the political preconditions of an 'international police force', in which he analyses the post-Westphalian Holy Roman Empire as an archetypal international society-cum-international organisation. In so doing, he thereby extends the range of precursors of international organisations extant before the UN, as well as expanding the units of analysis from which collective management of security in decentralised political systems might be considered. Morgenthau is worth quoting at length here:

> the Diet [of the Holy Roman Empire], similar to the United Nations, could only request member states to put money and armed contingents at the disposal of the Empire, taking what the member states were willing to give; it could no longer, as it once did, enforce the 'matricula' specifying the quota of contingents each state was obligated to furnish to the imperial army. Thus the Holy Roman Empire developed in a way which is the reverse of the development many expect the United Nations to take starting as supranational organisation, it ended as a federation of sovereign states. (Morgenthau 1963: 398)

In the same paper, Morgenthau cycles through the problem of international policing and the forms this takes in various scenarios, from Cold War-style geopolitical competition through confederal political systems to actual world government. Indeed, Morgenthau's recounting of the disintegration of an imperial army at the 1757 Battle of Rossbach due to conflicting political interests, national loyalties, and differing confessional sympathies, makes UN blue helmet operations today seem paragons of harmonious functioning and seamless interoperability by comparison. Morgenthau's analysis of how 'police action' degenerates into straightforward coalition warfare may be usefully studied if we are indeed on the brink of a multipolar world in which supranational co-ordination in peacekeeping-style activities may become more difficult. 'The deficiencies of an international police force,' Morgenthau observes, 'are the deficiencies of the international order revealed in the perspective of a particular task' (Morgenthau 1963: 402).

Thus, in many ways, classical realism has much that the contemporary study of peacekeeping continues to lack, being rich, historically informed and concrete. Given its range, depth, and versatility there is plenty of reason to stretch classical realism to cover the institutional and conceptual innovation embodied in peacekeeping practice and which, as we have already seen, directly tackles fundamental questions of politics – the character of legitimate force, the construction of political order, the possibility of sustained international co-operation, the difference between peace and war – all in the laboratory of the nominally peripheral and marginal zones of the states system, such as Africa. This would seem to provide fertile ground for innovative use of classical realism.

Structural realism

Of the three varieties of realism identified in this chapter, structural realism would seem to have the least to offer the study of peacekeeping today. Focused firmly at the systemic level and dismissive of the capacities of international organisation to sustain collective co-operation in the realm of security, the expansion of peacekeeping would seem to be evidence of the incapacity of structural realism to explain so much of international politics. Mesmerised by shifting dynamics of great-power politics and recurrent patterns of international order, the analytical power of structural realism comes at the expense of considering the variety of the new forms that world politics consistently throws up – such as peacekeeping. Far less than a reliable international police force, and yet peacekeeping remains instrumental to understanding the actual dynamics of war and peace today in many of the world's war zones. As already indicated above, in light of the growth and sophistication of peacekeeping and its embeddedness in conflict, the explanatory insufficiency of structural realism would seem exposed in face of the expansive, global military footprint of blue helmet operations.

Yet caution might be in order here. It is a commonplace observation in the study of peacekeeping that peacekeeping operations boomed with the end of the Cold War. This shows that it is widely – even if only tacitly – accepted among scholars that peacekeeping is somehow tied to the overall distribution of power in the international system (although the precise character of those linkages is rarely spelled out, beyond the implied impact of the declining use of vetoes on the UN Security Council facilitating the spread of peacekeeping; e.g. Bellamy et al. 2010: 50–1). Inasmuch as structural realism is focused on the overall distribution of power in the international system, then peacekeeping could help us flesh out the security characteristics of different kinds of international system. That is to say, if the post-Cold War era has indeed been one of unipolarity (e.g. Monteiro 2012), we could hazard a working hypothesis that one of the features of unipolarity is peacekeeping operations (Cunliffe, forthcoming). If bipolarity has curbed the deployment of peacekeepers (e.g., Bellamy et al. 2010), unipolarity would seem propitious to extensive peacekeeping operations, as indicated by the boom in peacekeeping since the early 1990s after the implosion of the USSR. This could also lead us to expect a reconfiguration of the global peacekeeping footprint if there is to be a redistribution of power in the international system.

Perhaps there is already evidence of this in the difficulties over the extension of the mandate for the blue helmet mission in the Central African Republic (Plichta 2018). Geopolitical tussles here could be a harbinger of the potential for growing great-power tension and competition to erode the comity and co-operation needed to sustain peacekeeping. The self-referential character of peacekeeping studies runs the risk of leaving both the analysis and practice of peacekeeping blind-sided by a new distribution of power that is less propitious for the actual maintenance of a global peacekeeping system. Whatever the specific configuration of power in the future world order, we knew that bipolarity was less propitious for peacekeeping, so at the very least a new dispensation of geopolitical rivalry will have significant consequences for the structure and practice of peacekeeping. A related question concerns the relationship between UN and regional peacekeeping – whose interaction does not suggest any straightforward or obvious relationship, such as an inverse one. How might these inter-organisational relations be affected by a new dispensation of power at the global level? Peacekeeping could be a terrain on which to explore the predictive capacities of structural realism and to follow through the dynamics of system-level effects to new, hitherto overlooked outcomes in the field of international security.

Neoclassical realism

The final branch of realism to be dealt with here is neoclassical realism (henceforward NCR). The basic claim of NCR is to offer conceptual bridges between the structural or systemic effects that are patterned by structural realists, and the unit-level or state-level behaviour that was supposedly the realm of classical realists. Thus outcomes can be traced in a consistent, empirically demonstrable and causally sufficient way from the internal workings of states right through to the international system itself. NCR was largely a response to intellectual demands that were thrown up by realism itself, with NCR emerging as a means of reconciling intellectual contradictions within the theory of structural realism and its refusal to supply a theory of foreign policy (Lobell et al. 2009; Waltz 1996). The parsimony and explanatory power of structural realism could not be squeezed down and then threaded through state behaviour to explain foreign policies, with the result that the analytical grip of structural realism was actually too loose to grasp the shifting patterns of international politics. Thus the explanatory power of structural realism would seem to dissipate, incapable of explaining state behaviours that did not conform to a range of large, recurrent patterns in international politics.

Notwithstanding disputes over the conceptual coherence of NCR, it is perhaps the most immediately promising avenue for extending realism to the study of peacekeeping. Whilst there is a fairly extensive literature on case studies of peacekeeping by major and rising powers – studies that have perforce drawn attention to basic realist tropes such as power, interest, and so on (e.g. Stuenkel 2014; see also Kenkel and Cunliffe 2015) – few of these have been informed in any systematic way by realist theorising. A small academic cottage industry sprang up around the topic of 'BRICS peacekeeping' and military intervention, before the global economic crash washed over these economies too, with much discussion, for instance, of the short-lived Brazilian initiative, the Responsibility while Protecting (McDougall 2014). While this literature was insightful and productive, little of it was rooted in paying close attention to underlying power capacities or any strong claims about systemic shifts in the balance of power. Much of it was foreign-policy-focused, thereby avoiding any strong claims about a shift in systemic polarity. Perhaps therefore it overestimated the capacities of some of these states. More attention might have been paid to the political and economic shifts that would eventually disintegrate the 'BRICS' (Brazil-Russia-India-China-South Africa) grouping.

Changing economic fortunes have undercut Brazil and South Africa, and the lack of any strategic or military structures to help prop up the BRICS has led to the fading of a term that was, after all, a catchy acronym designed to grab investors' attention rather than intended for geopolitical analysis. Had more attention been paid to systemic questions, then the foreign policies of intervention, peacekeeping, and new aid policies pursued by some of these states might not have been overblown into systemic shifts in the global redistribution of power. Nonetheless, peacekeeping as a major military activity by states could become a fertile terrain to test the propositions of neoclassical realism. NCR also has the potential to help tighten up and structure studies of states' peacekeeping behaviour, helping to articulate the various agencies and chains of causal connections that otherwise risk being blended away in large-n studies.

Conclusion

In conclusion, it is worth summarising here the intellectual benefits of realist theorising for the study of peacekeeping. While the scale of peacekeeping makes it a tableau that is useful to explore and test and extend the various branches of realism, realist concepts and theories should alert us to at least several phenomena of particular significance for peacekeeping at this particular point in time.

Most obviously, realism focuses attention on power politics – and not just the trite insights on the enduring reality of self-interest in decision-making but rather the more fundamental point that politics itself is fundamentally about shifting dynamics of competition for power. While any analyst of peacekeeping would accept this basic proposition at the level of, say, ethnic conflict and the design of peace settlements after civil wars, all too frequently these same analysts would remain oblivious to this insight when applied to the level of states – where it registers perhaps only as the behaviour of units in the field, or in collisions between conflicting chains of command cutting across peacekeeping headquarters in New York and various national capitals. Competition for power *through* peacekeeping and *over* peacekeeping should be foregrounded as a core dynamic of the politics of peacekeeping. More than this, realism offers a means of conceptually integrating and synthesising the study of peacekeeping with other types of state behaviour in the realm of state security and military power – a synthesis that would push scholars and students outside the realm of internally oriented micro-theory.

Thus realism allows us to connect the dynamics of peacekeeping to great-power competition. Africa, one such likely theatre of competition, is also that continent that is host to the largest and most important peacekeeping operations today. Great-power competition through and over peacekeeping is one obvious means by which peacekeeping may be directly hooked up to the central 'macro-theoretical' stream of the discipline. Conversely, peacekeeping as a form of military intervention and as an arena in which great powers jockey for status and prestige and seek to project themselves into the centre of international politics, would be an excellent means of extending realist theorising to new forms of international security. Finally, and linked to the question of whether we are entering a multipolar world, the question of polarity in the international system is perhaps the single most important point for the study of peacekeeping. As it is firmly established that peacekeeping is dependent on the polarity of the international system, a switch in polarity at the systemic level may have the farthest-reaching implications for the study of peacekeeping. The international system may go through cycles of recurrence and repetition, but the structure of peacekeeping operations and global peacekeeping deployments change profoundly in response to changes in international order.

Philip Cunliffe

Note

1 I will not be differentiating between offensive and defensive structural realism, as this subdivision within structural realism does not seem to me to have significant implications for how realists might address peacekeeping.

References

Bellamy, Alex J., Paul D. Williams, and Stuart Griffin (2010), *Understanding Peacekeeping* (Cambridge: Polity).
Bove, Vincenzo, and Leandro Elia (2011), 'Supplying peace: Participation in and troop contribution to peacekeeping missions', *Journal of Peace Research*, 48:6, 699–714.
Cunliffe, Philip (forthcoming), 'Changing the polarity: Peacekeeping and multipolarity'.
Gaibulloev, Khusrav, Todd Sandler, and Hirofumi Shimizu (2009), 'Demands for UN and non-UN peacekeeping: Nonvoluntary versus voluntary contributions to a public good', *Journal of Conflict Resolution*, 53:6, 827–52.
James, Alan (1990), *Peace-keeping in International Politics* (London: Palgrave Macmillan).
Karlsrud, John (2015), 'The UN at war: Examining the consequences of peace-enforcement mandates for the UN peacekeeping operations in the CAR, the DRC and Mali', *Third World Quarterly*, 36:1, 40–54.
Kenkel, Kai M., and Philip Cunliffe (eds) (2015), *Brazil as a Rising Power: Intervention Norms and the Contestation of Global Order* (Abingdon and New York: Routledge).
Kupchan, Charles A., and Clifford A. Kupchan (1995), 'The promise of collective security', *International Security*, 20:1, 52–61.
Lobell, S.E., N.M. Ripsman, and J.W. Taliaferro (2009), *Neoclassical Realism, the State and Foreign Policy* (Cambridge: Cambridge University Press).
MacQueen, Norrie (2006), *Peacekeeping and the International System* (Abingdon and New York: Routledge).
McDougall, Derek (2014), 'Responsibility while Protecting: Brazil's proposal for modifying responsibility to protect', *Global Responsibility to Protect*, 6:1, 64–87.
Mearsheimer, John J. (1994), 'The false promise of international institutions', *International Security*, 19:3, 5–49.
Mearsheimer, John J., and Stephen Walt (2013), 'Leaving theory behind: Why simplistic hypothesis-testing is bad for International Relations', *European Journal of International Relations*, 19:3, 427–57.
Monteiro, Nuno P. (2012), 'Unrest assured: Why unipolarity is not peaceful', *International Security*, 36:3, 9–40.

Morgenthau, Hans J. (1963), 'The political conditions for an international police force', *International Organization*, 17:2, 392–403.

Morgenthau, Hans J. (1983), *Politics among Nations: The Struggle for Power and Peace* (New York: Alfred A. Knopf).

Neack, Laura (1995), 'UN peace-keeping: In the interest of community or self?', *Journal of Peace Research*, 32:2, 181–96.

Paris, Roland (2000), 'Broadening the study of peace operations', *International Studies Review*, 2:3, 27–844.

Plichta, Marcel (2018), 'France and Russia fiddle while the Central African Republic burns', *World Politics Review*, 28 November.

Richmond, Oliver P., and Roger Mac Ginty (2015), 'Where now for the critique of the liberal peace?', *Cooperation and Conflict*, 50:2: 171–89.

Scheuerman, William E. (2011), *The Realist Case for Global Reform* (Cambridge: Polity).

Scheuerman, William E. (2013), *Morgenthau* (New York: John Wiley and Sons).

Stuenkel, Oliver (2014), 'Regulating intervention: Brazil and the responsibility to protect', *Conflict, Security and Development*, 14:4, 379–402.

Waltz, Kenneth (1996), 'International politics is not foreign policy', *Security Studies*, 6:1, 54–7.

Zolo, Danilo (1997), *Cosmopolis: Prospects for World Government* (Cambridge: Polity).

2

Liberal institutionalism

Carla Monteleone and Kseniya Oksamytna

Liberal institutionalism emerged as a major alternative to (neo) realism and played a prominent role in the literature on international institutions, regimes, and regional integration in the 1980s and 1990s.[1] Scholars chose to challenge neorealism in its own turf, so liberal institutionalism combines the belief in the possibility of change and improvement with some traditional realist assumptions. Its contribution to the analysis of international relations and its influence on policy-makers remain of high relevance, but they both have witnessed significant variations over time. Likewise, the perceived crisis of institutions such as the UN or, at the regional level, the EU has given new credit to alternative explanations.

Although UN peacekeeping fits the definition of an 'international institution', liberal institutionalism has been applied only to its specific aspects, such as coalition-building in the UN Security Council, domestic pressures for intervention, and troop contributions. The difficulty of applying liberal institutionalism to the analysis of Security Council bargaining is linked to the secretive nature of the negotiations: the key decisions are reached in private consultations and the majority of peacekeeping resolutions are adopted by consensus. Scholars have therefore sought creative ways of overcoming this hurdle, for example, by looking at sponsoring rather than voting behaviour to detect the existence and evolution of dominant coalitions in the Council.

Liberal institutionalism: An overview

Liberal institutionalism[2] brings attention to the role of domestic and international institutions in facilitating co-operation. Building on the liberal tradition, liberal institutionalism has real-world roots in the experience of the two post-World War systems and in the increasing institution-building effort that led, among other things, to the creation of the League of Nations and the United Nations (Johnson and Heiss 2018). The 1970s and 1980s strand (often referred to as neoliberalism) was also heavily influenced by the pluralist literature that emerged in the 1960s and 1970s pointing at the increasing relevance of non-state actors, and by the research on the importance of domestic institutions in international politics. This led Keohane (1989: 2), one of the leading liberal institutionalist scholars, to assert that 'state actions depend to a considerable degree on prevailing institutional arrangements'. The focus shifted towards institutions, that is the 'persistent and connected sets of rules (formal and informal) that prescribe behavioural roles, constrain activity, and shape expectations' (Keohane 1989: 3). Institutions can take the form of formal intergovernmental organisations, such as the UN, but also of international regimes, that is 'principles, norms, rules, and decision-making procedures around which actor expectations converge in a given issue-area' (Krasner 1982: 185), such as the Bretton Woods international monetary regime, and conventions, that is 'informal institutions with implicit rules and understandings, that shape the expectations of actors' (Keohane 1989: 4). All three institutional forms create expectations on states' behaviour, reducing the uncertainty inherent to the anarchic system.

Liberal institutionalism shares with neorealism the assumption that the international system is anarchic, that states are the leading actors and that they behave rationally to promote their self-interest, and that co-operation in an anarchic system is not an easy task, especially in the security field (Sterling-Folker 2016: 89; Stein 2008: 208). However, it also believes that formal and informal institutions can help reduce uncertainty and therefore overcome some of the hurdles of co-operation in an anarchic system. Institutions provide stable forums in which states can regularly exchange information and negotiate; they monitor states' compliance and increase the cost of defecting; they form expectations on others' behaviour and create bonds. Repeated interaction can encourage co-operation even in an anarchic system (Axelrod 1984), so, within institutions, policy-makers learn about each other's preferences and intentions, and they can discover common interests, knowing that cheating can be sanctioned, and a loss of reputation can occur. In this respect, institutions can help in solving collective action problems (Janik and Sterling-Folker 2011).

Not surprisingly, the issue of compliance has received significant consideration. Although states are by and large compliant with the international agreements they enter, scholars are divided on whether compliance can be measured on and the reasons behind states' compliance (Chayes and Chayes 1993; Downs et al. 1996). Some scholars have pointed out that states comply when they perceive the rule as legitimate (Franck 1990) or because over time they internalise the identity and norms of the appropriate behaviour (Koh 1997). Other scholars have indicated that states comply as a result of a cost-benefit analysis, entering into agreements that do not demand major changes in the behaviour they would have otherwise adopted (what Downs et al. 1996 refer to as selection bias). Other researches have shown that states tend to comply when the agreement reflects the government's electoral leverage and the informational status of domestic constituencies (Dai 2005), and it is also possible that states entering an agreement want to tie their hands to resist demands coming from domestic groups (Raustiala and Slaughter 2002: 551).

On the one hand, this has led scholars to explore whether and how variation in institutional design can influence co-operation.

Three aspects have been explored in-depth: bargaining, defection, and autonomy (Sterling-Folker 2016; Koremenos et al. 2001). On the other hand, consistently with the liberal tradition, greater attention has been paid to the interaction between the domestic and the international system. Domestic preferences and domestic politics have received greater attention in the analysis of decision-making processes. But how international institutions may influence domestic ones has come under scrutiny too (Stein 2008: 214–15).

Institutions and states are not seen as in a zero-sum game, nor is states' power considered irrelevant. On the contrary, in building institutions, states promote their interests. States enter into agreements voluntarily and they reduce the transaction costs associated with the continuous organisation of a coalition of the willing to solve collective problems (Stein 2008: 209). Moreover, the support of hegemonic states may be needed to create international organisations and regimes (Young 1982). And the states creating an international institution exercise a form of power by altering the status quo and the available options and by excluding non-members from benefits (Stein 2008: 211; Downs et al. 1998). Indeed, as Richardson (2008: 227) remarks, although the term 'co-operation' remains positively connotated, states co-operate to maximise gains and minimise losses, so institutions remain 'of the privileged, by the privileged, and all too often for the privileged' (Keohane 2002: 256). But in their absence, powerful states would be even less restrained. Once institutions are created, they become more autonomous from power to the point that they are capable of surviving power shifts (Keohane 1984).

Richardson (2008) notes a different conception of liberal institutionalism by Ruggie and Ikenberry, both looking at the character of the contemporary institutional order. Ruggie (1982 and 1993) focuses on state–society relations and relates the multilateral character of international institutions and their rise after the Second World War not to US *hegemony* but to *US* hegemony. That is, the domestic characters (in particular, the democratic regime) and the preferences of the hegemon – rather than the hegemonic structure – have influenced the selection of the institutional form and the embedded liberalism of the post-Second World War international order. Ikenberry (2001 and 2011) focuses on the increasing institutionalisation of the post-1945 US-led hegemonic order, stressing its liberal and constitutional character. For Ikenberry too, the organisation given to the international system reflected the domestic liberal preferences of the US. The order was also coalition-based, and this guaranteed wider support and greater involvement in system-maintenance activities. That is, through institutions, the US accepted voluntary restraints on its rule to make it more acceptable to subordinate countries, and this guaranteed the persistence of the order.

Liberal institutionalism and UN peacekeeping

Since peacekeeping is an international institution, one could expect liberal institutionalism to be the dominant perspective on its evolution and functioning. However, the applications of this theory have focused only on selected aspects of peacekeeping policy-making, such as peacekeeping negotiations in the Security Council and the provision of troops for peacekeeping operations, which are reviewed below. Studies that look at the domestic origins of UN member states' decisions on peacekeeping also draw on liberal institutionalist assumptions, at least implicitly.

Like the rest of the volume, this chapter does not primarily address the question of whether or how peacekeeping works, although liberal institutionalist concepts have been widely used in that literature, for example in the analysis of the international community's bargaining leverage over the host government (Doyle and Sambanis 2006; Fortna 2008; Ruggeri et al. 2013; Howard 2019: chapter 3). We also do not concentrate on the use of peacekeeping in bargaining over other policy goals, which can take place both at domestic and at international levels. Internationally, for instance, China has vetoed the extension of the UN Preventive Deployment Force in Macedonia (UNPREDEP) as a punishment for Macedonia establishing diplomatic relations with Taiwan (Tardy 2015). Domestically, a government can send a costly signal to rebels to reassure them of its intention to abide by the peace agreement by inviting a peacekeeping operation (Fortna and Martin 2009). Below, we look at peacekeeping as an institution rather than an instrument or signal. Finally, we do not address the extensive critique of 'liberal peace', which is covered by Lucile Maertens in Chapter 7 below.

Security Council negotiations

The UN Security Council is less researched than other intergovernmental bodies, such as the UN General Assembly or the Council of the EU. One of the reasons is the secrecy and informality of Security Council negotiations: despite the recent efforts to enhance transparency and inclusiveness, 'much of the Council's business continues to be conducted in informal consultations, or "informals," closed to all non-Council members and most Secretariat staff and leaving no formal record' (von Einsiedel et al. 2015: 836). The voting record, which in other organisations constitutes a valuable resource for analysis and is used regularly in the case of the General Assembly (see, among others, Alker and Russett 1965; Kim and Russett 1996; Voeten 2000), is of limited utility: most peacekeeping resolutions are adopted by consensus, despite the increasing use of the veto in other situations on the Council's agenda. Analysing Council's negotiations requires extensive familiarity with, and access to, its opaque proceedings. For this reason, the majority of studies of the institution's dynamic have been qualitative.

Security Council policy-making can be driven by informal groups of states with an interest in a particular conflict or peacekeeping operation. Such groups, referred to as Groups of Friends of the Secretary-General or Core Groups, keep the Council's attention focused on the conflict, assist the Secretariat in negotiating with the host government, and supplement missions' activities with bilateral initiatives. Such groups have convened around UN peacekeeping missions in Namibia, El Salvador, Guatemala, Haiti, Western Sahara, Georgia, Kosovo, and East Timor. Prantl (2006) applies the concept of exit, voice, and loyalty in his extensive study of such groups, a concept which has initially been developed in the context of comparative politics (Hirschman 1970) but is increasingly finding applications in the literature on international institutions (see, for example, Kentikelenis and Voeten 2018). In Whitfield's (2007) view, these groups represent 'variable geometry' in Security Council decision-making – another familiar concept from the liberal institutionalist literature. Indeed, these groups embody the tension between minilateralism and multilateralism.

In recent years, these groups have been partially replaced by the practice of penholdership. One member (sometimes two or more) of the Council 'owns' a thematic or conflict-specific issue and pens draft resolutions, which are then negotiated with the rest of the Council membership. The majority of conflict-specific issues on the Council's agenda, including peacekeeping operations, are the domain of the three Western permanent members: France, the UK, and the US. So far, penholdership has been analysed mostly through the lenses of practice theory (Ambrosetti 2012; Pouliot 2016; Ralph and Gifkins 2017).

Domestic preferences and UN peacekeeping

The study of domestic origins of states' positions and strategies in international organisations straddles the boundary between International Relations (IR) and foreign policy analysis. Yet the idea of 'two-level games' (Putnam 1988) has been a staple of liberal institutionalist theorising. Domestic considerations shape UN members' policies on two principal peacekeeping-related decisions: first, launching an operation, and second, contributing – or ceasing to contribute – to it. Domestic-level motivations for contributing peacekeeping troops are reviewed below; in this subsection, we look at the domestic pressure to 'do something' about a conflict (especially when it is driven by emotive coverage of civilian suffering), and the decision to withdraw from a peacekeeping operation. Colloquially, the former is known as the 'CNN effect' and the latter is referred to as the 'Black Hawk down' syndrome.

Jakobsen (2002) argued that the post-Cold War expansion and transformation of peacekeeping are due to globalisation: instead of the conventional realist end-of-bipolarity explanation, he put forward both liberal institutionalist (interdependence and the 'CNN effect') and constructivist (the diffusion of human rights and democracy norms) arguments to explain it. However, with regard to interventions in general, scholars have disputed the significance of the 'CNN effect' as compared with other factors in the policy-making process (Robinson 2002).

Peacekeeping operations that are driven by domestic or global public opinion can lack the staying power necessary to bring them to successful completion, as exemplified by the US's withdrawal from the UN mission in Somalia after its military taskforce lost 18 soldiers and two helicopters in a battle with a Somali warlord. Like the 'CNN effect', the casualty aversion hypothesis has been disputed: Burk (1999) studied US public opinion of the UN mission in Somalia (UNOSOM II) and found that the deaths of American soldiers had little effect on the (already negative) perception of the operation. Raes et al. (2019) empirically assessed the role of casualty aversion in OECD countries and found that casualties due to malicious acts played no role in the decision to discontinue contributions to UN peacekeeping missions. These findings might need to be revisited in the future in case of a sharp rise in peacekeeping fatalities.

Supplying peace

Domestic conditions, like casualty tolerance, also affect the decision to contribute troops to a UN peacekeeping operation in the first place (Bove and Elia 2011). This strand of the literature has drawn explicitly on liberal institutionalist concepts, like public and private goods, burden-sharing, and free-riding. Since the question of 'where peacekeepers are sent' is briefly covered in the Introduction, we concentrate here on states' decision to volunteer troops for UN operations. The motivations for supplying peacekeeping troops are often classified according to whether they produce benefits for the international community or individual troop-contributing countries (TCCs). The benefits for the international community include addressing human suffering and stemming negative externalities, such as conflict spillover, terrorism, and refugee flows. Externalities are greater for neighbours of the conflict-affected country, which may motivate troop contributions (Uzonyi 2015; Bove and Elia 2011; Passmore et al. 2018).

Other interests that states seek to realise by contributing troops include the desire to enhance prestige or legitimacy (Victor 2010; Bellamy and Williams 2013), offer national militaries operational training (Gaibulloev et al. 2009), benefit from UN reimbursements (for a summary of the debate and the scope conditions of these benefits, see Coleman and Nyblade 2018), please allies or accrue side payments (Henke 2016; Ward and Dorrussen 2016), keep militaries away from domestic politics (Kathman and Melin 2017), and enhance links with the host country (Passmore et al. 2018). TCCs vary in the capacity to contribute peacekeepers, which is affected by the size of the military, commitment to other missions, and internal security needs (Victor 2010; Bove and Elia 2011). Capacities and interests affect not only the decision to contribute troops to peacekeeping but also the speed with which contributions are deployed (Lundgren et al. 2020).

Coalitions in the Security Council

The importance of institutionalised relations among states is evident in the Security Council, where the analysis of the decision-making process reveals the presence of coalitions of states capable of persisting over time, exercising a significant influence on peacekeeping resolutions.[3] States in a coalition do not just share homogeneous preferences, but coalitions create bonds and expectations on the other members' behaviour as well as substantive and procedural norms to manage internal conflicts and disagreements. Whilst their interests and strategies tend to converge, they also normally share an affinity in their domestic systems, engage in collective decision-making among themselves, and, despite the absence of enforcement mechanisms, tend to act as a single unit even when some members have little stake in the outcome. However, they are less binding and formalised than alliances (Monteleone 2015: 45–6).

Besides the fact that Security Council decisions are usually taken by consensus, as discussed above, a hidden veto can block proposals. Moreover, the Council's composition (five permanent members with veto power and ten rotating members elected for two-year terms) gives its members different voting power and does not allow for long-term comparisons. Thanks to their veto power, the five permanent members have an ability to prevent action (Coleman 1973 and 1986). However, the presence of a coalition creates expectations and therefore can change how states will vote, altering the distribution of voting power (O'Neill 1996: 221). Moreover, veto use has become more costly from a political point of view, and the widespread opposition to it by non-veto-holding states and civil society has led the two European permanent members to refrain from using it, and France to present a proposal (so far unsuccessful) to forbid its use in case of mass atrocities. Finally, the habit of holding informal consultations makes of this non-formal venue the place where decisions are actually made. For these reasons, sponsoring behaviour, which indicates that a state is behind or supports a specific proposal, provides a more accurate picture of the positions held by states in the Security Council. Indeed, collective sponsoring is politically important because normally one sponsor is enough to activate the decision-making process, so by co-sponsoring states want to signal their – and be seen as acting in – support of a proposal and/or its proponents.

However, information on voting behaviour can be helpful too: in a coalition, states are expected not only to co-sponsor but also to jointly oppose proposals presented by competing coalitions. In this respect, although formally abstentions do not block the approval of resolutions, they signal a political distance from the proponents. Combining information on sponsoring with information on voting behaviour is, therefore, useful to detect coalitions in the Security Council, that is groups of two or more states that tend to act together over the long period, exhibiting regular patterns of sponsoring (and opposing) draft resolutions collectively.

Previous analyses have shown that in the Security Council in the 1993–2012 period there was a dominant coalition composed of the US and European states, but also that this coalition was evolving. Signs of a potential coalition in the making centred on Russia and China were also found (Monteleone 2015). However, the analysis did not focus specifically on peacekeeping. To be clear, peacekeeping operations dominate the agenda of the Council. In 2018, out of 61 draft resolutions, 31 concerned peacekeeping operations.[4] Moreover, Monteleone (2011) argued that the co-operation between the US and the EU and European states was – at least in the 1991–2008 period – an enabling factor when it comes to peacekeeping operations. The factors that played a role included financial, troop, and logistical resources and the critical mass of political support made available, as well as European states' ability to build on the support of the EU network. This was facilitated by the institutional arrangements that made the EU states capable of creating a caucus incorporating the EU mission and the frequent contacts with the US delegation, both in New York and in any arena in which discussions on peacekeeping took place. The multilayered interaction process and the dense networks of contacts between the US and the EU and its member states allow several access points to each other's decision-making process and give information and voice to members of the caucus that would otherwise be excluded. In the Security Council, this persistent grouping is reflected in the cohesion of the three Western permanent members (P3), which is also capable of attracting 'like-minded' countries such as Japan, South Korea, Australia, etc.

If we look at the sponsors of draft resolutions on peacekeeping in 2013 (previous analyses went up to 2012), we find that previously identified trends are still evident (see Table 2.1). With the exception of draft resolution S/2013/27, which has no sponsors, the draft resolutions on peacekeeping in 2013 are sponsored by the transatlantic dominant coalition with the support of like-minded states. Russia is hardly present, co-sponsoring with the transatlantic coalition three draft resolutions, one on the UN Mission for the Referendum in Western Sahara (MINURSO) and two on the UN Disengagement Observer Force (UNDOF), but never sponsoring alone. Despite its increasing activism in the field, China was never a sponsor of draft resolutions on peacekeeping. While Russia and China maintain their role as veto players, it is the transatlantic coalition that sets the agenda. And it does so effectively, considering that, except for the two resolutions on the UN Peacekeeping Force in Cyprus on which Azerbaijan and Pakistan abstained, all the draft resolutions are approved unanimously. The unanimous approval confirms that, when the US and the European states decide to support a peacekeeping operation, their persistent grouping becomes capable of attracting other Security Council members and of increasing the political cost of using the veto for the other permanent members. As for the geographical distribution, it is interesting to observe that the bulk of peacekeeping operations take place in Africa. This chapter is not the place for an analysis of the determinants of

Table 2.1   Sponsors of draft resolutions on peacekeeping in the Security Council in 2013 (excludes draft resolution S/2013/348)

Sponsor(s)	Issue
Australia, France, Luxembourg, Rwanda, Togo, United Kingdom, and United States	African Union Mission to Somalia
France, Togo, United Kingdom, and United States	African Union Mission to Somalia
Congo, France, Gabon, Luxembourg, Morocco, Republic of Korea, Rwanda, Togo, United Kingdom, and United States	Central African Republic
France, United Kingdom, and United States	Côte d'Ivoire
Australia	International Security Assistance Force
Rwanda, Togo and United States	Liberia
France, Russia, Spain, and United States	United Nations Mission for the Referendum in Western Sahara
Australia, France, Luxembourg, Morocco, Republic of Korea, Rwanda, Togo, United Kingdom, and United States	United Nations Multidimensional Integrated Stabilisation Mission in Mali
France, Togo, and United States	United Nations Organisation Stabilisation Mission in the Democratic Republic of Congo
Australia	United Nations Assistance Mission in Afghanistan
Togo and United Kingdom	United Nations–African Union Mission in Darfur
Australia, France, Luxembourg, Russia, United Kingdom, and United States	United Nations Disengagement Observer Force
Australia, France, Russia, United Kingdom, and United States	United Nations Disengagement Observer Force
France, United Kingdom, and United States	United Nations Peacekeeping Force in Cyprus *(Abstaining: Azerbaijan)*
United Kingdom and United States	United Nations Peacekeeping Force in Cyprus *(Abstaining: Azerbaijan, Pakistan)*
France and Spain	United Nations Interim Force in Lebanon

Table 2.1 Sponsors of draft resolutions on peacekeeping in the Security Council in 2013 (excludes draft resolution S/2013/348) (Continued)

Sponsor(s)	Issue
France, Morocco, Rwanda, Togo, United Kingdom, and United States	United Nations Mission in Liberia
Australia, Luxembourg, Republic of Korea, and United States	United Nations Mission in South Sudan
Australia, France, Luxembourg, Republic of Korea, Rwanda, Togo, United Kingdom, and United States	United Nations Mission in South Sudan
France, Togo, United Kingdom, and United States	United Nations Operation in Côte d'Ivoire
Australia, France, Luxembourg, Republic of Korea, Rwanda, Togo, United Kingdom, and United States	United Nations Assistance Mission in Somalia
Non sponsored – according to prior consultations	On highlighting the role of multidimensional peacekeeping missions (S/2013/27)

peacekeeping operations. However, it may be worth highlighting that, in line with liberal institutionalist expectations, although decisions are made by states, the institutional framework makes it possible to produce results that do not necessarily reflect their immediate interests. Interventions in an area of little economic and strategic concern of the most active permanent members seem to find a justification in the attention towards world stability and peace as a global public good (see Monteleone 2011: 278; and Gailbulloev et al. 2009: 831).

Whilst the previously analysed dynamics can also be found in the following years, since 2016 the number of sponsors has dropped significantly. Looking at 2018 (Table 2.2), and excluding draft resolution S/2018/667 (a thematic resolution on children and armed conflict), and draft resolution S/2018/1109 (on integration of UN

Table 2.2   *Sponsorship of draft resolutions on peacekeeping in the Security Council in 2018 (excludes draft resolution S/2018/667)*

Sponsor(s)	Number of draft resolutions	Issue
United States	11	United Nations Mission in South Sudan; United Nations Mission for the Referendum in Western Sahara; United Nations Interim Security Force for Abyei; United Nations Mission for Justice Support in Haiti; United Nations Assistance Mission for Iraq; S/2018/853 on comprehensive and integrated performance *(S/2018/394 on United Nations Mission for the Referendum in Western Sahara: China, Ethiopia and Russia abstained; S/2018/970 on United Nations Mission for the Referendum in Western Sahara: Bolivia, Ethiopia and Russia abstained S/2018/286 on United Nations Mission for Justice Support in Haiti: China and Russia abstained)*
United Kingdom	8	United Nations–African Union Mission in Darfur; United Nations Peacekeeping Force in Cyprus; United Nations Assistance Mission in Somalia; African Union Mission to Somalia; European Union Force Bosnia and Herzegovina

Table 2.2 Sponsorship of draft resolutions on peacekeeping in the Security Council in 2018 (excludes draft resolution S/2018/667) (Continued)

Sponsor(s)	Number of draft resolutions	Issue
France	7	United Nations Multidimensional Integrated Stabilisation Mission in the Central African Republic; United Nations Interim Force in Lebanon; United Nations Organisation Stabilisation Mission in the Democratic Republic of Congo; United Nations Multidimensional Integrated Stabilisation Mission in Mali; Democratic Republic of Congo; Central African Republic
Netherlands	1	United Nations Assistance Mission in Afghanistan
Russia and United States	2	United Nations Disengagement Observer Force
Côte d'Ivoire, Equatorial Guinea, Ethiopia, France, Netherlands, Peru, Poland, Sweden, United Kingdom, and United States	1	S/2018/1109 on integration of UN support of police, justice and correctional sectors

support of police, justice, and correctional sectors), all the resolutions on peacekeeping are sponsored by one state only – or two in the case of UNDOF. Whilst they are no longer sponsored collectively, draft resolutions on peacekeeping are still presented mostly by the US and European states, with the US playing the role of top sponsor, followed by the UK and France. Russia is hardly present, with the exception of the two resolutions on UNDOF co-sponsored with the US, and China is not an active sponsor. The focus on Africa is less present, while particular interests of the sponsoring countries seem to gain new prominence. As in 2013, in 2018 all draft resolutions on peacekeeping were approved, pointing to the US and European influence on both the agenda and decision-making stages. However, Russia and China distanced themselves more from these peacekeeping initiatives, abstaining together in the cases of MINURSO and MINUJUSTH, always on draft resolutions sponsored by the US. Russia abstained three times and attracted support of other Security Council members. Owing to the change in the US administration under President Trump that caused the tensions in transatlantic relations, the UK's decision to leave the EU that reduced its role as a transmission belt of EU states' interests, and an increase in competition within the international system, a reduction in the strength and coherence of the transatlantic coalition in the Security Council lowered the political cost of opposing the US's proposals for Russia and China.

Conclusion

The application of liberal institutionalism to peacekeeping has shed light on several important questions regarding why member states support the deployment of a specific operation, how they build support for their position, whether domestic preferences influence their strategies in the Security Council, and why they volunteer troops for peacekeeping. Whilst the latter question benefited from the availability of data on the number of soldiers that each country provides, decision-making in the Security Council has been more difficult to analyse due to the limited utility of the official voting record. Sponsorship records have been a more useful source for researching coalition-building on peacekeeping.

There are several future research avenues. As non-permanent members and regional organisations seek to (re)claim a more prominent role in peacekeeping decision-making (on the EU, see

Monteleone 2011), their role deserves greater attention. A promising avenue is the analysis of peacekeeping resolutions' content. Whilst systematic data on all mandated tasks have become available only recently (Di Salvatore et al. 2020), specific aspects of peacekeeping resolutions – such as bias in favour of the government or rebels (Benson and Kathman 2014) – have already been studied, and more studies of that nature are likely to be published in the near future. As the second decade of the twenty-first century draws to a close and multilateralism becomes increasingly contested, the need for high-quality research on the basis, scope, and nature of international co-operation is hard to overestimate.

Notes

1   This chapter is the result of a joint effort. However, Carla Monteleone is responsible for the sections 'Liberal institutionalism: An overview' and 'Coalitions in the Security Council', while Kseniya Oksamytna wrote the introduction, the paragraph 'Liberal institutionalism and UN peacekeeping', and the conclusion.
2   No differenciation will be made here between liberal institutionalism and neoliberal institutionalism (Keohane 1989) or institutional liberalism (Keohane 2012) as these labels have been variously used over time by liberal institutionalist scholars themselves.
3   The analysis builds on Monteleone (2011 and 2015).
4   Data here and in subsequent tables are from the UN digital library. The search has followed the selection 'subjectheading:[PEACEKEEPING OPERATIONS]' 'Security Council' 'draft resolutions and decisions' and year: https://digitallibrary.un.org/ (accessed 14 August 2019).

References

Alker, Hayward R., and Bruce M. Russett (1965), *World Politics in the General Assembly* (New Haven and London: Yale University Press).

Ambrosetti, David (2012), 'The diplomatic lead in the United Nations Security Council and local actors' violence: The changing terms of a social position', *African Security*, 5:2, 63–87.

Axelrod, Robert (1984), *The Evolution of Cooperation* (New York: Basic Books).

Bellamy, Alex J., and Paul D. Williams (eds) (2013), *Providing Peacekeepers: The Politics, Challenges and Future of United Nations Peacekeeping Contributions* (Oxford: Oxford University Press).

Benson, Michelle, and Jacob D. Kathman (2014), 'United Nations bias and force commitments in civil conflicts', *Journal of Politics*, 76:2, 350–63.

Bove, Vincenzo, and Leandro Elia (2011), 'Supplying peace: Participation in and troop contribution to peacekeeping missions', *Journal of Peace Research*, 48:6, 699–714.

Burk, James (1999), 'Public support for peacekeeping in Lebanon and Somalia: Assessing the casualties hypothesis', *Political Science Quarterly*, 114:1, 53–78.

Chayes, Abram, and Antonia Chayes (1993), 'On compliance', *International Organization*, 47:2, 175–205.

Coleman, James S. (1973), 'Loss of power', *American Sociological Review*, 38:1, 1–17.

Coleman, James S. (1986), 'Control of collectivities and the power of a collectivity to act', in James S. Coleman: *Individual Interests and Collective Action* (Cambridge: Cambridge University Press).

Coleman, Katharina, and Benjamin Nyblade (2018), 'Peacekeeping for profit? The scope and limits of "mercenary" UN peacekeeping', *Journal of Peace Research*, 55:6, 726–41.

Dai, Xinyuan (2005), 'Why comply? The domestic constituency mechanism', *International Organization*, 59:2, 363–98.

Di Salvatore, Jessica, Magnus Lundgren, Kseniya Oksamytna, and Hannah M. Smidt (2020), 'Introducing the peacekeeping mandates (PEMA) dataset', working paper.

Downs, George W., David M. Rocke, and Peter N. Barsoom (1996), 'Is the good news about compliance good news about cooperation?', *International Organization*, 50:3, 379–406.

Downs, George W., David M. Rocke, and Peter N. Barsoom (1998), 'Managing the evolution of multilateralism', *International Organization*, 52:2, 397–419.

Doyle, Michael W., and Nicholas Sambanis (2006), *Making War and Building Peace: United Nations Peace Operations* (Princeton, NJ: Princeton University Press).

Fortna, Virginia Page (2008), *Does Peacekeeping Work? Shaping Belligerents' Choices after Civil War* (Princeton, NJ: Princeton University Press).

Fortna, Virginia Page, and Lisa Martin (2009), 'Peacekeepers as signals: The demand for international peacekeeping in civil wars', in Helen V. Milner and Andrew Moravcsik (eds), *Power, Interdependence, and Nonstate Actors in World Politics* (Princeton, NJ: Princeton University Press), 87–108.

Franck, Thomas M. (1990), *The Power of Legitimacy among Nations* (New York: Oxford University Press).

Gaibulloev, Khusrav, Todd Sandler, and Hirofumi Shimizu (2009), 'Demands for UN and non-UN peacekeeping: Nonvoluntary versus voluntary contributions to a public good', *Journal of Conflict Resolution*, 53:6, 827–52.

Henke, Marina E. (2016), 'Great powers and UN force generation: A case study of UNAMID', *International Peacekeeping*, 23:3, 468–92.

Hirschman, Albert (1970), *Exit, Voice, and Loyalty: Responses to Decline in Firms, Organizations, and States* (Cambridge. MA: Harvard University Press).

Howard, Lise Morjé (2019), *Power in Peacekeeping* (Cambridge: Cambridge University Press).

Ikenberry, G. John (2001), *After Victory: Institutions, Strategic Restraint, and the Rebuilding of Order after Major Wars* (Princeton, NJ: Princeton University Press).

Ikenberry, G. John (2011), *Liberal Leviathan: The Origins, Crisis, and Transformation of the American World Order* (Princeton, NJ: Princeton University Press).

Jakobsen, Peter Viggo (2002), 'The transformation of United Nations peace operations in the 1990s: Adding globalization to the conventional "end of the Cold War explanation"', *Cooperation and Conflict*, 37:3, 267–82.

Janik, Laura, and Jennifer Sterling-Folker (2011), 'Neoliberal institutionalism', in Bertrand Badie, Dirk Berg-Schlosser, and Leonardo Morlino (eds), *International Encyclopedia of Political Science* (Thousand Oaks, CA: Sage), 1673–6.

Johnson, Tana, and Andrew Heiss (2018), 'Liberal institutionalism', in Thomas G. Weiss and Rorden Wilkinson (eds), *International Organization and Global Governance* (Abingdon: Routledge), 123–34.

Kathman, Jacob M., and Molly D. Melin (2017), 'Who keeps the peace? Understanding state contributions to UN peacekeeping operations', *International Studies Quarterly*, 61:1, 150–62.

Kentikelenis, Alexander, and Erik Voeten (2018), 'Exit, voice, and loyalty towards liberal international institutions: Evidence from United Nations speeches 1970–2017', paper presented at the International Political Economy Society conference, Massachusetts Institute of Technology, Cambridge, MA, 2–3 November.

Keohane, Robert O. (1984), *After Hegemony* (Princeton, NJ: Princeton University Press).

Keohane, Robert O. (1989), 'Neoliberal institutionalism: A perspective on world politics', in Robert O. Keohane, *International Institutions and State Power* (Boulder, CO: Westview), 1–20.

Keohane, Robert O. (2002), *Power and Governance in a Partially Globalized World* (London: Routledge).

Keohane, Robert O. (2012), 'Twenty years of institutional liberalism', *International Relations*, 26:2, 125–38.

Kim, Soo Y., and Bruce Russett (1996), 'The new politics of voting alignments in the United Nations General Assembly', *International Organization*, 50:4, 629–52.

Koh, Harold H. (1997), 'Why do nations obey international law?', *Yale Law Journal*, 106:8, 2598–659.

Koremenos, Barbara, Charles Lipson, and Duncan Snidal (2001), 'The rational design of international institutions', *International Organization*, 55:4, 761–99.

Krasner, Stephen D. (1982), 'Structural causes and regime consequences: Regimes as intervening variables', *International Organization*, 36:2, 185–205.

Lundgren, Magnus, Kseniya Oksamytna, and Katharina P. Coleman (2020, forthcoming), 'Only as fast as its troop contributors: Incentives, capabilities, and constraints in the UN's peacekeeping response', *Journal of Peace Research*.

Monteleone, Carla (2011), 'The enabling factor: The influence of US–EU cooperation on UN peace operations', *European Security*, 20:2, 265–89.

Monteleone, Carla (2015), 'Coalition building in the UN Security Council', *International Relations*, 29:1, 45–68.

O'Neill, Barry (1996), 'Power and satisfaction in the United Nations Security Council', *Journal of Conflict Resolution*, 40:2, 219–37.

Passmore, Timothy J.A., Megan Shannon, and Andrew F. Hart (2018), 'Rallying the troops: Collective action and self-interest in UN peacekeeping contributions', *Journal of Peace Research*, 55:3, 366–79.

Pouliot, Vincent (2016), *International Pecking Orders: The Politics and Practice of Multilateral Diplomacy* (Cambridge: Cambridge University Press).

Prantl, Jochen (2006), *The UN Security Council and Informal Groups of States: Complementing or Competing for Governance?* (Oxford: Oxford University Press).

Putnam, Robert D. (1988), 'Diplomacy and domestic politics: The logic of two-level games', *International Organization*, 42:3, 427–60.

Raes, Steffi, Cind Du Bois, and Caroline Buts (2019), 'Supplying UN peacekeepers: An assessment of the body bag syndrome among OECD nations', *International Peacekeeping*, 26:1, 111–36.

Ralph, Jason, and Jess Gifkins (2017), 'The purpose of United Nations Security Council practice: Contesting competence claims in the normative context created by the Responsibility to Protect', *European Journal of International Relations*, 22:3, 630–53.

Raustiala, Kal, and Anne-Marie Slaughter (2002), 'International law, international relations and compliance', in Walter Carlsnaes, Thomas Risse, and Beth A. Simmons (eds), *Handbook of International Relations* (London: Sage), 538–58.

Richardson, James L. (2008), 'The ethics of neoliberal institutionalism', in Christian Reus-Smit and Duncan Snidal (eds), *The Oxford Handbook of International Relations* (Oxford: Oxford University Press), 222–33.

Robinson, Piers (2002), *The CNN Effect: The Myth of News, Foreign Policy and Intervention* (London: Routledge).

Ruggeri, Andrea, Theodora-Ismene Gizelis, and Han Dorussen (2013), 'Managing mistrust: An analysis of cooperation with UN Peacekeeping in Africa', *Journal of Conflict Resolution*, 57:3, 387–409.

Ruggie, John Gerard (1982), 'International regimes, transactions, and change: Embedded liberalism in the postwar economic order', *International Organization*, 36:2, 379–415.

Ruggie, John Gerard (1993), *Multilateralism Matters: The Theory and Praxis of an Institutional Form* (New York: Columbia University Press).

Stein, Arthur A. (2008), 'Neoliberal institutionalism', in Christian Reus-Smit and Duncan Snidal (eds), *The Oxford Handbook of International Relations* (Oxford: Oxford University Press), 201–21.

Sterling-Folker, Jennifer (2016), 'Neoliberalism', in Tim Dunne, Milja Kurki, and Steve Smith (eds), *International Relations Theories* (Oxford: Oxford University Press), 88–106.

Tardy, Thierry (2015), 'United Nations Preventive Deployment Force (UNPREDEP-Macedonia)', in Joachim Koops, Norrie MacQueen, Thierry Tardy, and Paul D. Williams (eds), *The Oxford Handbook of United Nations Peacekeeping Operations* (Oxford: Oxford University Press), 500–10.

Uzonyi, Gary (2015), 'Refugee flows and state contributions to post-Cold War UN peacekeeping missions', *Journal of Peace Research*, 52:6, 743–57.

Victor, Jonah (2010), 'African peacekeeping in Africa: Warlord politics, defense economics, and state legitimacy', *Journal of Peace Research*, 47:2, 217–29.

Voeten, Erik (2000), 'Clashes in the Assembly', *International Organization*, 54:2, 182–215.

von Einsiedel, Sebastian, David M. Malone, and Bruno Stagno Ugarte (2015), 'Conclusion: The Security Council and a world in crisis', in Sebastian von Einsiedel, David M. Malone, and Bruno Stagno Ugarte (eds), *The UN Security Council in the 21st Century* (Boulder, CO: Lynne Rienner), 827–76.

Ward, Hugh, and Han Dorussen (2016), 'Standing alongside your friends: Network centrality and providing troops to UN peacekeeping operations', *Journal of Peace Research*, 53:3, 392–408.

Whitfield, Teresa (2007), *Friends Indeed? The United Nations, Groups of Friends, and the Resolution of Conflict* (Washington, DC: US Institute of Peace).

Young, Oran R. (1982), 'Regime dynamics: The rise and fall of international regimes', *International Organization*, 36:2, 177–297.

3

Rational choice institutionalism

Yf Reykers

Increasingly robust mandates and deployment to high-risk environments are ever more pressing concerns in discussions about the future of UN peacekeeping. They illustrate the conflicts of interest among UN members and within the UN bureaucracy. Likewise, allegations of abuse and human rights violations by UN blue helmets have in recent years led to a debate about the UN's efforts to monitor troops in the field and hold them accountable. Ultimately, most of these discussions can be classified into two more generic categories: the *politics of mandating* and the *politics of control* of UN peacekeeping operations. In light of these discussions, it is remarkable that rational choice institutionalist theorisation, and principal-agent modelling in particular, have to date been applied only infrequently to UN peacekeeping.

This chapter applies a rational choice institutionalist approach to UN peacekeeping and shows that the principal-agent model can offer valuable insights for analysing the most pressing challenges. These include questions such as: Why are UN peacekeeping operations deployed to one crisis and not another? Why are Western peacekeepers an exception rather than the rule? How autonomous is the UN Department of Peace Operations (DPO) from the UN Security Council (UNSC)? How much leeway do deployed forces enjoy in implementing the increasingly forceful mandates? Can the UN hold accountable non-UN forces with enforcement mandates? And under what conditions are mandates extended, revised, or concluded? Answering these questions requires paying attention to the preference heterogeneities among UNSC members, information asymmetries between the UNSC, DPO, and troops in the field, as well as to the capacity and willingness of the UN machinery to install credible and effective monitoring mechanisms.

This chapter starts by outlining the core assumptions of the rational choice institutionalist school and zooms in on the principal-agent model. Next, it discusses the state of the art of principal-agent theorisation in UN studies. In the third section, the chapter highlights the model's heuristic value for gaining a better understanding of the politics of control in the increasingly complex web of agents in UN peacekeeping. In doing so, it focuses on two challenges in particular: first, information flows between the UN headquarters in New York and the missions in-theatre; and, second, the difficulty that comes with the increased involvement of regional organisations in peace operations.

From cost-benefit calculations to delegation

From discussing the behaviour of member states within the UN to explaining the persistence of UN peacekeeping over time, rational choice institutionalists (would) adopt an economic understanding of decision-making which is generally flagged as a *logic of consequences* (e.g. Barkin 2015). As part of the new institutionalist agenda in International Relations, they treat international political actors as eventually rational, behaving instrumentally (Hall and Taylor 1996: 939). In so doing, rational choice institutionalists often build upon Oliver Williamson's argument that organisational structures are developed or used by these political actors on the basis of transaction-cost considerations, which implies that institutions are created or used only when it lowers the costs compared with acting unilaterally (Williamson 1978, 1985).

Three assumptions form the backbone of the rational choice institutionalist approach (see e.g. Hall and Taylor 1996; Pollack 1997). First, states are treated as the primary political actors. Although this does not imply that international organisations, such as the UN, and their bureaucracies are seen as 'passive mechanisms with no independent agendas of their own' (Barnett and Finnemore 1999: 705), they have traditionally not been treated as the primary units of analysis. Second, state preferences are expected to be exogenously given and fixed. And third, states are assumed to behave in a functionalist manner to attain their policy goals.

Whilst a large part of the rational choice institutionalist literature is devoted to explaining the creation and design of formal international organisations (Koremenos et al. 2001; Dijkstra 2017), many scholars have also looked into when and why these organisations are used. Most influential in that regard has been the work by Abbott and Snidal (1998), who claimed that states decide to work through an international organisation only after having rationally evaluated the costs and benefits of doing so compared to alternatives, such as unilateral action. Following the transaction-cost logic, they theorise that states tend to use international organisations for their capacity of 'centralisation', which is defined as the ability to provide 'a concrete and stable organizational structure and an administrative apparatus managing collective activities', and for their 'independence', referring to an organisation's neutrality and authority to act autonomously (Abbott and Snidal 1998: 9). Abbott and Snidal mention UN peacekeeping as an example of such transaction-cost-driven behaviour, not only referring to the UN's principle of neutrality and bureaucratic expertise but also claiming that 'UN peacekeeping allows powerful states to support conflict reduction without being drawn into regional conflicts and discourages other powers from taking advantage of their inaction' (Abbott and Snidal 1998: 19).

A dominant strand within the wider rational choice institutionalist literature is principal-agent modelling (Pollack 1997), to which the remainder of this chapter will be devoted. Following the rationalist take on political behaviour, the principal-agent model captures the relationship between a principal and an agent to whom a task is delegated. The model finds its origins in the neo-economic literature, where it was developed to study the relationship between a company's shareholders and its executive management (Jensen and Meckling 1976; Moe 1984; Ross 1973). It was first used in political science in analyses of American Congressional behaviour, serving as an approach to study, among other things, congressional oversight of its executive and regulatory agencies (Ferejohn and Shipan 1989; McCubbins and Schwartz 1984; Weingast and Moran 1983). Over the years, the model's application has been expanded to international relations, becoming a dominant heuristic device for understanding delegation from states to international organisations. In general, principal-agent scholars focus either on pre-delegation, identifying motivations behind delegation and explaining the design of contracts, or on post-delegation, addressing questions about the principal's control and agent's autonomy (Delreux and Adriaensen 2018; Hawkins et al. 2006).

Principal-agent relations generally develop through an act of delegation, which can take the form of a formal contract or be more informal. The presence of such an act of delegation, or mandate, is a necessary prerequisite for a principal-agent relationship (Delreux and Adriaensen 2018). The first key question in the principal-agent literature is why delegation takes place. Generally speaking, delegation is assumed to be the result of careful transaction-cost analysis by the principal, whereby its benefits should outweigh its costs. Hawkins et al. (2006: 19) list the following benefits of delegation: specialisation, managing policy externalities, facilitating collective action, resolving disputes, increasing credibility, and, eventually, locking in policy bias.

Whilst delegation is conceived as the result of careful cost-benefit analysis by the principal, this does not at all imply that it always benefits the principal as originally intended. A core tenet of the principal-agent model is illustrated by Williamson's (1985: 30) claim that agents are 'self-interest seeking with guile'. The second main question in the principal-agent literature hence deals with the conditions under which there is room for *agency slack*, which is defined as 'independent action by an agent that is undesired by the principal' (Hawkins et al. 2006: 8). As a result, the concern of how to delegate a task to an agent without ceding too much control is central to many principal-agent studies (Nielson and Tierney 2003: 246). Key assumptions thus include a likely conflict of interests between a principal and an agent, as well as information asymmetries favouring the agent due to their capacity to hide information (Kiewiet and Mccubbins 1991; Miller 2005; Tallberg 2002).

A principal can anticipate undesired agency behaviour by installing control mechanisms (Hawkins et al. 2006; Pollack 2003). Frequently mentioned control mechanisms at the mandating stage involve, among other things, careful selection of the agent and the use of screening procedures, clearly defined boundaries for mandate implementation, institutional checks, and predefined reporting requirements. During and after mandate implementation, principals can try to control agency behaviour by installing monitoring mechanisms, and (threatening with) using sanctions, such as revising or revoking the agent's budget or mandate. Yet, even in spite of these control mechanisms, principals can nonetheless be challenged by undesired agency behaviour. Over the years, principal-agent scholars have identified a long list of factors which affect the likelihood of runaway agents and undesired agency behaviour (Epstein and O'Halloran 1999; Hawkins and Jacoby 2006; Hawkins et al. 2006; Pollack 2003, 2006; Waterman and Meier 1998). These relate to the availability of agents, the discretion agents enjoy in implementing their delegated tasks, the credibility and effectiveness of monitoring and sanctioning mechanisms, the presence of information asymmetries, and the extent of preferences divergence between the principal and the agent, as well as among individual members of collective principals and agents.

The principal-agent model and UN peacekeeping

Compared to other policy domains, the principal-agent model has made its way into the field of peace and security relatively late; its applications to UN peacekeeping are rare (Reykers 2017, 2018). In the following section, I will show that, whilst the model has gradually found entry into UN studies, there still exists a vast research agenda to which principal-agent insights can contribute, especially regarding the politics of control over UN and UN-mandated peacekeeping operations.

The principal-agent model was first used to understand delegation from states to financial organisations, such as the International Monetary Fund, the World Bank, the World Trade Organization, and multilateral development banks (Cortell and Peterson 2006; Graham 2014; Lyne et al. 2006; Martin 2006), as well as the EU (Pollack 1997, 2003). Regarding their limited application in UN studies, Alexander Thompson (2006: 254) was one of the first to suggest applications of the principal-agent model to the UN, stressing that principal-agent scholars had until then mainly looked into organisations with 'unusually large and influential bureaucracies'. Focusing on the UNSC and conceptualising it as an 'informative agent', he highlighted how international organisations can play a role as information providers to member states and their citizens about the intentions and actions of coercive actors.

Thompson's work reflects the traditional theorisation of international organisations as agents 'at the end of a long "chain of delegation"', which 'complicat[es] the transmission of demands from the ultimate principals to the IOs' (Nielson and Tierney 2003: 242; see also Bergman et al. 2000; Vaubel 2006). These chains of delegation involve voters, parliaments, governments, and ultimately international organisations. Yet, this approach does not focus on delegation from the UNSC to the UN bureaucracy, leaving little room for the analysis of UN peacekeeping operations (Reykers 2017).

It is only recently that decision-making on UN peacekeeping has been studied from a principal-agent viewpoint, a development that has followed the growing scholarly interest in international secretariats. Theorising the UNSC as a principal of the UN Secretariat takes place within the wider recognition that international organisations and their secretariats can be conceived as actors in their own rights, with their own preferences. They can have an interest in maximising their budgets, gaining autonomy, and pursuing their own policy goals (Vaubel 1996). This follows Barnett and Finnemore's (1999) observation that the UN and its peacekeeping operations, like many other international institutions, might have their own agenda.

International secretariats are considered agents that provide benefits in terms of specialisation and expertise. Following this logic, assessments provided by DPO in the planning of UN peacekeeping operations are assumed to be more neutral than those coming from UNSC members with a stake in the conflict (Dijkstra 2012, 2015: 24). However, it is a trade-off: it gives the Secretariat an information asymmetry and room for potential self-interest-driven behaviour, necessitating the installation of credible control mechanisms by the principals. The fact that UN Secretariat officials, on the one hand, and UNSC members, on the other hand, might have different preferences contributes to the problematic nature of this principal-agent relationship. The ambition of peacekeeping mandates and the types of crises which should be addressed by blue helmets are examples of many issues over which a conflict of interests arose in the past decade. The autonomy of DPO vis-à-vis the UNSC has in that light become an increasingly studied topic. Most noteworthy in that regard are the studies by Dijkstra (2015, 2016) and Allen and Yuen (2014).

For example, Dijkstra (2015) introduces the concept of 'shadow bureaucracies', which is a control mechanism that member states individually install to prevent international secretariats from exploiting their information advantage. In his application of the principal-agent model to the UN Secretariat's role in the mandating process for the UN Mission in South Sudan (UNMISS), he illustrates how large UNSC members such as the US ignored the Secretariat's assessment, relying on their own assessments instead. Allen and Yuen (2014) extend their view from mandating to oversight in decision-making about UN peacekeeping. They highlight that most research on the UNSC and UN peacekeeping has focused on explaining where missions go, sometimes from a principal-agent perspective (see Chapman and Reiter 2004), which they see as 'a useful first step in gauging institutional independence' (Allen and Yuen 2014: 622). To examine the role of the UN Secretariat once missions are deployed, they quantitatively analysed how preference heterogeneity among the five permanent UNSC members explains DPO autonomy in defining and revising peacekeeping mandates. Short time limits in the mandates, short mandate extensions, and highly specified resolutions are all considered evidence of closer oversight. Their data suggest a positive correlation between UNSC oversight and the affinity between permanent UNSC members and the country hosting the peacekeeping operation. A positive correlation was also found between UNSC oversight and the difficulty of the conflict.

Following coverage of human rights abuse by peacekeeping forces, there has been growing scholarly attention to such misbehaviour and the UN's capacity to hold peacekeepers accountable. Although this can be considered a typical example of undesired agency behaviour, only a few authors have taken a principal-agent approach to human rights violations. In their dataset, Butler et al. show that sexual violence is less likely to occur when agents are under tight control and held closely accountable (Butler et al. 2007). Referring to examples from UN peacekeeping, they highlight the importance of tight monitoring by, amongst others, international NGOs, for reducing information asymmetries, as well as of training and recruiting which increases self-monitoring (Butler et al. 2007: 681). Nordås and Rustad (2013: 521) conducted a similar study, focusing specifically on peacekeeping operations by the UN, the

AU, ECOWAS, and NATO. Despite sharing the principal-agent expectation that individual peacekeepers' preferences are likely to prevail 'when leaders (principals) have limited capacity to monitor soldiers (agent)' they use the model only to generate hypotheses without further theorisation.

The principal-agent studies described above share some commonalities. First, a shift could be witnessed in the past years from treating the UNSC as an agent of its member states towards conceptualising it as a collective principal within a larger chain of delegation (Reykers 2018). This 'UNSC as collective principal' conceptualisation has been most influential in the study of the autonomy of the UN Secretariat, and DPO in particular. Most of these studies have taken a quantitative approach to issues of mandating and control in UN peacekeeping. Dijkstra (2015, 2016) offers some notable exceptions in that regard. However, he mainly focused on the *politics of mandating* in UN peacekeeping rather than oversight. In addition, he has looked at large member states, although this is a logical choice given his focus on states' unilateral control of international secretariats.

In sum, the principal-agent model is steadily gaining a foothold in UN studies. Yet, while the *politics of mandating* of UN peacekeeping has received some scholarly attention, this is less the case for the *politics of control*, and particularly control during mandate implementation. The relative dominance of quantitative approaches to UN oversight and monitoring has offered valuable insights, but it leaves us in the dark about how control, and oversight in particular, works in practice. What do preference divergences between or within UN bodies imply for actual reporting from the field to UN headquarters? Moreover, while UNSC oversight of DPO has been addressed, less attention has been paid to other principal-agent relationships beyond New York, for instance, the relationship between DPO and various peacekeeping field headquarters. Is the UN Secretariat always willing and able to monitor UN peacekeepers on the ground?

Will the ultimate agent please stand up?

As Breakey and Dekker (2014) rightfully highlight, UN peacekeeping consists of actors at the executive level (the UNSC), the administrative level (UN Secretariat), and the field level (local headquarters and soldiers in the theatre of operations). Given this plethora of actors involved, each with their own interests and expertise, it is remarkable that the principal-agent model has not been applied more widely in UN peacekeeping studies. This section highlights the model's heuristic value for gaining a deeper understanding of the politics of control in this increasingly complex web of agents. Two avenues for future research are identified: first, the ill-explored relationship of delegation between UN headquarters in New York and missions in the field; and, second, the difficulties that come with the increased involvement of regional organisations in peace operations.

Extending the chain of delegation

Much of the recent work focuses on the relationship between the UNSC, acting as a principal, and DPO, acting as an agent. What remains ill-addressed is the chain of command, or delegation, from New York to mission headquarters in the field. In fact, this is an observation about civil–military relations that goes well beyond the domain of UN peacekeeping. Principal-agent scholars have only rarely focused on the relationship between secretariats of multinational security organisations and their deployed military troops, with the notable exception of Auerswald and Saideman's (2014) study of NATO in Afghanistan. This knowledge gap is particularly remarkable in the light of accountability discussions, where effective oversight measures are considered necessary requirements to avoid problems of mandate implementation and human rights abuses. This is even more the case in situations where agents are given relatively ill-specified mandates, which is an often-voiced concern in light of the recent emphasis on protection of civilians in UN peacekeeping operations (UN 2015; Roberts 2016).

Few scholars of UN peacekeeping have taken a closer look at the relationship between New York and the missions. Focusing on information management in the context of the UN Mission in Liberia (UNMIL), Winckler (2014: 73) highlights how 'there is a disconnection between DPKO and the peacekeeping missions', whereby communication processes are used as a tool to guard one's organisational autonomy within the peacekeeping bureaucracy. Interestingly, he also identifies problems of 'constant shifting of responsibility and accountability' (Winckler 2014: 79), largely as a result of the strongly decentralised nature of UN peacekeeping decision-making. Dysfunctional communication and misunderstandings warrant closer attention as they are likely to impact control and autonomy, for which principal-agent models offer valuable heuristic tools.

A full conceptualisation of the chain of delegation in UN peacekeeping could shed new light on information flows and reporting lines from the missions to the UN Secretariat, and ultimately to the UNSC. For doing so, the principal-agent model differentiates between the *ultimate principal* and a *proximate principal*. The latter is the agent of the ultimate principal which aggregates the ultimate principal's demands and gives instructions to the agent. Proximate principals are expected to 'filter messages coming down the chain, so that erroneous or exaggerated information is not conveyed to the agent' (Nielson and Tierney 2003: 250). Through their double-hatted role, they are expected to play a crucial role in the flow of information from the agent in the field up the chain to the ultimate principal. Applying this conceptualisation to the chain of command in UN peacekeeping, the UNSC can be conceptualised as the ultimate principal which authorises an operation through an act of delegation, taking the form of a resolution. The UN Secretariat, in turn, and departments such as DPO, are hierarchically subordinate to the UNSC, but superior to the deployed mission command. In principal-agent terminology, it could be argued that DPO – in theory – acts as an agent of the UNSC, while simultaneously functioning as the proximate principal to mission leadership, including the Special Representative of the Secretary-General and the force commander. If one is to assess mandate compliance in UN peacekeeping operations, the UN Secretariat's departments and offices are an integral and crucial part of the chain of delegation. This theorisation hence calls attention to its role in processing and filtering information, which should not be left unexplored.

Interestingly, principal-agent scholars assume that the risk of information loss and agency problems increases with the length of the chain of delegation (Nielson and Tierney 2003: 251). According to this logic, information which the UNSC receives when reviewing peacekeeping operations might be incomplete, not only due to insufficient reporting from the field but perhaps also due to filtering within the Secretariat's bureaucracy. The most shocking illustration is General Romeo Dallaire's cable to New York in 1994, known nowadays as the 'genocide fax', wherein he unsuccessfully tried to warn the UN Secretariat about the impending genocide in Rwanda (Gourevitch 1998). Yet, to the author's knowledge, the practice of reporting – and, as a result, the effectiveness of the UN's monitoring mechanisms – has hardly been investigated, and for sure not from a principal-agent viewpoint.

In earlier work, I have shown how reporting requirements that are imposed in UNSC resolutions authorising non-UN forces with enforcement mandates are likely to be insufficient guarantees against mission creep or undesired agency behaviour (Reykers 2018). On the basis of the NATO-led intervention in Libya of 2011, which can be considered an extreme case of the problem of accountability of non-UN forces, it was shown that reporting by the implementing agent can become largely irrelevant in contexts where members of the principal are involved in mandate implementation. The investigated case reflects a general concern about accountability in operations wherein permanent UNSC members actively participate, hence reflecting a 'blurred distinction between principal and agent' (Reykers 2018: 548). Likewise, allowing implementation leeway or accepting information stovepipes in operations such as the African Union Mission in Somalia (AMISOM) can be considered by Western UNSC members as a price to pay for their own lack of political will to actively engage in some crises (Reykers 2017). However, these findings stem from research on non-UN operations, which differ from UN peacekeeping operations as the UN Secretariat is not (actively) involved in mission follow-up.

Apart from conceptualising the relationship between the UN Secretariat and the mission, fully grasping the chain of delegation also requires paying attention to the position and influence of individual actors. Breakey and Dekker (2014) show how the actor who is most conservative or hesitant in using force is likely to be decisive for the action that a peacekeeping mission will undertake. Likewise, Paddon Rhoads (2016: 136–7) highlighted how an ambiguous chain of command determined MONUC's inaction during the Bukavu crisis in 2004. Despite these remarkable observations, there has been little research into the role and influence of individual mission commanders or UN Special Representatives in the field. Since they monitor missions on behalf of the UN Secretariat and regularly brief the UNSC, they hold a crucial position with room for filtering information from the missions to their principals in New York (Karlsrud 2013; Winckler 2014). In sum, UN peacekeeping literature could benefit from applying the chain of delegation concept in order to study the politics of control *during mandate implementation* and *beyond the New York context*.

Expanding the range of agents

The 1992 Agenda for Peace set the scene for the increased involvement of regional organisations in peacekeeping, framing their value in terms of sharing the burden of maintaining international peace and security (UN 1992). While regionalisation of peace operations has led to a debate about the likelihood of success (Bellamy and Williams 2005), regional organisations have over the years become central actors in maintaining international peace and security (Diehl and Balas 2014). However, regional involvement in UN-authorised peace operations comes with challenges in terms of interest convergence and doctrinal alignment, control over mandate implementation, and, ultimately, accountability. The principal-agent model offers a valuable heuristic device for gaining deeper knowledge about each of these challenges.

For instance, African efforts to assist in maintaining peace and security have developed considerably in recent years. The AU–UN partnership is the most prominent example of the increased importance of regional organisations in sharing the burden of international peace and security. As de Coning (2017: 146) observes, 'Africa is currently the largest regional contributor to global peace operations', referring to contributions to both UN- and AU-led peace operations. He notices how 'a symbiotic division of work has developed between the AU and the UN', whereby stabilisation is provided by the AU and African sub-regional organisations, after which UN peacekeeping operations take over (de Coning 2017: 154).

Yet, this division of labour, with enforcement activities increasingly being implemented by regional organisations, creates a slippery slope for the UN. On the one hand, delegating responsibilities to regional organisations such as the AU is a necessity due to resource scarcity. On the other hand, although coercive activities fall outside the peacekeeping doctrinal framework, the UNSC maintains the primary responsibility for international peace and security. The UN hence faces the typical trade-off between delegating responsibilities and safeguarding sufficient control to avoid undesired agency behaviour. This tension is particularly present in the UN's relationship with the AU and African sub-regional organisations, where concerns about doctrinal differences resemble the general problem of preference divergence between principals and agents.

One of the most notable examples of peace enforcement within a UN peacekeeping operation is the Force Intervention Brigade (FIB) in the UN Stabilization Mission in the Democratic Republic of Congo (MONUSCO) in 2013 (Karlsrud 2015; Mandrup 2019). The FIB had its own leader and command and control system, yet it fell under the overall command of the MONUSCO Force Commander (de Coning 2017). Situations like this are likely to create ambiguity about lines of reporting, control, and accountability. In theoretical terms, this proliferation of implementing agents raises doubts about who the actual principal is, hence it is unclear who is responsible in case of undesired (agency) behaviour. Thinking in terms of principals and agents makes this complexity explicit. Mapping out implementing agents and their principals can serve as a heuristic tool to understand reporting and monitoring practices, as well as related interest divergences and information asymmetries.

The fact that African-led missions have a history of transforming into UN peacekeeping operations adds to this complexity. Following the principal-agent model's transaction-cost reasoning, this might logically lead to more strict reporting requirements in the mandates (Reykers 2017), particularly since preferences, doctrines, and rules of conduct might not match those of the UN. Likewise, resource scarcity of these regional organisations makes AU-led or ECOWAS-led operations, such as AMISOM, rely upon logistical and financial contributions from the UN and its (Western) members. The AU's desire to rely on UN assessed contributions to fund UNSC-mandated African peace operations (see de Coning et al. 2016) is likely to encourage UNSC members to call for tight oversight in order to limit information asymmetries. Yet, actual compliance with reporting requirements by these regional organisations has hardly been studied. This is remarkable, as accountability concerns around non-UN forces have gained traction. For instance, the Report of the

High-Level Independent Panel on United Nations Peace Operations (UN 2015: para. 269) suggested that '[w]hen the Security Council authorises non-UN forces, it should establish requirements for reporting and accountability to the Council'.

Overall, ongoing accountability discussions reveal an increased need for a more systematic assessment of the politics of control in UN peacekeeping at all levels of the decision-making complex. This can be achieved by mapping out the complex web of principals and agents, including their different preferences, as well as their potential to use information in their own interests.

Conclusion

This chapter discussed the value of rational choice institutionalism, and principal-agent modelling in particular, for expanding our understanding of the politics of UN peacekeeping, including both mandating and control in UN peacekeeping, and in peace operations more generally. Against the background of academic and policy debate on increasingly robust peacekeeping mandates, the division of labour with (sub-)regional organisations, and accountability concerns, the principal-agent model offers a valuable heuristic device for more systematic analysis. Meanwhile, however, the principal-agent model has to date mainly been applied to the issue of mandating UN peacekeeping operations. Many aspects of control remain underexplored. A crucial avenue for future research would be to explore the relationship between the UN Secretariat and troops in the field. Mapping actors in this extensive chain of delegation, identifying their preferences, and analysing their capacity to shape information flows would be a welcome addition to the debates on accountability of UN peacekeeping operations. Another avenue is the relationship between the UN and regional organisations. While the division of labour might come with benefits in terms of burden-sharing, principal-agent insights highlight how it creates ambiguity about who is holding whom accountable.

Yet, the functionalist logic that underpins rational choice theorisation, and thus also the principal-agent model, has not been without criticism. The understanding of political behaviour as driven by utility-maximisation has been critisised from various perspectives, such as sociological institutionalism. Sociological institutionalists claim that the rationalist oversimplification and abstraction of political behaviour ignores the impact of social rules or normative motivations (e.g. Barnett and Finnemore 1999; Schepsle 2008). While rational choice institutionalists have gradually enriched their take on political behaviour with insights from other traditions, becoming more pragmatic (see Abbott and Snidal 1998; Ferejohn 1991), the rationalist perspective is still far from dominant in the study of UN peacekeeping. While principal-agent modelling might not fill all the gaps in our understanding of the politics of UN peacekeeping, it opens up opportunities for more systematic research on key concerns in this increasingly complex web of principals and agents.

References

Abbott, Kenneth W., and Duncan Snidal (1998), 'Why states act through formal international organizations', *Journal of Conflict Resolution*, 42:1, 3–32.

Allen, Susan Hannah, and Amy T. Yuen (2014), 'The politics of peacekeeping: UN Security Council oversight across peacekeeping missions', *International Studies Quarterly*, 58:3, 621–32.

Auerswald, David P., and Stephen M. Saideman (2014), *NATO in Afghanistan: Fighting Together, Fighting Alone* (Princeton, NJ: Princeton University Press).

Barkin, J. Samuel (2015), 'On the heuristic use of formal models in international relations theory', *International Studies Review*, 17:4, 617–34.

Barnett, Michael N., and Martha Finnemore (1999), 'The politics, power, and pathologies of international organizations', *International Organization*, 53:4, 699–732.

Bellamy, Alex J., and Paul D. Williams (2005), 'Who's keeping the peace? Regionalization and contemporary peace operations', *International Security*, 29:4, 157–95.

Bergman, Torbjörn, Wolfgang C. Müller, and Kaare Stroslash (2000), 'Introduction: Parliamentary democracy and the chain of delegation', *European Journal of Political Research*, 37:3, 255–60.

Breakey, Hugh, and Sidney Dekker (2014), 'Weak links in the chain of authority: The challenges of intervention decisions to potect civilians', *International Peacekeeping*, 21:3, 307–23.

Butler, Christopher K., Tali Gluch, and Neil J. Mitchell (2007), 'Security forces and sexual violence: A cross-national analysis of a principal-agent argument', *Journal of Peace Research*, 44:6, 669–87.

Chapman, Terrence L., and Dan Reiter (2004), 'The United Nations Security Council and the rally 'round the flag effect', *Journal of Conflict Resolution*, 48:6, 886–909.

de Coning, Cedric (2017), 'Peace enforcement in Africa: Doctrinal distinctions between the African Union and United Nations', *Contemporary Security Policy*, 38:1, 145–60.

de Coning, Cedric, Linnea Gelot, and John Karlsrud (2016), *The Future of African Peace Operations: From the Janjaweed to Boko Haram* (Chicago: The University of Chicago Press/Zed Books).

Cortell, Andrew P., and Susan Peterson (2006), 'Dutiful agents, rogue actors, or both? Staffing, voting rules, and slack in the WHO and the WTO', in Darren G. Hawkins, David A. Lake, Daniel L. Nielson, and Michael J. Tierney (eds), *Delegation and Agency in International Organizations* (Cambridge: Cambridge University Press), 255–80.

Delreux, Tom, and Johan Adriaensen (2018), 'Twenty years of principal-agent research in EU politics: How to cope with complexity?', *European Political Science*, 17:2, 258–75.

Diehl, Paul F., and Alexandru Balas (2014), *Peace Operations* (Cambridge: Polity Press).

Dijkstra, Hylke (2012), 'Efficiency versus sovereignty: Delegation to the UN secretariat in peacekeeping', *International Peacekeeping*, 19:5, 581–96.

Dijkstra, Hylke (2015), 'Shadow bureaucracies and the unilateral control of international secretariats: Insights from UN peacekeeping', *Review of International Organizations*, 10:1, 23–41.

Dijkstra, Hylke (2016), *International Organizations and Military Affairs* (London: Routledge).

Dijkstra, Hylke (2017), 'The rational design of relations between intergovernmental organizations', in Rafael Biermann and Joachim A. Koops (eds), *The Palgrave Handbook of Inter-organizational Relations in World Politics* (London: Palgrave Macmillan), 97–112.

Epstein, David, and Sharyn O'Halloran (1999), *Delegating Powers: A Transaction Cost Politics Approach to Policy Making Under Separate Powers* (Cambridge: Cambridge University Press).

Ferejohn, John A. (1991), 'Rationality and interpretation: Parliamentary elections in early Stuart England', in Kristen Renwick Monroe (ed.), *The Economic Approach to Politics* (New York: Harper Collins), 279–305.

Ferejohn, John A., and Charles Shipan (1989), 'Congressional influence on administrative agencies: A case study of telecommunications policy', in

Lawrence Dodd and Bruce Oppenheimer (eds), *Congress Reconsidered*, 4th ed. (Washington, DC: Congressional Quarterly Press), 393–410.

Gourevitch, Philip (1998), 'The genocide fax', *The New Yorker*, 11 May 1998, 42.

Graham, Erin R. (2014), 'International organizations as collective agents: Fragmentation and the limits of principal control at the World Health Organization', *European Journal of International Relations*, 20:2, 366–90.

Hall, Peter A., and Rosemary C. Taylor (1996), 'Political science and the three new institutionalisms', *Political Studies*, 44:5, 936–57.

Hawkins, Darren G., and Wade Jacoby (2006), 'How agents matter', in Darren G. Hawkins, David A. Lake, Daniel L. Nielson, and Michael J. Tierney (eds), *Delegation and Agency in International Organizations* (Cambridge: Cambridge University Press), 199–228.

Hawkins, Darren G., David A. Lake, Daniel L. Nielson, and Michael J. Tierney (eds) (2006), *Delegation and Agency in International Organizations* (Cambridge: Cambridge University Press).

Jensen, Michael C., and William H. Meckling (1976), 'Theory of the firm: Managerial behavior, agency costs and ownership structure', *Journal of Financial Economics*, 3:4, 305–60.

Karlsrud, John (2013), 'Special Representatives of the Secretary-General as norm arbitrators? Understanding bottom-up authority in UN peacekeeping', *Global Governance*, 19:4, 525–44.

Karlsrud, John (2015), 'The UN at war: Examining the consequences of peace-enforcement mandates for the UN peacekeeping operations in the CAR, the DRC and Mali', *Third World Quarterly*, 36:1, 40–54.

Kiewiet, Roderick D., and Matthew D. Mccubbins (1991), *The Logic of Delegation* (Chicago: University of Chicago Press).

Koremenos, Barbara, Charles Lipson, and Duncan Snidal (2001), 'The rational design of international institutions', *International Organization*, 55:4, 761–99.

Lyne, Mona M., Daniel L. Nielson, and Michael J. Tierney (2006), 'Who delegates? Alternative models of principals in development aid', in Darren G. Hawkins, David A. Lake, Daniel L. Nielson, and Michael J. Tierney (eds), *Delegation and Agency in International Organizations* (Cambridge: Cambridge University Press), 41–76.

Mandrup, Thomas (2019), 'Multinational rapid response forces in the Democratic Republic of Congo – another example of winning battles, but losing the peace?', in John Karlsrud and Yf Reykers (eds), *Multinational Rapid Response Mechanisms: From Institutional Proliferation to Institutional Exploitation* (London: Routledge).

Martin, Lisa L. (2006), 'Distribution, information, and delegation to international organizations: The case of IMF conditionality', in Darren G. Hawkins, David A. Lake, Daniel L. Nielson, and Michael J. Tierney (eds), *Delegation and Agency in International Organizations* (Cambridge: Cambridge University Press), 140–64.

McCubbins, Mathew D., and Thomas Schwartz (1984), 'Congressional oversight overlooked: Police patrols versus fire alarms', *The American Journal of Political Science*, 28:1, 165–79.

Miller, Gary J. (2005), 'The political evolution of principal-agent models', *Annual Review of Political Science*, 8:1, 203–25.

Moe, Terry M. (1984), 'The new economics of organization', *American Journal of Political Science*, 28:4, 739–77.

Nielson, Daniel L., and Michael J. Tierney (2003), 'Delegation to international organizations: Agency theory and World Bank environmental reform', *International Organization*, 57:2, 241–76.

Nordås, Ragnhild, and Siri C.A. Rustad (2013), 'Sexual exploitation and abuse by peacekeepers: Understanding variation', *International Interactions*, 39:4, 511–34.

Paddon Rhoads, Emily (2016), *Taking Sides in Peacekeeping: Impartiality and the Future of the United Nations* (Oxford: Oxford University Press).

Pollack, Mark A. (1997), 'Delegation, agency, and agenda setting in the European Community', *International Organization*, 51:1, 99–134.

Pollack, Mark A. (2003), *The Engines of European Integration: Delegation, Agency, and Agenda Setting in the EU* (Oxford: Oxford University Press).

Pollack, Mark A. (2006), 'Delegation and discretion in the European Union', in Darren G. Hawkins, David A. Lake, Daniel L. Nielson, and Michael J. Tierney (eds), *Delegation and Agency in International Organizations* (Cambridge: Cambridge University Press), 165–96.

Reykers, Yf (2017), 'Constructive ambiguity or stringent monitoring? Towards understanding UN Security Council oversight over non-UN-led forces', *Global Affairs*, 3:1, 17–29.

Reykers, Yf (2018), 'Holding accountable UN-authorized enforcement operations: Tracing accountability mechanisms', *International Peacekeeping*, 25:4, 528–53.

Roberts, Adam (2016), 'The use of force: A system of selective security', in Sebastian von Einsiedel, David M. Malone, and Bruno Stagno Ugarte (eds), *The UN Security Council in the 21st Century* (Boulder, CO: Lynne Rienner), 349–72.

Ross, Stephen A. (1973), 'The economic theory of agency: The principal's problem', *The American Economic Review*, 63:2, 134–9.

Schepsle, Kenneth A. (2008), 'Rational choice institutionalism', in Sarah A. Binder, R.A.W. Rhodes, and Bert A. Rockman (eds), *The Oxford Handbook of Political Institutions* (Oxford: Oxford University Press), 23–38.

Tallberg, Jonas (2002), 'Delegation to supranational institutions: Why, how, and with what consequences?', *West European Politics*, 25:1, 23–46.

Thompson, Alexander (2006), 'Screening power: International organizations as informative agents', in Darren G. Hawkins, David A. Lake, Daniel L.

Nielson, and Michael J. Tierney (eds), *Delegation and Agency in International Organizations* (Cambridge: Cambridge University Press), 229–54.

United Nations (1992), 'An Agenda for Peace: Preventive diplomacy, peacemaking and peace-keeping', A/47/277 – S/24111.

United Nations (2015), 'Report of the High-Level Independent Panel on Peace Operations (HIPPO) on Uniting Our Strengths for Peace: Politics, Partnership and People', A/70/95 – S/2015/446.

Vaubel, Roland (1996), 'Bureaucracy at the IMF and the World Bank: A comparison of the evidence', *The World Economy*, 19:12, 195–210.

Vaubel, Roland (2006), 'Principal-agent problems in international organizations', *The Review of International Organizations*, 1:2, 125–38.

Waterman, Richard W., and Kenneth J. Meier (1998), 'Principal-agent models: An expansion?', *Journal of Public Administration Research and Theory*, 8:2, 173–202.

Weingast, Barry R., and Mark J. Moran (1983), 'Bureaucratic discretion or congressional control? Regulatory policymaking by the Federal Trade Commission', *The Journal of Political Economy*, 91:5, 765–800.

Williamson, Oliver E. (1978), *Markets and Hierarchies: Analysis and Antitrust Implications* (New York: Free Press).

Williamson, Oliver E. (1985), *The Economic Institutions of Capitalism: Firms, Markets, Relational Contracting* (New York: Free Press).

Winckler, Joel Gwyn (2014), 'Protectionism within the organization of United Nations peacekeeping: Assessing the disconnection between headquarters and mission perspectives', *Journal of International Organizations Studies*, 5:1, 71–84.

4

Sociological institutionalism

Sarah von Billerbeck

Sociological institutionalism has been applied to UN peacekeeping only in a limited fashion. Indeed, most peacekeeping scholarship examines the policies, practices, processes, and effects of peacekeeping, but neglects the internal institutional environment in which the UN exists and in particular the internal preferences, interests, and motivations of staff within the UN. In this way, the UN's organisational identity, preferences, and goals are often considered epiphenomenal and thus treated as contextual factors that merit only description but not analysis in their own right.

Sociological institutionalism, like other forms of 'new' institutionalism, is based upon the claim that the institutional environment in which organisations exist matters because it provides, first, material resources that enable an organisation to act and, second, legitimacy that gives it the authority to do so (Weaver 2008: 4; Barnett and Finnemore 2004). Within this tradition, sociological institutionalism emphasises the role of norms, rules, and culture in not only shaping behaviour but also constituting the identities and self-images of actors. In contrast to rational choice institutionalism, which holds that political actors respond rationally to their institutional environment and act largely as utility maximisers (Weaver 2008: 5; Saurugger 2017; Hall and Taylor 1996; Reykers, Chapter 3 above), sociological institutionalism focuses on actors as social agents whose behaviour is culturally specific and constructed around ideas of appropriateness (March and Olsen 1998; Schmidt 2014; Lowndes and Roberts 2013). In this way, sociological institutionalism presents an endogenous account of the preferences, interests, and behaviours of political actors through an examination of discourse, myth, and ceremony *within* organisations.

In this chapter, I apply a sociological institutionalist lens to UN peacekeeping. First, I outline what sociological institutionalism is, contextualising it within other institutionalist theories, and outlining its take on how institutions delineate what is considered appropriate and feasible behaviour in organisations and how organisational change is deeply tied to socially constructed conceptions of legitimacy. Second, I discuss the limited application of sociological institutionalism to UN peacekeeping to date, which I ascribe to a general tendency to ignore the UN's own perceptions of its legitimacy and values, and I demonstrate how this leaves gaps in our understanding of UN peacekeeping. Finally, I provide an empirical discussion of how sociological institutionalism helps us to understand the form that UN peacekeeping takes through a case study of local ownership in peacekeeping, demonstrating how UN staff engage in inefficient or outright contradictory behaviours because of their own need to perceive that their actions are appropriate and legitimate.

Sociological institutionalism

As outlined in the Introduction to this volume, sociological institutionalism is one of several strands of 'new institutionalisms' or neo-institutionalism. The latter emerged in the 1970s and 1980s to challenge the behavioural and rational choice bias in political science at the time, and it sought to clarify the role of institutions in bringing about observed political outcomes (March and Olsen 1984; Hysing and Olsson 2018: 28). Beyond this shared acceptance of the importance of institutions however, there is little convergence between the main strands of neo-institutionalism, including rational choice, historical, and sociological institutionalism.[1] Indeed, sociological institutionalism evolved concurrently with, but largely independently of, its fellow new institutionalisms, emerging primarily out of sociology and organization studies (Hall and Taylor 1996: 946; Bevir and Rhodes 2010: 27).[2]

Sociological institutionalism argues for the powerful influence of social context on political actors. It focuses on the socially constructed nature of institutional structures, rules, and norms and asserts that this institutional environment shapes, constrains, and constitutes the identities and goals of actors within it (Schmidt 2006, 2014; Schofer et al. 2012; March and Olsen 1984; Finnemore 1996; Meyer and Rowan 1977; Lowndes and Roberts 2013). More specifically, sociological institutionalism posits that the institutional environment both socialises political actors into particular roles, thus 'constituting' them, and also causes them to 'internalize the norms associated with these roles', in turn influencing their behaviour and thus reinforcing the norms and rules of the environment (Hall and Taylor 1996: 948). In this way, institutions and individual actors are mutually constituted and mutually constituting, and institutions determine what is possible, conceivable, and meaningful in social life. The institutional environment – that is, institutional norms, rules, symbols, and images – thus both produces the identities and self-images of actors *and* delineates what actions are appropriate, imaginable, and legitimate for them by providing 'scripts [and] templates' that enable actors to recognise and respond to events (Hall and Taylor 1996: 948).

Within organisations, March and Olsen (1998) have depicted such behaviour – that is, behaviour guided by institutional rules and norms – as aligned with action taken according to a 'logic of appropriateness' as opposed to a 'logic of expected consequences', where the former highlights the importance of ideas and identities and the latter stresses material factors. According to the logic of appropriateness, policy choices are most accurately seen as 'the application of rules associated with particular identities to particular situations' (March and Olsen 1998: 951). In this regard, efficiency is only one of many considerations when organisations adopt policies and respond to events, and social legitimacy – that is, alignment with socially established institutional identities, norms, and rules – is often at least as important as, if not more important than, other considerations. As Saurugger (2017) notes, 'actors ... are motivated to act appropriately, seeking legitimacy from their peers' and 'cognitive scripts inside institutions establish what is appropriate'. In this way, the institutional environment delimits what is conceivable, feasible, and imaginable for staff within organisations.

Because of the limited nature of what is appropriate, several scholars have asserted that such behaviour in organisations can give rise to 'dysfunction' where irrational, inefficient, or even self-defeating policy choices are made (Hall and Taylor 1996; Barnett and Finnemore 2004). However, behaviour according to a logic of appropriateness does not imply that actors are not goal-oriented or that they behave irrationally; instead sociological institutionalism holds that 'rationality is socially constructed and culturally and historically contingent' (Schmidt 2006: 107). Rationality is thus not conceived of as entailing efficiency and utility maximisation measured against some exogenous, universal standard; instead, it is about defining goals and undertaking actions in ways that are 'valued within a broader cultural environment' (Hall and Taylor: 949) and are perceived to be legitimate according to the socially constructed standards of that environment. Indeed, judgements about the legitimacy or appropriateness of actions in organisations can and usually do prioritise both alignment with norms, values, and rules *and* utility maximisation, efficiency, and outputs because both are socially valued within the institutional setting; however, rationality is socially constructed in that institutional setting. Scholars have variously labelled rationality in this perspective as 'imperfect, bounded, or "garbage can"' (Saurugger 2017).[3] As Risse and Ropp (2013: 13) assert, 'the logic of consequences and the cost-benefit calculations of utility-maximising egoistic actors are often embedded in a more encompassing logic of appropriateness of norm-guided behavior'.

In this way, sociological institutionalism provides a particularly useful frame for understanding the contradictory and inefficient behaviour that is often observed in organisations. According to sociological institutionalism, actors are guided by both normative considerations of appropriateness *and* more utilitarian considerations of efficiency and outputs; where these clash, they often adopt contradictory policies or say one thing but do another in order to bring them both into alignment with the institutional environment. Brunsson (2002) has described this dynamic as 'organizational hypocrisy', where organisations face conflicts between institutional norms and demands for efficiency and effectiveness, both of which constitute sources of legitimacy for the organisation. Similarly, Krasner (1999: 65–6) posits that organised hypocrisy occurs when there is a conflict between the logic of appropriateness and the logic of consequences, and asserts that actors 'must honor, perhaps only in talk, certain norms but at the same time act in ways that violate these norms'.

A logical consequence of a sociological institutionalist approach is that change in organisations is about augmenting social legitimacy, rather than (only) maximising efficiency. As Hall and Taylor (1996: 949) assert, 'organizations often adopt a new institutionalist practice, not because it advances the means-ends efficiency of the organization but because it enhances the social legitimacy of the organization or its participants'. Of course, change *could* advance means–ends efficiency, but only if is valued within the organisation's institutional landscape, as noted, and does not simultaneously delegitimise other valued norms or standards. Similarly, Benner et al. (2011: 61–2) assert that 'the interpretive frames and cultural norms' of an organisation – what they call organisational culture – is one of a number of elements that set the scope for organisational learning. They add that organisational culture can vary within an organisation, and thus learning can become a competitive process of internal negotiation and bargaining in which actors must make convincing claims for how their proposed change is the most closely aligned with the existing norms and rules of the organisation.

In addition, this further implies that change proposals that seek to shift, address, or (selectively) eliminate the norms and rules of the institutional environment are likely to be highly contested and slow to be accepted, because those rules and norms are fundamental to the self-images of organisation staff. This in turn suggests that resistance to substantive change proposals will be high, which explains the difficulties most organisations have with reform efforts: because reform may threaten the very rules and norms that constitute organisational actors and that frame their understanding of the world, those actors are likely to perceive it as an existential threat.

Sociological institutionalism and UN peacekeeping

There is a relative paucity of sociological institutionalist analyses of UN peacekeeping. This is partly the result of a general neglect of international organisations more broadly in sociological institutionalist studies, which have focused primarily on private firms and local government agencies, and only rarely on large international, intergovernmental organisations (Benner et al. 2011: 53; von Billerbeck 2019). In addition, as mentioned, there is a tendency to assess and analyse UN peacekeeping as policy, rather than as an institution. More specifically, most scholarship on peacekeeping examines the actors, decision-making procedures, effectiveness, and impact of peacekeeping, but neglects the institutional environment in which these exist, treating it as epiphenomenal and secondary. Indeed, the tendency to orient the study of peacekeeping towards evaluation of outcomes is one of the reasons that it is under-theorised in general, which is, of course, a state of affairs that this volume seeks to counter.

Sociological institutionalism

In spite of this, there have been several attempts to use sociological institutionalism to analyse and understand UN peacekeeping, efforts that turn the lens 'inwards' to identify and understand the institutional characteristics that give rise to contradictory behaviour, inefficiency, failures, and the conditions for organisational learning. Among the first and best known is *Rules for the World* by Barnett and Finnemore (2004). In this seminal volume, the authors argue that international organisations frequently become overly focused on rule-making and therefore produce inefficient and even self-defeating outcomes – what they call 'pathological' behaviour or 'dysfunction'. These suboptimal outcomes are partly a result of the institutional environment in which these organisations exist – that is, the rules that govern what is appropriate and inappropriate and thus delimit the realm of what is possible, acceptable, and legitimate for the organisation. As Barnett and Finnemore (2004: 37) note, '[international organisation] behavior might be only remotely connected to the efficient implementation of its goals and more closely coupled to legitimacy criteria that come from the cultural environment', an environment that they further specify is characterised by 'often conflicting functional, normative, and legitimacy imperatives' (2004: 37).

They illustrate their argument with the case of UN peacekeeping in Rwanda in 1994. They argue that the organisation's failure to respond to the unfolding genocide was a result not of reluctance by member states – the most commonly offered explanation for UN inaction – but instead the UN's own peacekeeping culture, in which long-established rules of peacekeeping relating to consent and impartiality designated increased and more robust intervention inappropriate and dangerous, both to the operation and the UN as an organisation (Barnett and Finnemore 2004: 142). Particular courses of action were considered a risk to the UN's identity as an organisation, and thus were 'off-limits' because they did not align with the internal institutional environment of the organisation. In this way, organisational culture 'shaped DPKO's understanding of appropriate responses' (2004: 142) and constrained its perceived policy options, even in the face of external circumstances that overwhelmingly spoke in favour of a more robust course of action. According to Barnett and Finnemore, this case shows that the UN's failure to respond to the Rwandan genocide demonstrates how organisation staff 'tend to use the available scripts and rules to interpret information' and that they tend 'to cling to preexisting beliefs' in doing so, making change a highly contested process because it imperils fundamental elements of self-understanding (2004: 155).

Second, Lipson (2007) attempts to explain the expansion – in terms of both scope and frequency – of peacekeeping after the Cold War by applying Kingdon's adaption of Cohen, March, and Olsen's Garbage Can Model to UN peacekeeping. He stresses that this outcome was based not upon the 'rational fitting of solutions to problems' or a 'clear means to well-defined ends' (2007: 82) but upon instead the linking of an available solution to an existing problem by policy entrepreneurs during an open policy window.[4] He notes that this process of 'linkage' or 'coupling' of solutions to problems takes place according to three criteria: 'technical feasibility, consistency with the policy community's values, and judgements about what is acceptable in the larger political system' (2007: 84), which in turn are heavily influenced by organisational culture (2007: 85). Lipson further argues that peacekeeping did not represent an entirely new choice but instead a 'mutation and recombination' of existing policies. This more broadly suggests that change, even seemingly dramatic change, may only consist of the reorganisation and recombination of old options and their 'assignment' to problems to which they had not previously been assigned. In this way, change in organisations and in peacekeeping tends to be limited in scope, constrained within the institutional environment of the UN, with its particular rules, norms, and procedures. That said, Lipson concedes that the international normative environment was also shifting at the time with 'the acceptance of liberal democracy as the standard of legitimate governance' (2007: 89), thus recognising that the expansion of peacekeeping was perhaps as dramatic as it was due to both the garbage can process that he describes *and* the existence of a broader permissive environment.

Third, Autesserre (2010) argues how a dominant peacekeeping culture precluded particular courses of action in the UN's peacekeeping mission in the Democratic Republic of Congo, MONUC. Specifically, she asserts that the UN's institutional environment is characterised by a bias towards national- and regional-level understandings and policies, and how this rendered local-level solutions inappropriate and therefore beyond consideration. However, according to Autesserre, the conflict in Congo was primarily fuelled by local-level disputes over land, resources, and power, and thus the UN's fixation on national and regional dynamics has contributed directly to its failure to secure a durable peace in Congo. In other words, the UN's organisational culture – its 'ideologies, rules, rituals, assumptions, definitions, paradigms, and standard operating procedures' (2010: 11) – created a 'mismatch' between the problem and the solution, similar to Lipson's analysis, because it pre-emptively designated particular policy options as inconceivable, unnatural, and inappropriate to the UN's identity.

Whilst Barnett and Finnemore, Lipson, and Autesserre focus on questions of organisational culture, Benner et al. (2011) and Howard (2008) zero in on the question of organisational learning in UN peacekeeping, describing how this is both constrained and enabled by the institutional environment. According to Benner et al. (2011: 55), organisational learning entails 'a knowledge-based process of questioning and changing organizational rules to change organizational practice'. In the context of peacekeeping then, because rules are *prior* to practice, changes in peacekeeping practice can come about only because of a change in organisational rules, which regulate and constitute the social world within the UN (Benner et al. 2011: 54). The authors note that temporary changes in practice can occur without changes in rules, but stress that learning – that is the institutionalisation of change – occurs only when rules are amended; equally, however, they note that new rules are not always fully implemented, leading to incomplete learning.

In peacekeeping, they consider this process to be highly contested, because there are a plethora of knowledge sources within the UN, and thus there needs to be a phase of advocacy – similar to Lipson's policy entrepreneurs – in order to progress to institutionalisation (Benner et al. 2011: 55–8). They note, however, that peacekeeping learning often stalls during the advocacy and institutionalisation phases, as a result either of weak political support or of weak learning infrastructure. Their conclusions are not wholly negative, though: they point out that successful learning can and does occur, a welcome contrast to much of the literature on organisational change, which suggests that learning is usually either a partial or a failed enterprise. Still, institutional rules are the *sine qua non* of organizational learning, and those rules are limited and limiting because they exist within 'the interpretive frames and cultural norms' of the organisation (Benner et al. 2011: 61).

Howard (2008) also addresses learning in UN peacekeeping, though her intention is to evaluate more the drivers of success and failure in peacekeeping than organisational learning itself, and her study draws selectively upon sociological institutionalism rather than adopting the approach entirely. She divides learning into two levels: one that occurs within individual peacekeeping operations and one that occurs between operations and headquarters. Examining ten cases of multidimensional post-Cold War peacekeeping, she concludes that, whilst there has been some first-level learning *within* missions, learning *between* missions has lagged behind. She does not characterise this as 'full' second-level organisational dysfunction – that is, 'when sections of the organization work at cross-purposes with one another, important general insights from one operation are not adequately transferred to other operations, actions are at odds with the fundamental principles of the organization, and there is no systematic evaluation of problems, goals, or methods'

(2008: 330). Instead, she labels what she observes as 'incremental adaptation', in which practices are transferred from one mission to another without regard for contextual specificities or any broader, holistic strategy. Like the other authors covered in this section, Howard ascribes much of the responsibility for this relative failure in learning to the UN Secretariat, rather than the more oft-blamed Security Council (2008: 340), in short, due to limited internal imagination about the potential for transfer of knowledge and adaptation of new procedures.

All of these studies stress, in various ways, the critical importance of the institutional environment of UN peacekeeping and add helpful insights into our understanding of why peacekeeping takes the form that it does, including both why contradictory policies are adopted in practice, leading to often cataclysmic failures, and why the UN subsequently fails to learn lasting lessons from these experiences. However, as a body of scholarship on peacekeeping, they remain remarkably disparate, and the sociological institutionalist approach has remained secondary to other approaches to the study of peacekeeping. In the next section, I apply sociological institutionalism to the concept of local ownership in peacekeeping, in a further addition to this growing literature.

Local ownership and UN peacekeeping

Adding to the literature outlined in the previous section, I here use a sociological institutionalist frame to understand the UN's persistent emphasis on local ownership in peacekeeping, in spite of the fact that it is only sporadically implemented and often represents, at least in the short term, an inefficient policy option. I argue that the UN's dedication to local ownership in peacekeeping is based not upon its perceived efficiency or ability to contribute to the rapid and cost-effective achievement of stated objectives but instead upon its alignment with the norms, principles, and self-images of UN staff. Local ownership represents an approach to peacekeeping that is appropriate to the UN's identity, and thus – whether or not it is actually implemented in practice or, where it is implemented, whether it enables the UN to more efficiently achieve its goals – it is the right policy choice. In this way, local ownership provides an excellent illustration of how policy choices are informed and bounded by the institutional environment and self-perceptions of organisational identity and how the institutional environment can give rise to seemingly contradictory behaviour within organisations.

The term 'local ownership' was adopted into peacekeeping in the early 2000s from international development, where the involvement of beneficiaries had been advocated as an effective approach to aid starting in the 1980s (von Billerbeck 2017: 28–30). Since then, discourse surrounding local ownership has reached the level of orthodoxy within peacekeeping, and it is widely advocated not only as an efficient way to do peacekeeping but – more importantly – as the *right* way to do peacekeeping. In 2011, the Security Council called local ownership 'a moral imperative', a sentiment echoed in a number of other documents (UN 2011b: 2; see also UN 2011a: 10). This enthusiasm is based upon the belief that peacekeeping processes that are locally owned will be more legitimate – that is, they allow the UN to remain aligned with principles and values that are key elements of its organisational identity (von Billerbeck 2017).

More specifically, peacekeeping is an endeavour that necessitates deep intrusion into national and local processes, processes that would not normally be open to external interference, in order to bring about meaningful conflict transformation. However, such intrusion directly contravenes highly valued norms relating to self-determination and non-imposition within the UN, and UN peacekeeping staff thus often face situations where they must violate their stated principles in order to achieve their stated goals. This creates an uncomfortable situation for peacekeeping staff, because they view themselves as standard bearers for principles of appropriate behaviour in the international system, principles that are enshrined in the UN Charter and that serve as key boundaries of the organisation's institutional environment.

As a result, peacekeeping staff seek out policies and approaches to peacekeeping that enable them to remain aligned with the principles and norms of their institutional environment, even if those policies and approaches are inefficient or unlikely to lead to success. Local ownership – that is, involving a variety of national actors at various stages and in various ways in peacekeeping activities – is perceived to lessen intrusion and ensure that actions are not imposed but instead jointly agreed upon, thus rendering them appropriate within the institutional bounds of the UN. As one former senior UN official asserted,

> There is a deep-seated political bias in the UN that the UN stands for self-determination rather than externally-imposed, neo-imperial forms of governance. Local ownership fits that view nicely. This is an important part of the UN's self-perception.[5]

In this way, local ownership is considered an appropriate, correct, and legitimate approach to peace operations, one that enables the UN to reconcile the contradictions between its operational obligations and its institutional norms and rules.

Importantly, this is the case even if local ownership is inefficient in a particular context or time period, weakens the chances of peacekeeping success, or slows the delivery of outputs.[6] Indeed, many UN staff assert that local ownership in peacekeeping delays or even prevents efficient action by the UN because it implies that the UN will need to share responsibility for decision-making and implementation with actors who either have weak capacities or maintain illiberal, divisive, or authoritarian postures that run counter to those in the UN's mandate (von Billerbeck 2017). One senior UN official described how the involvement of local actors in its peace operation, MONUC, 'slowed everything down to no end',[7] and another described how a large number of local actors 'are not strong and they play a small role'.[8] Such assessments suggest that local ownership is not considered a particularly effective approach to peacekeeping by UN staff. Nevertheless, they continue to advocate local ownership on the basis of its alignment with norms and rules relating to self-determination and non-imposition, which are key elements of the institutional environment and of the UN's self-perception of its identity. In short, local ownership remains *the right thing to do*, even if it is not *the efficient thing to do*.

In addition, because of its alignment with institutional norms and principles, local ownership is also viewed as *universally* appropriate, and discourse surrounding local ownership reveals little effort to differentiate between contexts or thematic areas. Rarely is local ownership deemed appropriate in one mission setting but not another or in some operational areas – such as political institution building or civil society strengthening – but not others – such as security sector reform or disarmament, demobilisation, and reintegration programmes. Instead, local ownership is portrayed as suitable everywhere and at all times. Indeed, local ownership is not simply one among many possible approaches to peace operations, but has been elevated to the status of a principle of peacekeeping in the UN. Documents ranging from the *United Nations Peacekeeping Operations: Principles and Guidelines*, known as the 'Capstone Doctrine' (UN DPKO 2008), to the DPO/DOS *Core Pre-Deployment Training Materials* (United Nations 2017) now list local ownership as a key principle of peacekeeping alongside the traditional troika of consent, impartiality, and the non-use of force. And of course, as a principle of peacekeeping, local ownership by definition cannot be only appropriate sometimes and in some places.

Critically, however, peacekeeping staff are also motivated by more utilitarian considerations of outputs and results. This is because, within the institutional environment of the UN, effective action and delivery against stated objectives is also a social good valued by staff, alongside alignment with norms and principles. Rational behaviour within this institutional setting therefore dictates that staff will attempt both to comply with norms and rules *and* to realise goals and outputs. In this sense, local ownership is problematic, because it is largely considered to be inefficient by UN staff and to imperil the delivery of their stated objectives. As a result, local ownership ends up becoming primarily a discursive tool for UN staff, one that enables them to *portray* their actions as locally owned, even if, in practice, they are not.

Indeed, significant amounts of research have shown that local ownership is in fact rarely implemented or is only implemented partially: while the UN persistently invokes the discourse of local ownership, it does little to coherently define local ownership, provides no guidance on how local ownership should be realised in practice, and fails to monitor whether local actors actually feel any sense of ownership of the peacekeeping processes in their countries. Instead, it remains largely discursive – that is, local ownership constitutes, as noted above, a 'script [or] template' for explaining otherwise inappropriate behaviour in a way that is normatively appropriate. As one DPO official in New York explained, the UN should aim for 'national ownership at the strategic level, but at the operation[al] and funding level, [it] must be more cautious because the [host] government doesn't have the capacity or neutrality [for implementation]', and the UN thus tends to slip into a 'direct execution mentality'.[9] This was echoed by other officials, both in field locations and in New York. One stated that 'we have ownership in mind, but we just do things for [local actors] sometimes because there is a pressure to deliver',[10] and another noted that giving national actors ownership in peace operations can result in 'delaying and complicating the achievement of [our] objectives'.[11]

At the same time, UN peacekeeping staff continue to invoke local ownership to legitimise their behaviour and demonstrate their compliance with the standards and expectations of their institutional environment, in what Lipson (2010: 274) calls decoupling, where 'practices that are legitimized within an organizational field but are not conducive to operational performance will be maintained for their symbolic function, but decoupled from actual behavior'.

As one UN official remarked, local ownership 'sounds politically correct'[12] and another noted that local ownership is about 'signalling non-imposition'.[13] These sentiments are shared by staff in the field, who insist that it is an 'imperative'[14] and granting ownership to local actors is 'doing the right thing'.[15] In this way, the rhetoric and reality of local ownership do not match: the UN invokes the language of local ownership because it aligns with institutional norms and values in an activity that may contradict those norms and values, but simultaneously fails to systematically implement local ownership because of its perceived deleterious effect on results and the social legitimacy derived from delivering results. In short, local ownership illustrates both the organised hypocrisy that Krasner (1999: 65–6) describes, in which organisations use 'talk only' to reconcile conflicting institutional imperatives, and the contradictory behaviour often observed in organisations in which they say one thing and do another. More broadly, it illustrates, first, how peace-keeping staff are socialised by their environment to view certain policy choices as acceptable, appropriate, and natural because they align with institutional principles like self-determination and non-imposition and how they use templates and frames to explain and demonstrate how behaviour, even contradictory behaviour, aligns with that institutional identity.

Conclusion

As this chapter has demonstrated, sociological institutionalist approaches to the study of peacekeeping provide key insights into the practices, policy choices, and failures of UN peacekeeping. By examining the perceptions of UN peacekeeping staff, sociological institutionalism shows how the latter are constrained by the insti-tutional environment in which they operate, where principles and norms like consent, impartiality, and non-use of force (Barnett and Finnemore 2004) or self-determination and non-imposition (von Billerbeck 2017) inform what is considered appropriate, feasible, and right and constitute key elements of their self-images. As noted, this does not imply that peacekeeping staff are not concerned with effectiveness and delivery; on the contrary, these are highly valued within the social environment of peacekeeping. However, the maximisation of efficiency and results exists within and is informed by the broader framework of the UN's institutional environment. There is thus no contradiction between more rational, material motivations and more normative ones; instead there is only a trade-off between behaviour that aligns with institutional imperatives and behaviour that does not. Because of this, UN staff use discursive templates, symbols, and scripts – like 'local ownership' – to explain, portray, and justify their behaviour.

In spite of the existing studies outlined above that have adopted this approach or elements of it, internal institutional considerations tend to be overlooked in studies of UN peacekeeping, which instead focus on evaluating outcomes and effectiveness. In so doing, they miss out on a rich layer of insight that helps to explain much of the contradictory behaviour observed in peacekeeping; the adoption of policies that are blatantly inefficient or highly likely to fail; and the slowness of or resistance to change, learning, and reform in peacekeeping. More importantly, the failure to include sociological institutionalist approaches results in a neglect of the perspectives of UN staff themselves, thereby omitting valuable 'insider' insights into peacekeeping. Sociological institutionalism thus offers a useful addition to ongoing analyses of peacekeeping, and one that merits increased inclusion in future research into UN peacekeeping.

Notes

1 Some scholars also add normative, discursive, and constructivist institutionalism to this list (Hysing and Olsson 2018; see also Jenson and Mérand 2010).
2 Indeed, some scholars consider the term 'neo-institutionalism' to be not only a misnomer but ontologically misleading, as it implies greater similarity between strands than actually exists (Bevir and Rhodes 2010; Schmidt 2014; Hall and Taylor 1996).

3 The 'garbage can model' is explained in detail in the next section.
4 According to Kingdon, there are two types of windows: policy and problem (Lipson 2007: 83).
5 Author interview with senior UN official, Oxford, October 2011.
6 Local ownership can, in some circumstances, facilitate the delivery of outputs, in particular where it bestows legitimacy on or generates popular buy-in for UN-initiated activities (see von Billerbeck 2017; Whalan 2013). Still, most UN officials admit that this usually comes at a temporal or financial price, due to the often lengthy vetting process involved in identifying effective and acceptable national partners and the cost involved in building their capacities, where necessary.
7 Author interview with senior UN official, Geneva, May 2011.
8 Author interview with DPO official, Kinshasa, March 2011.
9 Author interview with DPO official, New York, December 2010.
10 Author interview with DPO official, Kinshasa, March 2011.
11 Author interview with senior UN official, New York, December 2010.
12 Author interview with UN official, New York, November 2009.
13 Author interview with senior UN official, New York, December 2010.
14 Author interview with UN official, New York, November 2009.
15 Author interview with UN official, New York, November 2009.

References

Autesserre, Séverine (2010), *The Trouble with the Congo: Local Violence and the Failure of International Peacebuilding* (Cambridge: Cambridge University Press).

Barnett, Michael N., and Martha Finnemore (2004), *Rules for the World: International Organizations in Global Politics* (Ithaca, NY: Cornell University Press).

Benner, Thorsten, Stephan Mergenthaler, and Philipp Rotmann (2011), *The New World of UN Peace Operations: Learning to Build Peace?* (New York: Oxford University Press).

Bevir, Mark, and R.A.W. Rhodes (2010), *The State as Cultural Practice* (Oxford: Oxford University Press).

von Billerbeck, Sarah B.K. (2017), *Whose Peace? Local Ownership and United Nations Peacekeeping* (Oxford: Oxford University Press).

von Billerbeck, Sarah B.K. (2019), '"Mirror, mirror, on the wall": Self-legitimation by international organizations', *International Studies Quarterly*, doi: 10.1093/isq/sqz089.

Brunsson, Nils (2002), *The Organization of Hypocrisy: Talk, Decisions and Actions in Organizations*, 2nd ed. Translated by Nancy Adler (Oslo: Abstrakt Forlag).

Finnemore, Martha (1996), 'Norms, culture, and world politics: Insights from sociology's institutionalism', *International Organization*, 50:2, 325–47.

Hall, Peter A., and Rosemary C. Taylor (1996), 'Political science and the three new institutionalisms', *Political Studies*, 44:5, 936–57.

Howard, Lise Morjé (2008), *UN Peacekeeping in Civil Wars* (Cambridge: Cambridge University Press).

Hysing, Erik, and Jan Olsson (2018), *Green Inside Activism for Sustainable Development: Political Agency and Institutional Change* (Cham: Palgrave Macmillan).

Jenson, Jane, and Frédéric Mérand (2010), 'Sociology, institutionalism and the European Union', *Comparative European Politics*, 8:1, 74–92.

Krasner, Stephen D. (1999), *Sovereignty: Organized Hypocrisy* (Princeton, NJ: Princeton University Press).

Lipson, Michael (2007), 'A "garbage can model" of UN peacekeeping', *Global Governance*, 13:1, 79–97.

Lipson, Michael (2010), 'Performance under ambiguity: International organization performance in UN peacekeeping', *Review of International Organizations*, 5:3, 249–84.

Lowndes, Vivien, and Mark Roberts (2013), *Why Institutions Matter: The New Institutionalism in Political Science* (Houndsmill: Palgrave Macmillan).

March, James G., and Johan P. Olsen (1984), 'The new institutionalism: Organizational factors in political life', *The American Political Science Review*, 78:3: 734–49.

March, James G., and Johan P. Olsen (1998), 'The institutional dynamics of international political orders', *International Organization*, 52:4: 943–69.

Meyer, John W., and Brian Rowan (1977), 'Institutionalized organizations: Formal structure as myth and ceremony', *American Journal of Sociology*, 83:2: 340–63.

Risse, Thomas, and Stephen C. Ropp (2013), 'Introduction and overview', in Thomas Risse, Stephen C. Ropp, and Kathryn Sikkink (eds), *The Persistent Power of Human Rights: From Commitment to Compliance* (Cambridge: Cambridge University Press).

Saurugger, Sabine (2017), 'Sociological institutionalism and European integration', in William R. Thompson (ed.), *Oxford Research Encyclopedia of Politics*, available at: http://politics.oxfordre.com/view/10.1093/acrefore/9780190228637.001.0001/ acrefore-9780190228637-e-179 (accessed 31 July 2019).

Schmidt, Vivien (2006), 'Institutionalism', in Colin Hay, Michael Lister, and David Marsh (eds), *The State: Theories and Issues* (Houndmills: Palgrave Macmillan), 98–117.

Schmidt, Vivien (2014), 'Institutionalism', in Michael T. Gibbons (ed.), *The Encyclopedia of Political Thought* (London: John Wiley and Sons), 1–4.

Schofer, Evan, Ann Hironaka, David John Frank, and Wesley Longhofer (2012), 'Sociological institutionalism and world society', in Edwin Amenta, Kate Nash, and Alan Scott (eds), *The Wiley-Blackwell Companion to Political Sociology* (Chichester: Blackwell Publishing), 57–68.

United Nations (2011a), 'Civilian Capacity in the Aftermath of Conflict', A/65/747-S/2011/85.

United Nations (2011b), 'Proces-Verbaux of 6630th Meeting [provisional]: Maintenance of international peace and security', S/PV.6630.

United Nations (2017), *Core Pre-deployment Training Materials* (New York: United Nations).

United Nations Department of Peacekeeping Operations (UN DPKO) (2008), *United Nations Peacekeeping Operations: Principles and Guidelines* ('Capstone Doctrine') (New York: United Nations).

Weaver, Catherine (2008), *Hypocrisy Trap: The World Bank and the Poverty of Reform* (Princeton, NJ: Princeton University Press).

Whalan, Jenni (2013), *How Peace Operations Work: Power, Legitimacy, and Effectiveness* (Oxford: Oxford University Press).

5

Constructivism

Marion Laurence and Emily Paddon Rhoads

Constructivism differs from some of the other theories explored in this volume because it is not a substantive theory of International Relations (IR), *per se*. Unlike realism, for example, it does not rest on explicit claims about which actors matter most in international politics, nor does it advance specific predictions about how those actors will behave (Finnemore and Sikkink 2001: 393). Instead, constructivism is a social theory, an approach to studying international relations that takes seriously the 'dynamic, contingent, and culturally based condition of the social world' (Adler 2013: 114). Like any group of scholars, constructivists disagree about exact definitions and the relative importance of core concepts. Still, they share a belief that the material world is not independent of our interpretations – that actors are shaped by their social milieu and that interests and identities cannot be taken for granted (Finnemore and Sikkink 2001: 394). They also share an analytical toolbox, which includes concepts like norms, culture, and identity.

Constructivism's focus on 'the social' and particularly the role of norms explains why those who study UN peacekeeping have drawn extensively on insights offered by the approach. As discussed in the Introduction, UN peacekeeping has changed dramatically since it was 'invented' in the 1950s. It is impossible to make sense of these changes without paying close attention to the social, historical, and ideational context in which missions are deployed. What is more, international organisations (IOs) serve as both norm followers and norm promoters (Barnett and Finnemore 2004: 33; Park 2006: 343). Since the end of the Cold War, for example, the UN has embraced liberal norms around democracy and human rights (Paris 2004: 35). In addition to respecting the core peacekeeping norms of impartiality, consent, and the non-use of force except in self-defence, blue helmets are supposed to uphold cross-cutting thematic norms like gender equality, children's rights, and the protection of civilians (PoC) (UN DPKO 2008: 16). It makes sense, then, that peacekeeping scholars frequently use the constructivist toolbox to analyse the form, function, and activities of UN missions. These efforts have improved our understanding of the material and ideational factors that shape UN peacekeeping over time and within particular mission contexts. In this chapter we argue, however, that there is still unrealised potential here.

We begin with a brief discussion of constructivism's distinguishing characteristics and of how it has informed the existing literature on UN peacekeeping. We then use evidence from the UN mission in the Democratic Republic of Congo (MONUSCO) to illustrate three areas in which constructivism can deepen and enrich understanding of UN peacekeeping, and to demonstrate how the study of UN peace operations can contribute to wider debates in the field of IR. The first area is a micro-level focus on how peacekeepers interpret and implement norms in practice. The second area emphasises interactions between UN missions and surrounding communities, especially peacekeepers' effect on local norms, identities, and cultures. The third involves macro-level analyses of peacekeeping's prospects and place in a shifting global order.

What is constructivism?

Constructivism is a social theory rather than a substantive theory of IR in so far as it does not rest on explicit claims about which actors matter most in international politics, nor does it advance predictions about how those actors will behave (Finnemore and Sikkink 2001: 393). Moving beyond the precepts of rationalism's methodological individualism, constructivism emerged in the late 1980s to advance a social understanding of international politics and rapidly staked out a place of prominence in the discipline.

Constructivists are united in their belief that 'we can't understand people, their interests, their discourses or behavior in isolation from their social context' (Barkin 2010: 58). Their scholarship is based on a deep appreciation for the intersubjective nature of reality and the ways in which agents and structures are interdependent and co-constitutive; 'that is, individuals and groups create and maintain these structures through their shared beliefs, practices and interactions. Critically, the observation of the socially constructed nature of reality provides a lens through which to understand political change' (Jackson 2009: 175). Indeed, it is precisely a belief in and desire for change that draws so many to constructivism. Consequently, scholars adopting this approach often focus on people-centred issues, like peacekeeping, and work at the 'hard edge of human misery' to identify conjectures propitious for change (Reus-Smit 2002: 500).

This emphasis on the social realm and the possibilities for change means that constructivist scholars focus on both the *regulative* effects of norms – how they order behaviours – and their *constitutive* effects.[1] The latter refers to the ways in which norms shape actors' identities and interests, 'create ... certain kinds of activity' and 'foster group identification' that allows for 'the coordination of ... social power' (Hurrell 2002: 145). This concern with the constitutive effects of norms is reflected in the definition of a norm adopted by most constructivists – 'collective expectations for the proper behavior of actors with *a given identity*' (Checkel 1998: 334).

Despite sharing core assumptions about the social nature of reality, constructivist scholarship displays considerable heterogeneity.

A common distinction is between 'positivist' and interpretivist or 'post-positivist' approaches.[2] The positivist approach emerged in the 1990s as a direct challenge to rationalism. Those who adopt a positivist epistemology maintain 'that the socially constructed international system contains patterns that are amenable to generalisation and [to] falsifiable hypotheses' (Hurd 2008: 307). Consequently, scholars within this approach tend to conceive of norms as stable. They focus on the structuring power of norms: how they emerge and shape state interests and behaviour. To establish that the 'logic of appropriateness' is as important as the 'logic of consequences', scholars of this approach have tended to select 'hard' test cases, such as state security, in pursuit of which actors arguably have a strong material interest to act one way, but instead opt to behave according to what is deemed morally appropriate.[3] By adopting a positivist epistemology, scholars within this approach were able to enter successfully into debates with rationalists, catapulting them to a place of prominence within mainstream IR.

The assumptions adopted by positivists in order to explain behaviour – namely, that norms are stable and unchanged by the interpreter – has however attracted criticism from fellow constructivists who contend that a social ontology is incongruent with an epistemology that rests on a separation between an external world and interpretations of that world by individuals (Fierke 2007). To that end, interpretative or post-positivist constructivism, the second approach, has been less concerned with engaging rationalists. Those who subscribe to this approach eschew the goal of causal explanation. Instead they trace the instability of norms across contexts, as well as the malleability of social understandings and structures. They reconceptualise the interplay between institutions, identities, and interests to give greater prominence to individual agency. The focus is more on processes of interpretation and the fact that the intersubjective dimension of norms may produce changes in the meaning of a norm or in strengthening or weakening of the norm itself.

Constructivism and UN peacekeeping

When constructivism first 'arrived' in the field of IR, scholars looked primarily at how norms, identity, and culture shape the behaviour of states (see Finnemore and Sikkink 1998: 893; Jepperson et al. 1996: 33–4). Over time, though, they expanded their focus to encompass IOs, treating them as actors deserving of attention in their own right (Barnett and Finnemore 1999: 700). This, in turn, led them to explore the ways in which ideational factors shape IO-led activities like UN peacekeeping.[4] To date, these analyses have usually followed one of two paths. Some scholars focus on pressures emanating from outside the UN – on the ways in which norms, culture, and identity shape peacekeeping from the outside in. Others focus on intersubjective knowledge within the UN itself, analysing how it affects the form, function, and activities of UN peacekeeping missions.[5] Examples of the former include Roland Paris's work on UN peace operations and the rise of liberal peacebuilding. Paris argues that 'global culture' shapes peacekeeping in fundamental ways. Peacekeeping actors and member states are 'predisposed to develop and implement strategies that conform with the norms of global culture, and they are disinclined to pursue strategies that deviate from those norms' (Paris 2003: 442–3). In substantive terms, this means that peacekeeping agencies demonstrate a marked preference for political and economic liberalisation. Paris finds that, after the end of the Cold War, liberal democracy emerged as the only mode of governance with broad ideological legitimacy. Peacekeeping policy mirrored this cultural shift, and peacekeepers became active proponents of liberal democratic institutions and values (Paris 2003, 2004).

Paris is not the only scholar to look at how norms emanating from outside the UN affect the behaviour of peacekeepers. Annika Björkdahl (2006: 214) takes a similar approach, arguing that UN missions provide the international community with channels for norm diffusion. Whilst peacekeepers can challenge and transform prevailing norms through practice, a mission's form and function tend to reflect the 'international normative context' in which it is deployed.

Peacekeeping scholars have also drawn on constructivist insights to show how internal dynamics affect the form and function of UN peace operations.[6] Barnett and Finnemore were among the first to do this, showing that IO behaviour – including behaviour that seems dysfunctional – is often a product of 'internally generated cultural forces' (Barnett and Finnemore 1999: 702). They argue that IOs' bureaucratic character predisposes them to certain 'pathologies'. The UN's commitment to rule-following, for example, may lead peacekeepers to act in ways that are ultimately self-defeating. Barnett and Finnemore find that the Secretariat's commitment to consent and impartiality contributed to peacekeeping failures in Rwanda and the former Yugoslavia. Its unwavering commitment to these rules created an organisational culture where it was 'tolerable, and even desirable, to disregard mass violations of human rights' (Barnett and Finnemore 2004: 155).

Silke Weinlich (2014: 218–19) builds on findings like this by taking a closer look at how the Secretariat affects agenda-setting, policy formulation, and policy adoption in UN peace operations. Séverine Autesserre (2010: 30; 2009: 249; 2016) has also dissected the ways in which intersubjective knowledge circumscribes international peacebuilding. Drawing on evidence from the Democratic Republic of Congo (DRC), she shows that the dominant culture and 'discursive frames' among international peacebuilders shape their understanding of the strategies that are available to them. This undermines conflict-prevention efforts because it leads peacebuilders to ignore grassroots conflicts, even when they generate massive human-rights violations and fuel broader tensions. These scholars share a focus on ideational factors that operate within the UN bureaucracy or within communities of peacekeepers and peacebuilders.

This distinction between 'external' and 'internal' factors is analytically useful, but the divide is rarely clear or rigid in practice.

As Oksamytna and Karlsrud (Introduction, above) note, the governance of UN peacekeeping reflects the interests and priorities of many different actors. Cross-cutting norms like PoC – and expectations about how they should affect peacekeepers' day-to-day practices – also tend to evolve through a complex iterative process where 'external' actors interact with 'internal' ones (Karlsrud 2013a: 14–15). Some peacekeeping scholars bridge this divide by looking at how external factors interact with internal ones. For example, Karlsrud (2016: 2) uses the concept of 'linked ecologies' to explain how actors moving between posts with the UN, think tanks, non-governmental organisations (NGOs), academia, and member states can form 'policy alliances' and drive normative change in peace operations. More recently, Andersen has looked at normative disagreements between member states and the UN's peace bureaucracy, linking them to wider changes in the 'global political *Zeitgeist*' (Andersen 2018: 9). She finds that international civil servants are 'pushing back' against member states' attempts to 'militarise' peacekeeping – a move they view as a challenge to the 'foundational assumptions that underpin the identity of the UN peace bureaucracy and its understanding of the "proper" role of UN peacekeeping' (Andersen 2018: 2, 6). These internal disagreements are, in her view, symptoms of shifting norms and a global order that is 'increasingly in flux' (Andersen 2018: 19). Both of these scholars draw on constructivist concepts – including norms and identity – to explore interactions between the many internal and external actors who affect the form, functions, and evolution of UN peacekeeping.

It should be clear from the discussion above that peacekeeping scholars have been drawn to the tools and concepts offered by constructivism to improve our understanding of UN missions. Still, we argue that there are areas where constructivism remains especially relevant. Heeding Paris's call for peacekeeping research that investigates dynamics at both the macro- and micro-levels, in what follows we identify three directions for future research using the

UN mission in the DRC (MONUSCO) as an illustrative case study (Paris 2014: 501).

UN peacekeeping in the Democratic Republic of Congo

The United Nations Mission in the DRC (MONUC/MONUSCO) was first deployed in late 1999, three years before the formal end of Congo's epic war.[7] The mission is the UN's largest and most expensive peacekeeping operation to date, and over the last two decades it has been at the forefront of new peacekeeping practices and norms (e.g. protection of civilians, stabilisation). Its ambition and authorised robustness have steadily increased, largely in response to continued violence and instability in the country. In 2008, under Resolution 1856, MONUC became the first mission to operate with a mandate that designated PoC as the highest priority.[8] And in 2013, the Council deployed the Force Intervention Brigade (FIB), a specialised unit within MONUSCO, authorised to take offensive military action to 'neutralise' and 'disarm' rebel groups (UN Security Council 2013: 7–8). The mission has also been a driving force behind the development of innovative peacekeeping practices, and operational mechanisms and guidance developed by MONUC/MONUSCO have been replicated in other mission contexts.[9]

Yet these ambitious plans and policies have been inconsistently implemented in practice: as much as the mission has been lauded for its innovation and celerity, it has been lambasted for what many have seen as its ineffectiveness, impotence, and inconsistent implementation of its mandate. After two decades of UN involvement, both the country and the mission are in a precarious state. An array of armed groups remains deeply ensconced in the eastern part of the country and continues to threaten civilians whom peacekeepers are charged with protecting. Armed conflict and intercommunal tensions have arisen in previously stable areas.[10] Peacekeepers have been killed and injured in some of the worst attacks against the UN in recent history.[11] And the government has spent much of the last two years in the throes of a constitutional crisis as Kabila's oppressive regime clings to power, forestalling elections that were due to take place in 2016 (Human Rights Watch 2018). For millions of Congolese, the future is bleak.

The protracted nature of instability in Congo, as well as the mission's scope and scale, has attracted scholarly interest. Nonetheless, there are still important issues worthy of study that are relevant to other missions, and for which constructivism provides analytical purchase.

First, at the more micro-level, gaps remain in our understanding of peacekeeping practice and specifically how norms get interpreted and implemented within and across the mission. Peacekeeping is supposed to be a quintessentially norm-governed activity. Yet the exact meaning and requirements of a norm are always contested (Krook and True 2010: 122–3; Wiener 2004: 191–2; Stimmer and Wisken 2019). Even a norm like impartiality – long part of the 'holy trinity' of guiding norms for peacekeeping – can be reinterpreted over time and in particular places (Paddon Rhoads 2016: 48–52). A constructivist lens can help us understand the process by which norms shape peacekeepers' day-to-day practices in Congo and beyond, and the ways in which those practices affect broader processes of norm contestation.[12]

This is particularly relevant in a context like Congo, where the record of peacekeeping practice is highly variable. The mission has, for example, used force to protect civilians at particular junctures throughout its history – sometimes for sustained periods of time. However, this stands in marked contrast to instances where peacekeepers with knowledge of an attack or imminent attack have failed to protect civilians within their area of deployment. What is more, certain troop-contributing countries (TCCs) appear to be more reluctant to engage in particular practices than others (Paddon Rhoads 2016: chapter 4). Over the last decade, the mission in Congo has seen the increasing prevalence of national caveats, a *de facto* dual line of command – such that the advice offered from TCCs' capitals conflicts with directives issued by senior mission officials such as the Force Commander.

These dynamics raise a series of questions that constructivism is well placed to shed light on. Why do certain TCCs scupper norm implementation and/or adopt their own alternative conception of norms such as protection? What is the role of national military culture? How much contestation is the result of contingent factors? Do some national peacekeeping contingents undergo a process of socialisation within particular missions such that their interpretation of a norm and related practices change over time? The increased involvement of regional states over the last five years as part of the FIB as well as the fact that several countries (e.g. India and Pakistan) have fielded forces in Congo for almost two decades potentially provides fruitful avenues for investigating these dynamics.

The mission in Congo also highlights the need for greater understanding of the role that particular individuals (e.g. Special Representatives of the Secretary-General and Force Commanders) have in shaping a mission's strategic culture and processes of norm development and implementation. According to Patrick Cammaert, a Dutch general who commanded UN troops in eastern Congo, rules of engagement provide general parameters but they 'do not cover each and every event or incident' (Cammaert 2007: 6). This means that senior mission leaders often serve as 'norm arbitrators' who must weigh competing norms and interpret their mandates accordingly (Karlsrud 2013b: 537). For example, Lieutenant-General Carlos Alberto dos Santos Cruz is known for his willingness to use force and his expansive interpretation of MONUSCO's protection mandate during his time as Force Commander (Jenks 2016: 719–21). This is an area where arguably peacekeeping has just as much to contribute to constructivist theorising. Kathryn Sikkink (in Checkel 2018: 154) is one of several prominent constructivist scholars to call for greater 'agentic constructivism', a theoretical approach 'concerned with the micro-foundations of creating and constituting new actors and new conditions of possibility. It looks at those parts of social processes where new actors take on and challenge (and sometimes change) existing logics of appropriateness.'

Second, and related, is the issue of how peacekeepers shape the 'local' and the myriad effects of a mission like that in Congo on local norms, identities, and cultures. As constructivist scholars have aptly argued in recent years, actors in postcolonial states are not merely 'norm takers' despite often being portrayed as such. They are 'normative actors' as well. As Andrew Grant (2018: 255–63) notes, they 'have established, promoted, contested, modified, and resisted various transnational norms – thereby embedding themselves in the processes of international change'. What is more, they underscore the need to take seriously the local normative context and the ways in which it interacts with the transnational. For example, as the Congo mission has pursued more participatory and community-based approaches to protection, questions arise as to the impact of the UN's protection mandate on local protection norms and practices, including how people understand what it means to be safe. Has the mission's approach to protection influenced how individuals and communities self-protect? Similarly, how has the mission's mandate and peacekeeper engagement influenced armed group behaviour through, for example, processes of socialisation and/or norm instrumentalisation?

Finally, at the more macro-level, is the need for a deeper and more honest understanding of the mission, its prospects, and place in a shifting global order. Constructivism's attention to social and historical context is more important than ever, especially when it comes to understanding the present and future of missions like that in Congo. If peacekeeping reflects the prevailing *Zeitgeist*, scholars must have analytical tools that allow them to describe and track changes in that *Zeitgeist* while also taking material considerations into account. After two decades of deployment and the mission's emphasis on strengthening the capacity of the state, scholars would do well to interrogate the nature of the state in Congo. Are order and stability prioritised over more liberal conceptions of the state that emphasise political and civil rights? What are the consequences of this shift? Is it a reflection of global power shifts in an era of resurgent sovereignty? If, as Roland Paris states, peacekeeping is 'constitutive of emerging global norms', how does the mission in the DRC shed light on global order? How does the involvement of particular actors like China, which is a rising peacekeeping player in Congo and beyond, shape dynamics? Similarly to Finnemore's (2003: 4) seminal constructivist study of norms related to military intervention, peacekeeping scholars should assess the seemingly 'obvious' motivations and interests that guide UN peace operations in light of the evolving normative context in which missions are deployed. Those studying the UN's shift towards 'stabilisation' operations – and peacekeepers' increasing focus on the restoration of state authority – have started down this path (de Coning et al. 2017: 4–6). Karlsrud (2019: 1) argues, for example, that experiences like the 2008 financial crisis and long military engagements in Afghanistan have undermined Western states' commitment to liberal peacebuilding and made them more willing to task peacekeepers with *de facto* counter-insurgency operations. Questions persist, however, about the degree to which peacekeeping practices mirror shifting power dynamics and normative changes at the macro-level and this remains an important direction for future research.

Conclusion

Constructivism includes a diverse array of positivist and interpretivist scholarship, but its adherents share a belief that people, their interests, and their behaviour are shaped by social context (Finnemore and Sikkink 2001: 393). Constructivists explore the ways in which agents and structures are interdependent and co-constitutive, and their work highlights the impact of norms, culture, and identity in international politics. This historical focus on norms – and on the processes by which they emerge, spread, and evolve over time – helps explain why scholars have drawn extensively on constructivist insights when studying UN peace operations. Peacekeeping is a norm-governed activity *par excellence*. Blue helmets are expected to uphold core peacekeeping norms like consent, impartiality, and non-use of force except in self-defence. They are also tasked with implementing cross-cutting norms like gender equality and protection of civilians, even if they often fall short in practice (UN DPKO 2008: 16; Beber et al. 2016: 1). To date, most peacekeeping scholars have used constructivist insights to study external pressures like 'global culture', to explore the impact of intersubjective knowledge within the UN itself, or to look at interactions between the two and at how they inhibit and enable certain patterns of action among peacekeepers (Barnett and Finnemore 1999: 702; Paris 2003: 441).

Existing scholarship has enriched our understanding of UN peacekeeping in many ways, but there are three areas where constructivism remains especially relevant. First, gaps remain in our understanding of the relationship between peacekeepers' day-to-day practices and the norms that guide UN peace operations. Peacekeeping scholars should devote more attention to the manifold ways in which mission personnel implement – and reinterpret – norms at the micro-level. Second, the constructivist toolkit is well-suited to answering questions about how UN peace operations interact with the communities that host them. Specifically, it can shed light on the many ways in which a peacekeeping mission reshapes local norms, identities, and cultures, and vice versa. Finally, constructivism's attention to social and historical context helps scholars study the ways in which peacekeeping practices mirror – and contribute to – shifting power dynamics and normative changes at the macro-level. Together, these areas for future research suggest that a constructivist lens will continue to yield important insights about the form, function, and purpose of UN peace operations.

Notes

1 The distinction between regulatory norms and constitutive norms has a long lineage in philosophy and jurisprudence. E.g. Rawls (1955).

2 A plethora of labels exist to capture this epistemological distinction: 'modern' versus 'postmodern', 'naturalists' versus 'anti-naturalists', 'conventional' versus 'consistent' or 'critical', 'thin' versus 'thick'. See Klotz (2001: 223–5); Price and Reus-Smit (1998: 259– 94).

3 'Logic of appropriateness' is behaviour that occurs in accordance with legitimated norms. 'Logic of consequences' is behaviour that is based on cost-benefit calculations to maximise individual utility. March and Olsen (1989).

4 Constructivists do not deny of impact of material factors; they often look at how material and ideational factors interact. Within the field of IR, however, constructivists' focus on intersubjective knowledge distinguishes them from scholars whose explanations are materialist and individualist. Finnemore and Sikkink (2001: 393).

5 This two paths mirror Barnett and Finnemore's (1999: 717) distinction between theories of IO behaviour that focus on internal or organisational factors and those that privilege external or 'environmental' factors.

6 There is considerable overlap between this strand of constructivism and sociological institutionalism. See von Billerbeck (Chapter 4 above) for a more detailed discussion of the latter.

7 In 2010, the mission was renamed the UN Organisation Stabilisation Mission in the Democratic Republic of Congo (MONUSCO).

8 The Resolution was also unprecedented in specifically authorising the use of force to ensure the protection of civilians 'under imminent threat of physical violence … from *any* of the parties engaged in the conflict' (UN Security Council 2008).

9 For example, both the Joint Protection Teams and the Community Liaison Assistants were developed in Congo to improve the mission's ability to understand and respond to threats against civilians. Additionally, the UN's Human Rights Due Diligence Policy was based on guidance developed by the mission in Congo. See, for example, UN (2013).

10 For information on armed group activity, see The Kivu Security Tracker, a joint project of the Congo Research Group, based at New York University's Center on International Cooperation, and Human Rights Watch: https://kivusecurity.org/map.

11 Al Jazeera, 'Seven UN peacekeepers killed in fight against DRC rebels', 15 November 2018, available at: www.aljazeera.com/news/2018/11/peacekeepers-killed-fight-drc-rebels-181115191128456.html; Samuel Oakford, 'What one of the deadliest ever attacks on UN peacekeepers means for Congo', 8 December 2017, IRIN News, available at: https://www.irinnews.org/news/2017/12/08/

Constructivism

what-one-deadliest-ever-attacks-un-peacekeepers-means-congo; Colum Lynch, 'Congolese cover-up', 27 November 2018, available at: https://foreignpolicy.com/2018/11/27/congolese-cover-up-un-congo-murder-zaida-catalan-michael-sharp (all accessed 30 January 2020).

12 In some cases, this may mean incorporating insights from practice theory. See Bode (Chapter 6 below).

References

Adler, Emanuel (2013), 'Constructivism in international relations: Sources, contributions, and debates', in Walter Carlsnaes, Thomas Risse, and Beth A. Simmons (eds), *Handbook of International Relations*, 2nd ed. (London: Sage), 112–44.

Andersen, Louise Riis (2018), 'The HIPPO in the room: The pragmatic push-back from the UN peace bureaucracy against the militarization of UN peacekeeping', *International Affairs*, 94:2: 1–19.

Autesserre, Séverine (2009), 'Hobbes and the Congo: Frames, local violence, and international intervention', *International Organization*, 63:2: 249–80.

Autesserre, Séverine (2010), *The Trouble with the Congo: Local Violence and the Failure of International Peacebuilding* (Cambridge and New York: Cambridge University Press).

Autesserre, Séverine (2016), 'The responsibility to protect in Congo: The failure of grassroots prevention', *International Peacekeeping*, 23:1: 29–51.

Barkin, Samuel (2010), *Realist Constructivism: Rethinking International Relations Theory* (Cambridge: Cambridge University Press).

Barnett, Michael N., and Martha Finnemore (1999), 'The politics, power, and pathologies of international organizations', *International Organization*, 53:4, 699–732.

Barnett, Michael N., and Martha Finnemore (2004), *Rules for the World: International Organizations in Global Politics* (Ithaca, NY: Cornell University Press).

Beber, Bernd, Michael J. Gilligan, Jenny Guardado, and Sabrina Karim (2016), 'Peacekeeping, compliance with international norms, and transactional sex in Monrovia, Liberia', *International Organization*, 71:1: 1–30.

Björkdahl, Annika (2006), 'Promoting norms through peacekeeping: UNPREDED and conflict prevention', *International Peacekeeping*, 13:2, 214–28.

Cammaert, Patrick (2007), *Learning to Use Force on the Hoof in Peacekeeping: Reflections on the Experience of Monuc's Eastern Division* (Pretoria: Institute for Security Studies).

Checkel, Jeffrey (1998), 'The constructivist turn in International Relations theory', *World Politics*, 50:2: 324–48.

Checkel, Jeffrey (2018), 'Methods in constructivist approaches', in Alexandra Gheciu and William C. Wohlforth (eds), *The Oxford Handbook of*

International Security, available at: www.oxfordhandbooks.com/view/10.1093/oxfordhb/9780198777854.001.0001/oxfordhb-9780198777854-e-11 (accessed 31 July 2019).

de Coning, Cedric, Chiyuki Aoi, and John Karlsrud (2017), 'Towards a United Nations stabilization doctrine - stabilization as an emerging UN practice', in Cedric de Coning, Chiyuki Aoi, and John Karlsrud (eds), *UN Peacekeeping Doctrine in a New Era: Adapting to Stabilization, Protection and New Threats* (Abingdon: Routledge), 288–310.

Fierke, Karin M. (2007), 'Constructivism', in Tim Dunne, Milja Kurki, and Steve Smith (eds), *International Relations Theories: Discipline and Diversity* (Oxford: Oxford University Press), 166–84.

Finnemore, Martha (2003), *The Purpose of Intervention: Changing Beliefs about the Use of Force* (Ithaca, NY, and London: Cornell University Press).

Finnemore, Martha, and Kathryn Sikkink (1998), 'International norm dynamics and political change', *International Organization*, 52:4, 887–917.

Finnemore, Martha, and Kathryn Sikkink (2001), 'Taking stock: The constructivist research program in International Relations and comparative politics', *Annual Review of Political Science*, 4, 391–416.

Grant, Andrew (2018), 'Agential constructivism and change in world politics', *International Security Review*, 20:2, 255–63.

Human Rights Watch (2018), 'DR Congo: Opposition under assault', 28 August 2018, available at: www.hrw.org/news/2018/08/28/dr-congo-opposition-under-assault (accessed 28 January 2020).

Hurd, Ian (2008), 'Constructivism', in Christian Reus-Smit and Duncan Snidal (eds), *The Oxford Handbook of International Relations*, vol. 5 (Oxford: Oxford University Press), 298–316.

Hurrell, Andrew (2002), 'Norms and ethics in International Relations', in Walter Carlsnaes, Thomas Risse-Kappen, and Beth Simmons (eds), *Handbook of International Relations* (London: Sage), 137–56.

Jackson, Richard (2009), 'Constructivism and conflict resolution', in Jacob Bercovitch, Victor Kremenyuk, and I. William Zartmann (eds), *The Sage Handbook on Conflict Resolution* (London: Sage), 172–89.

Jenks, Chris (2016), 'United Nations peace operations: Creating space for peace', in Geoffrey S. Corn, Rachel E. VanLandingham, and Shane R. Reeves (eds), *U.S. Military Operations: Law, Policy, and Practice* (Oxford and New York: Oxford University Press), 691–728.

Jepperson, Ronald L., Alexander Wendt, and Peter Katzenstein (1996), 'Norms, identity, and culture in national security', in Peter Katzenstein (ed.), *The Culture of National Security: Norms and Identity in World Politics* (New York: Columbia University Press), 33–75.

Karlsrud, John (2013a), 'Responsibility to protect and theorising normative change in international organisations: From Weber to the sociology of professions', *Global Responsibility to Protect*, 5:1, 3–27.

Constructivism

Karlsrud, John (2013b), 'Special Representatives of the Secretary-General as norm arbitrators? Understanding bottom-up authority in UN peacekeeping', *Global Governance*, 19:4, 525–44.

Karlsrud, John (2016), *Norm Change in International Relations: Linked Ecologies in UN Peacekeeping Operations* (Abingdon: Routledge).

Karlsrud, John (2019), 'From liberal peacebuilding to stabilization and counterterrorism', *International Peacekeeping*, 26:1: 1–21.

Klotz, Audie (2001), 'Can we speak a common language?', in Karin M. Fierke and Knud Erik Jørgensen (eds), *Constructing International Relations: The Next Generation* (Armonk, NY: M.E. Sharpe), 223–35.

Krook, Mona Lena, and Jacqui True (2010), 'Rethinking the life cycles of international norms: The United Nations and the global promotion of gender equality', *European Journal of International Relations*, 18:1, 103–27.

March, James G., and Johan P. Olsen (1989), *Rediscovering Institutions: The Organizational Basis of Politics* (New York: The Free Press).

Paddon Rhoads, Emily (2016), *Taking Sides in Peacekeeping: Impartiality and the Future of the United Nations* (Oxford: Oxford University Press).

Paris, Roland (2003), 'Peacekeeping and the constraints of global culture', *European Journal of International Relations*, 9:3, 441–73.

Paris, Roland (2004), *At War's End: Building Peace after Civil Conflict* (New York: Cambridge University Press).

Paris, Roland (2014), 'The geopolitics of peace operations: A research agenda', *International Peacekeeping*, 21:4, 501–8.

Park, Susan (2006), 'Theorizing norm diffusion within international organizations', *International Politics*, 43:3: 342–61.

Price, Richard, and Christian Reus-Smit (1998), 'Dangerous liaisons? Critical international theory and constructivism', *European Journal of International Relations*, 4:3: 259–94.

Rawls, John (1955), 'Two concepts of rules', *The Philosophical Review*, 64:1: 3–32.

Reus-Smit, Christian (2002), 'Imagining society: Constructivism and the English School', *The British Journal of Politics and International Relations*, 4:3, 487–509.

Stimmer, Anette, and Lea Wisken (2019), 'Symposium introduction – The dynamics of dissent: When actions are louder than words', *International Affairs*, 95:3, 515–33.

United Nations (2013), *Lessons Learned: Report on the Joint Protection Team (JPT) Mechanism in Monusco. Strengths, Challenges, and Considerations for Replicating JPTs in Other Missions* (New York: DPKO/DFS-OHCHR).

United Nations Department of Peacekeeping Operations (UN DPKO) (2008), *United Nations Peacekeeping Operations: Principles and Guidelines* ('Capstone Doctrine') (New York: United Nations).

United Nations Security Council (2008), 'Resolution 1856', S/RES/1856.

United Nations Security Council (2013), 'Resolution 2098', S/RES/2098 (2013).

Weinlich, Silke (2014), *The UN Secretariat's Influence on the Evolution of Peacekeeping* (Basingstoke: Palgrave Macmillan).

Wiener, Antje (2004), 'Contested compliance: Interventions on the normative structure of world politics', *European Journal of International Relations*, 10:2: 189–234.

6

Practice theories

Ingvild Bode

Analysing peacekeeping from the vantage point of practice theories comes across as almost intuitive. After all, peacekeeping has long been understood as a *practice*, meaning that it is not grounded in the UN Charter but has evolved and continues to evolve in changing social and historical contexts and how they are interpreted and performed by various actors across the UN and its member states. This has led to significant shifts in our understanding of what peacekeeping means and what its main purpose is, frequently captured with the image of succeeding yet overlapping generations of peacekeeping. Therefore, peacekeeping is a prime example of a 'patterned action in social context' (Leander 2008: 18), to use a definition of practices.

Still, applications of practice theories to analyse peacekeeping in its multiple facets have only recently made conceptual headway. The reasons for this are threefold: first, scholarly literature on peacekeeping was initially theory-averse and later on primarily concerned with questions of effectiveness, which do not lend themselves neatly to the kind of critical, sociologically inspired analysis that practice theories are grounded in. Second, practice theories are a comparatively recent addition to the International Relations (IR) canon and are still in the process of being recognised as a diverse and dynamic theoretical programme. As I will argue, only once practice theory was increasingly understood as practice theories to denote their plural theoretical heritage and areas of application, thereby going beyond its initial exclusive association with tight readings of Pierre Bourdieu's works, did contributions based on their insights start to gain significant ground in analyses of peacekeeping. And third, practice theories seem to correspond particularly well to trends of analytically invested studies of peacekeeping starting with critical accounts of liberal peacebuilding, the local turn, and the growing interest in micro-dynamics of peacekeeping missions.

What is further remarkable about this attention spurt is that practice theories seem to speak in particular to scholars with practitioner backgrounds in peacekeeping, highlighting the significance of background knowledge. Indeed, as Autesserre argues, they appear to capture the fluid associations of competence and change that are at the heart of understanding what peacekeeping is (2014a) and allow us to go beyond 'armchair analysis' towards analysing social life outside of discourse (Neumann 2002: 628).

In the following, I provide a brief summary of practice theories and their core assumptions and then move on towards demonstrating how practice theories have been used to understand such diverse processes in peacekeeping as its implementation across different peacekeeping contexts, how it intersects with norm research to understand evolving understandings of fundamental peacekeeping principles (e.g. impartiality), and more fundamental problems associated with the phenomenon of background knowledge and knowledge hierarchies. I will then turn towards a more detailed case study of the protection of civilians in peacekeeping mandates to demonstrate and finish with offering a critical conclusion.

A very brief introduction to practice theories

Practice theories are firmly rooted in the constructivist research programme of IR. Indeed, constructivists have long considered practices as fundamental for understanding the make-up of social life: 'the international system, usually described as being anarchical because it lacks a central government, is still a system whose rules are made and reproduced by human *practices*' (Guzzini 2000: 155). Despite this constructivist provenance, practices have arguably remained analytically underspecified before becoming the central concept of IR's 'practice turn' from the mid-2000s onwards. Drawing on sociological and social theories, practice theories have developed into a dynamic and diverse theoretical agenda directing attention to the processes sustaining and therefore constituting international relations (Bode 2018a). In this, practice theories promise to offer novel accounts of the perennial questions of continuity and change in IR by concentrating on 'what makes the world hang together' in the everyday (Bueger and Gadinger 2015: 449). They focus on showcasing what (individual) diplomats, soldiers, UN officials, and NGO representatives are *doing*, how they are doing it, and why.

A focus on what is performative and practical in international politics as opposed to what is said, discursively represented, or even purely materially defined is fundamental to all iterations of practice theories. Yet, practice theories have likewise become increasingly diverse and multifaceted, depending on which aspects of social theory they draw most inspiration from. Commonly used approaches range, for example, from the praxeology of Bourdieu (Adler-Nissen 2013; Pouliot 2010; Bigo 2007; Leander 2011), to communities of practice (Adler 2005, 2008; Bueger 2013), and narrative takes on practice (Gadinger 2016; Bode 2014; Neumann 2012). Further, practice theories can be usefully differentiated into critical and pragmatic schools with the former concentrating primarily on repetition or reproduction and the latter on fluctuation or contingency (Bueger and Gadinger 2015: 456). While some scholars refer to them as '(international) practice theory', I seek to highlight the inherent diversity of this conceptual programme by referring to practice theories in the plural.

An early influential attempt at synthetising practice theories in the critical tradition defined practices as 'socially meaningful patterns of action, which, in being performed more or less competently, simultaneously embody, act out, and possibly reify background knowledge and discourse in and on the material world' (Adler and Pouliot 2011: 4). Two key notions included in this definition merit closer examination as they have come to feature prominently in early conceptualisations of practices: background knowledge and competence or competent performance.

In 'situat[ing] knowledge in practice' (Bueger and Gadinger 2015: 453), practice theories foreground background knowledge as essential for informing how and why actors engage in patterned actions. Practices are therefore considered to be routine ways of doing things based on actualising forms of habitual, background knowledge in context. Rather than originating in deliberative and reflective processes of decision-making, this reflexive element of practices highlights that actors are often hard-pressed to formulate on what basis they decide to engage in specific practices. Different forms of background knowledge are inherently connected to being part of particular (professional or cultural) communities and contexts. Acquired largely unconsciously over long stretches of times, different types of suitable background knowledge specific to social settings allow actors to perform practices *competently* – in other words, recognised as socially meaningful and 'appropriate'. The competent performance of practices therefore rests on actors' background knowledge, their 'inarticulate feel for the game' (Pouliot 2016: 73; see also Bueger and Gadinger 2015: 453; Kuus 2015: 369). This reasoning is closely connected to sociologist Pierre Bourdieu's analytical notion of habitus. Habitus is embodied personal history, social background and culture, working as an internalised 'generating principle of practices' (Bourdieu 1996: 161). Deeply ingrained in the actors, it functions 'unthinkingly', suggesting 'fitting' practices for actors to perform if they dispose of the necessary, incorporated background knowledge (Bode 2015: 37–8). Therefore, habitus represents a negative freedom as the range of competent practices actors can perform is limited: 'Habitus makes it possible to freely produce all thoughts, all perceptions and all actions which are inscribed within the inherent limits of its particular conditions of production' (Bourdieu 1980: 92). The functioning of this pre-reflexive habitus is often illustrated with sports situations where players exhibit an intuitive sense for the 'immanent necessity of the game' (Bourdieu 1987: 81).

Habitus as the incorporation of various forms of useful capital (e.g. social, cultural, economic, or symbolic capital) turned into background knowledge (Bourdieu 1986) and its connection to competent performances also foregrounds the unequal distribution of resources and, as a consequence, opportunities. In other words, they help us in 'identify[ing] relations of power' (Holmes 2019: 58). Actors performing practices are therefore not placed on an equal playing field but are, instead, embedded within socially ingrained positional hierarchies. While this does not mean that actors occupying a position of lower status are passive, they are at a disadvantage in terms of being seen as competent performers (Bode 2018b: 296; Holmes 2019: 59).

Practice theories are therefore to be credited with bringing competent performances based on background knowledge to the wide attention of IR scholarship, not least because many empirical observations point to the veracity or applicability of this argument (Hopf 2010: 539–40). Yet, the 'enchanted' relationship that results from actors performing practices *purely* on the basis of background knowledge has also been rightly criticised. The 'feel for the game' imagery prioritises one type of social situation at the expense of others that require actors to reflectively deliberate within a longer time frame (Bode 2018b: 296). In other words, instances of deliberation persist in how actors perform practices. We would thus do greater justice to taking the practical element of IR seriously if we recognised practices as based on both reflexive and reflective reasoning (Ralph and Gifkins 2017; Bode and Karlsrud 2019; Engell 2018).

Practices can be analysed at different levels of aggregation, that is as the output of collective or individual actors. As practices are patterned actions, their competence is typically negotiated in *relational* conceptions of agency: 'practices are social possessions and their skilful performance has to be recognized by a community of reference' (Pouliot 2016: 56; see also Bueger 2015: 5). At the same time, pragmatic versions of practice theories are also interested in creative adaptiveness of (Adler-Nissen 2014; Zarakol 2011) as well as the 'critical capacity of ordinary actors' (Gadinger 2016: 188; see also Boltanski 2011; Certeau 1984). As it makes a vast difference who performs practices, it is logical to take these considerations down to the individual level. When we consider individual socialisation processes as varied and therefore background knowledge as heterogeneous, we can therefore consider the competence of individual performers of practices as influenced by how well they are able to activate different context-based and situated-based parts of that knowledge (Bode 2018b: 299).

In sum, practice theories turn our attention to the day-to-day enactment of international politics through its actors – and allow us to capture how these practices contribute to making up all significant social structures and processes from order to change, from power to knowledge. They allow us to access competent performances of reflexive and reflective practices in hierarchically structured social fields by individual and collective actors.

Practice theories and peacekeeping literature

The basic premises of practice theories as a bottom-up approach are in line with the objectives of both the critical literature on the local turn in peacebuilding literature and the connected, increasing interest in investigating micro-dynamics of the peacekeeping arrangement at both field and headquarters levels.

The local turn arguably already started with critical investigations of peacebuilding in the mid-1990s. In its second generation, an ever-expanding range of tasks assigned to peacekeepers from election monitoring in Namibia to providing an interim state-like international administration in East Timor brought UN peacekeepers into much more substantial and longer-term contact with local populations in host countries. Further, in contrast to the restricted, often purely military activities of acting as a buffer between previously warring state parties that had characterised peacekeeping's first generation, peacebuilding now came with a distinct liberal democratic agenda. This changing character of peacekeeping expanded the actors involved in peacekeeping beyond the military to the police but also a range of civilians including diplomats, civil society representatives, and UN officials. With the introduction of the protection of civilians as a further key norm for peacekeepers to implement from 1999 onwards, peacekeeping became increasingly diversified. We currently see the coexistence of peacekeeping operations attached to the different generations, and studies point to a wide range of different dynamics when it comes to implementing (often vague, 'Christmas tree') mandates issued by the UN Security Council. To give an example, a 2009 study on the protection of civilians in UN peace-keeping operations found that 'the UN Secretariat, troop- and police-contributing countries, host states, humanitarian actors, human rights professionals, and the missions themselves continue to struggle over what it means for a peacekeeping operation to protect civilians, in definition and practice' (Holt and Taylor 2009: 4). Such dynamics lend themselves to be studied through the lens of practice theories. In particular, practice theories have allowed scholars to capture the multitude of often fragmented perspectives and understandings that make up peacekeeping. Further, in bringing in considerations about fields of power and hierarchies, practice theories enable scholars to understand peacekeeping as a deeply political activity rather than as a technical policy instrument (Paddon Rhoads 2016: 8).

More specifically, notions such as background knowledge have been usefully deployed by scholars such as Autesserre to demonstrate the disconnects between UN headquarters understanding of peacekeeping and the field. Her influential book *Peaceland* details the adverse effects of a unified, hierarchically superiorly positioned background knowledge that international peacekeepers share (Autesserre 2014b). The background knowledge *peacelanders* share is full of cross-cutting comparisons across conflict zones and the never-ending search for a one-size-fits-all approach and 'best practices' that are applicable across the range of conflict settings that the UN is involved in. This systematically serves to undermine and devalue the kind of local and contingent knowledge of specific conflict contexts Autesserre identifies as fundamentally necessary to contribute to durable conflict resolution. Conceiving of peacekeeping as a practice that is negotiated in the everyday, Autesserre (2014b: 6) is primarily interested in how standard practices, that is 'routine activities that are socially meaningful and have an unthought character, shared habit, and dominant narratives, stories that people create to make sense of their lives and environments' shape peacekeeping and its effectiveness from the bottom up.

Many shared practices that have come to be definitive for what peacekeepers do (such as socialising only with international expatriates, living in compounds, having no knowledge of the local language, and high staff turnover) are shared across staggeringly different countries and conflict settings. They primarily serve to reinforce social positional hierarchies present between international peacekeepers and the local population in host countries. Autesserre therefore investigates how power is deeply embedded within the performance and interplay of peacekeeping practices by demonstrating the politics and adverse consequences of what is considered competent (background) knowledge in peacekeeping settings.

Other studies bring practice theories into conversation with (critical) norms research to understand and critically examine the practical application or implementation of fundamental peacekeeping norms (Karlsrud 2016; Laurence 2019; Paddon Rhoads 2016, 2019; Holmes 2019; Bode and Karlsrud 2019). This analytical conversation between practice theories and norms research has likewise gained significant attention within the wider IR literature as a dynamic approach to studying the emergence and evolution of normative content and meaning (Bode and Huelss 2018; Wiener 2018). Norms can be defined as an intersubjective standard of appropriate behaviour (based on Finnemore 1996: 22–3; Klotz 1995: 451; Zimmermann 2016: 98) that, in this case, guides peacekeeping, such as impartiality, consent, the protection of civilians, or human rights.

In a well-cited study, Paddon Rhoads examines the increasingly contested practices attached to impartiality and how they are gradually transforming this norm's basic meaning over time across the shift towards assertive liberal internationalism: 'Claims to impartial authority are no longer based exclusively on terms to which all parties consent. Instead, they are premised on a more ambitious and expansive set of human-rights-related norms, around which consensus is presumed but not always secured' (2016: 2). Following an unpacking of impartiality as a composite norm integrating substantive and procedural dimensions, Paddon Rhoads (2019: 3) studies how 'deep divisions on the substantive dimensions of the norm' come out in practices, analysed by way of rich interview material gathered with military and civilian peacekeeping personnel.

Studying norms via practices therefore makes visible the discontents that result from typically deeply ambiguous international norms at the heart of peacekeeping. Laurence's work on impartiality takes this a step further in arguing that looking towards practices 'also means recognizing that a norm's meaning is malleable and embedded in social practice' (2019: 4), leading to a practical proliferation of 'ways of being impartial' (Laurence 2019: 20). This supports critical scholarship on norms in IR (Krook and True 2012; Sandholtz 2008; Huelss 2017), as we see normative content manifesting and emerging through implementation practices, rather than considering norms (like the protection of civilians) as already 'fixed' or shared once they have been adopted and institutionalised in UNSC resolutions or other official UN documents. Laurence is able to show how the meaning of impartiality, as well as what counts as competent practices associated with the impartiality norm, are negotiated in practices across different UN field operations. This can help us to both understand and conceptualise the current uncertainty around pinning down the precise content of impartiality, as well as ongoing transformations of impartiality as a constitutive norm of UN peacekeeping.

Holmes's account of gender mainstreaming norms in peacekeeping training connects a conceptual focus on norms and practices with investigating the processes' inherent power dynamics (Holmes 2019). Following an explicitly feminist praxiography, Holmes explores habitus by way of naturalised subject positions such as gender that 'dominant actors may use … to regulate subordinated actors within the field' (Holmes 2019: 6). Such hierarchically mediated subject positions are included in peacekeeping training, leading peacekeeping personnel to act in accordance with them upon deployment in order to be perceived as performing practices competently and appropriately (Holmes 2019: 14). Typically, the scripted subject positions available to female peacekeepers in peacekeeping training, as demonstrated by Holmes's study of Rwandan peacekeeping training, follow narrow instrumentalist readings of gender mainstreaming, expecting 'women to perform as "female peacekeepers" to deliver specific mission objectives' on account of their gender that they are not necessarily specifically trained for (Holmes 2019: 16). At the same time, Holmes is careful not to treat the peacekeeping personnel she engages with as passive subjects, highlighting instead their sense of agency: 'these subjects are both compelled and choose to engage in norm implementation' when it comes to gender mainstreaming norms (Holmes 2019: 26).

Combining practice theories and critical norms research therefore allows garnering novel insights into peacekeeping's deeply political and power-infused implementation processes from the headquarters to the field and the local level.

Unpacking the implementation of the protection-of-civilians norm via practices

In principle, the protection of civilians (PoC) plays an increasing role in UN peacekeeping since its doctrinal failure of the 1990s. Now, 90 per cent of UN peacekeeping operations are mandated to include measures up to the use of force to protect civilians 'under imminent threat of physical violence' (Security Council 1999: para. 14). While PoC as a norm has been firmly institutionalised in UN peacekeeping practice (Breakey 2014; Hultman 2012), its implementation on the ground varies greatly and is subject to a vast number of different and often conflicting understandings (Holt and Taylor 2009). Further, a 2014 report on the implementation of PoC mandates found that the use of force as a last resort to protect civilians had been applied particularly inconsistently (UN Office of Internal Oversight Services 2014: 14).

My joint research with John Karlsrud has investigated this variation in implementation, using a combination of critical norms research and practice theories, by way of making three arguments. First, the ambiguous formulations of many core international norms, such as the protection of civilians, enable the continued existence of different and often conflicting understandings of what the PoC norm means. While ambiguity is often necessary for achieving compromise, it ultimately does not and cannot resolve debate about normative meaning, which is instead relegated to practices.

Second, different understandings of norms will become visible in (diverging) implementation practices (Bode and Karlsrud 2019). This observation becomes even more complex when we consider that actions in a peacekeeping setting are informed not only by a single norm but within conflictual norm-scapes populated by different norms associated with disparate understandings of appropriateness (Karlsrud 2016). In this way, depending on how an actor understands the PoC norm, their understanding may come into conflict with the three other fundamental norms of peacekeeping: impartiality, the limited use of force, and consent.

Three, we studied an under-examined group of actors when it comes to implementing the PoC norm – military advisers to the permanent delegations of the UN in New York: 'Military advisers do not only provide advice and analysis to the UNSC and conduct most of the negotiations in developing the doctrine for UN peace-keeping, but they are also involved in the planning, budgeting, implementation, and evaluation of operations' (Bode and Karlsrud 2019: 461). By understanding norm implementation of PoC as deeply political processes, we consider how military advisers perform practices by relying on diverse forms of background knowledge and how they compete for being recognised as competent performers, that is putting forward implementation policies that are intersub-jectively recognised as appropriate.

To assess and apply these analytical arguments, we collected novel empirical material from military advisers under the Chatham House Rule through three methods: an online survey, a half-day workshop, and follow-up interviews. In the following, I will summarise five of our key findings.

First, military advisers have fundamentally different understand-ings of even basic features of the PoC norm such as the common phrase 'protecting civilians from the imminent threat of physical violence' that has been used in 11 different peacekeeping mandates since 1999 from for example Sierra Leone, to Liberia, South Sudan, Mali, and Lebanon. Although this phrase strongly suggests the use of force as a last resort, many military advisers' responses avoided referring to this explicitly and instead focused on defining contours of protection or reflecting on what counts as an imminent threat.

Second, there is significant divergence about the relative impor-tance of the use of force as an important option for peacekeeping aimed at protecting civilians. While some military advisers viewed this as fundamental to the overall legitimacy and credibility of any peacekeeping missions ('It is the primary condition for effective protection of civilians mandate implementation'), others thought about the use of force in much more restrictive terms, that is as a targeted response or strictly an option of last resort ('When there is no other way of protection and life is in danger'). These responses point to significant differences in understandings of what are appropriate practices for implementing the use of force, ranging from being based on highly selective case-by-case assessments to seeing it as a crucial obligation of peacekeeping with PoC mandates upon with the legitimacy of the entire operation rests.

Third, when asked what makes it difficult to decide whether force should be applied, many military advisers continued to point to limits on the use of force from their home countries and unclear rules of engagement (RoE). The latter have historically been an often-used explanation for rejecting the use of force in peacekeeping settings. As a consequence, the UN Secretary-General and the Department of Peace Operations have engaged in significant efforts to make RoE explicit and clear and addressing caveats that certain troop contributors might have before deployment. This has not only featured prominently in the so-called HIPPO report authored by the High-Level International Panel on Peacekeeping Operations (United Nations 2015) but has also been enforced through the repatriation of commanders and units from Darfur and South Sudan who did not meet performance expectations (United Nations 2016b, 2016a). The fact that such efforts continue to be thwarted and differences exist underlines the futility of seeking to reduce the ambiguity of the PoC norm: the troop-contributing countries, in particular, can secure their space for manoeuvre in interpreting the RoE and implementing the PoC norm only if ambiguity is retained.

Fourth, military advisers have diverging understandings on whether it is appropriate to use (primarily) defensive or offensive force to protect civilians in peacekeeping, while some indicated that their country does not even differentiate between offensive and defensive steps. While none of the military advisers we engaged with noted that their country would be reluctant to contribute to peacekeeping operations with explicit use of force elements, military advisers argued either for taking an overall 'robust posture' or for deciding on a case-by-case basis and considering the offensive use of force as inherently problematic in the context of peacekeeping. Therefore, arguments presented in favour of the defensive or offensive use of force can demonstrate how military advisers are positioned in a conflictual norm-scape, especially when it comes to impartiality. Whilst scholars from a rationalist perspective may argue that such differences stem from military advisers defending their countries' respective (national) interests, we could not find such evidence in our study. In fact, there was no disagreement among military advisers about the protection of civilians playing a vital role in current peacekeeping – what was contested, however, was precisely how the protection of civilians should best be done. Some advisers consider the shift in normative meaning towards assertive impartiality as appropriate and necessary: 'You can't go into peacekeeping saying "I am not ready to fight." Then don't do it. Don't provide contingents.' But others, retaining more traditional understandings of impartiality and consent, argue that 'offensive operations are part of the problem'.

Fifth, engaging with military advisers and their implementation practices also allowed us to observe them as a community where intersubjective assessments and competing competence claims regarding appropriate implementation practices are negotiated. This leads to instances of solidarity but also instances of contestation when considering their practices. On the one hand, military advisers expressed a shared sense of military identity and of being 'operators'. They frequently referred to a pragmatic, military way of thinking where 'issues are seen as more clear-cut' that is markedly distinct from what military advisers portrayed as a political or politicised viewpoint. On the other hand, military advisers do engage in contestation over what counts as appropriate and therefore competent implementation practices. A discussion about the *Kigali Principles*, a member-state initiative led by African states to improve how PoC is implemented by highlighting the readiness to use force, usefully illustrates this. While some states joined this process by indicating that they 'saw this as an opportunity', others criticised it as lacking inclusiveness as only nine states had been involved in drafting their text while all others were simply presented with a final draft. Military advisers therefore explained and defended both opposition to and support of the Kigali Principles as demonstrable engagement in appropriate and therefore competent practices.

In sum, this study of the implementation practices of military advisers when it comes to the military dimensions of the PoC underlines the analytical benefits of studying peacekeeping norms through the vantage point of practice theories. It allows for a deeper integration of typically ambiguous international norms as a means of understanding how diverging understandings of such pivotal norms as the protection of civilians are actualised and emerge in the context of conflictual norm-scapes.

Conclusion

This chapter started with the observation that practice theories are particularly well suited to making theoretical sense of peacekeeping operations because their analysis foregrounds 'what peacekeepers do'. Engaging with how competence, knowledge, and power are negotiated in practices therefore allows us to link micro and macro processes associated with peacekeeping. While practices have long been a staple concept of social constructivism, it has arguably been only with the introduction of practice theories that IR theory has been able to capture the full analytical promise of this important concept. Further, I argued that the growing recognition of practice theories' diverse location in social theory and sociology gives them deep analytical purchase, helping us access reasons for both situations of change and of persistent continuity. Engaging with both critical and pragmatic versions of practice theories also captures actors performing on the basis of reflexive background knowledge as well as reflective, creative decision-making.

Peacekeeping scholarship has already seen a growing number of applications of practice theories, often closely associated with critical thinking along the local and micro turns. Contributions by scholars I summarised underline the varied applications of practice theories: from focusing on the significant drawbacks of a hierarchically prioritised background knowledge inherent to international interventions practices performed by actors across the three United Nations (member state representatives, UN officials, and independent experts or NGOs), to critical combinations of practice theories and norm research around aspects of ambiguity.

Methodologically, doing research on peacekeeping via practice theories typically requires time-intensive amounts of fieldwork to conduct in-depth interviews, or engage in non-participant observation or anthropological study, as practices do not typically lend themselves to being studied via texts or discourse alone. In particular, scholars would find it hard to access practices based on reflexive background knowledge via textual analysis. The deep empirical understanding of particular instances of implementing peacekeeping operations and the positions of actors therein is a distinct advantage of practice theories. At the same time, this focus on gathering significant amounts of novel primary data to make sense of practices is time- and labour-intensive, therefore putting an empirical burden on scholars of peacekeeping. At the same time, scholars who work with pragmatic, reflective versions of practice theories argue that we can also study practices via textual ethnographies, focusing on the stories (former) individual peacekeepers tell in their own published works (Pingeot 2018: 373).

In sum, practice theories promise to deliver innovative, micro-level accounts of how peacekeeping and our understanding of it evolve through looking at its component parts. This makes practice theories particularly suitable for understanding the constant evolutionary aspects of peacekeeping doctrine, which is currently to a pragmatic turn, characterised by different conceptions in the same peacekeeping operation, making peacekeeping increasingly toolbox-like (de Coning

2018). As peacekeeping doctrine moves away from the liberal-peace agenda towards 'a multitude of embryonic and experimental approaches that in different ways promise to deliver more realistic, contextualised and/or effective forms of intervention' (Andersen 2018: 18), this will increase the room for manoeuvre for peacekeeping's implementing actors.

References

Adler, Emanuel (2005), *Communitarian International Relations: The Epistemic Foundation of International Relations* (London and New York: Routledge).

Adler, Emanuel (2008), 'The spread of security communities: Communities of practice, self-restraint, and NATO's post-Cold War transformation', *European Journal of International Relations*, 14:2: 195–230.

Adler, Emanuel, and Vincent Pouliot (2011), 'International practices', *International Theory*, 3:1: 1–36.

Adler-Nissen, Rebecca (ed.) (2013), *Bourdieu in International Relations: Rethinking Key Concepts in IR* (London: Routledge).

Adler-Nissen, Rebecca (2014), 'Stigma management in international relations: Transgressive identities, norms, and order in international society', *International Organization*, 68:1, 143–76.

Andersen, Louise Riis (2018), 'The HIPPO in the room: The pragmatic push-back from the UN peace bureaucracy against the militarization of UN peacekeeping', *International Affairs*, 94:2: 1–19.

Autesserre, Séverine (2014a), 'Going micro: Emerging and future peacekeeping research', *International Peacekeeping*, 21:4: 492–500.

Autesserre, Séverine (2014b), *Peaceland: Conflict Resolution and the Everyday Politics of International Intervention* (Cambridge: Cambridge University Press).

Bigo, Didier (ed.) (2007), *The Field of the EU Internal Security Agencies* (Paris: Harmattan).

Bode, Ingvild (2014), 'Storytelling in den Vereinten Nationen: Mahbub Ul Haq und Menschliche Entwicklung', in Frank Gadinger, Sebastian Jarzebski, and Taylan Yildiz (eds), *Politische Narrative: Konzepte – Analysen – Forschungspraxis* (Wiesbaden: Springer), 339–62.

Bode, Ingvild (2015), *Individual Agency and Policy Change at the United Nations: The People of the United Nations* (London: Routledge).

Bode, Ingvild (2018a), 'Expertise as social practice: The individual construction of experts', in Christian Henrich-Franke, Christian Lahusen, Robert Kaiser, and Andrea Schneiker (eds), *Transnational Expertise* (Baden-Baden: Nomos), 101–26.

Bode, Ingvild (2018b), 'Reflective practices at the Security Council: Children and armed conflict and the three United Nations', *European Journal of International Relations*, 24:2, 293–318.

Bode, Ingvild, and Hendrik Huelss (2018), 'Autonomous weapons systems and changing norms in international relations', *Review of International Studies*, 44:3, 393–413.

Bode, Ingvild, and John Karlsrud (2019), 'Implementation in practice: The use of force to protect civilians in United Nations peacekeeping', *European Journal of International Relations*, 25:2, 458–85.

Boltanski, Luc (2011), *On Critique: A Sociology of Emancipation*, English ed. (Cambridge and Malden, MA: Polity).

Bourdieu, Pierre (1980), *Le sens pratique* (Paris: Éditions de Minuit).

Bourdieu, Pierre (1986), 'The forms of capital', in John G. Richardson (ed.), *Handbook of Theory and Research for the Sociology of Education* (New York: Greenwood Press), 241–58.

Bourdieu, Pierre (1987), *Choses dites* (Paris: Éditions de Minuit).

Bourdieu, Pierre (1996), *The State Nobility: Elite Schools in the Field of Power* (Cambridge: Polity Press).

Breakey, Hugh (2014), 'Protection of civilians and law making in the Security Council', in Vesselin Popovski and Trudy Fraser (eds), *The Security Council as Global Legislator* (London: Routledge), 202–23.

Bueger, Christian (2013), 'Communities of security practice at work? The emerging African maritime security regime', *African Security*, 6:3–4, 297–316.

Bueger, Christian (2015), 'Making things known: Epistemic practices, the United Nations, and the translation of piracy', *International Political Sociology*, 9:1, 1–18.

Bueger, Christian, and Frank Gadinger (2015), 'The play of international practice', *International Studies Quarterly*, 59:3, 449–60.

de Certeau, Michel (1984), *The Practice of Everyday Life* (Berkeley, CA: University of California Press).

de Coning, Cedric (2018), 'Adaptive peacebuilding', *International Affairs*, 94:2, 301–17.

Engell, Troels Gauslå (2018), *Inside the United Nations Security Council: The Diplomatic Practices of Change in Global Security Governance* (Copenhagen: University of Copenhagen).

Finnemore, Martha (1996), *National Interests in International Society* (Ithaca, NY: Cornell University Press).

Gadinger, Frank (2016), 'On justification and critique: Luc Boltanski's pragmatic sociology and International Relations', *International Political Sociology*, 10:3, 187–205.

Guzzini, Stefano (2000), 'A reconstruction of constructivism in International Relations', *European Journal of International Relations*, 6:2, 147–82.

Holmes, Georgina (2019), 'Situating agency, embodied practices and norm implementation in peacekeeping training', *International Peacekeeping*, 26:1, 55–84.

Holt, Victoria, and Glyn Taylor (2009), *Protecting Civilians in the Context of UN Peacekeeping Operations. Successes, Setbacks and Remaining Challenges* (New York: United Nations).

Hopf, Ted (2010), 'The logic of habit in International Relations', *European Journal of International Relations*, 16:4, 539–61.

Huelss, Hendrik (2017), 'After decision-making: The operationalisation of norms in International Relations', *International Theory*, 9:3, 381–409.

Hultman, Lisa (2012), 'UN peace operations and protection of civilians: Cheap talk or norm implementation', *Journal of Peace Research*, 50:1, 59–73.

Karlsrud, John (2016), *Norm Change in International Relations: Linked Ecologies in UN Peacekeeping Operations* (Abingdon: Routledge).

Klotz, Audie (1995), *Norms in International Relations: The Struggle against Apartheid* (Ithaca, NY: Cornell University Press).

Krook, Mona Lena, and Jacqui True (2012), 'Rethinking the life cycles of international norms: The United Nations and the global promotion of gender equality', *European Journal of International Relations*, 18:1, 103–27.

Kuus, Merje (2015), 'Symbolic power in diplomatic practice: Matters of style in Brussels', *Cooperation and Conflict*, 50:3, 368–84.

Laurence, Marion (2019), 'An "impartial" force? Normative ambiguity and practice change in UN peace operations', *International Peacekeeping*, 26:3, 256–80.

Leander, Anna (2008), 'Thinking tools', in Audie Klotz and Deepa Prakesh (eds), *Qualitative Methods in International Relations: A Pluralist Guide* (Basingstoke: Palgrave Macmillan), 11–27.

Leander, Anna (2011), 'The promises, problems, and potentials of a Bourdieu-inspired staging of International Relations', *International Political Sociology*, 5:3, 294–313.

Neumann, Iver B. (2002), 'Returning practice to the linguistic turn. The case of diplomacy', *Millennium*, 31:2, 627–51.

Neumann, Iver B. (2012), *At Home with the Diplomats: Inside a European Foreign Ministry* (Ithaca, NY: Cornell University Press).

Paddon Rhoads, Emily (2016), *Taking Sides in Peacekeeping: Impartiality and the Future of the United Nations* (New York: Oxford University Press).

Paddon Rhoads, Emily (2019), 'Putting human rights up front: Implications for impartiality and the politics of UN peacekeeping', *International Peacekeeping*, 26:3: 281–301.

Pingeot, Lou (2018), 'United Nations peace operations as international practices: Revisiting the UN mission's armed raids against gangs in Haiti', *European Journal of International Security*, 3:3, 364–81.

Pouliot, Vincent (2010), *International Security in Practice: The Politics of NATO–Russia Diplomacy* (Cambridge: Cambridge University Press).

Pouliot, Vincent (2016), *International Pecking Orders: The Politics and Practice of Multilateral Diplomacy* (Cambridge: Cambridge University Press).

Ralph, Jason, and Jess Gifkins (2017), 'The purpose of United Nations Security Council practice: Contesting competence claims in the normative context created by the Responsibility to Protect', *European Journal of International Relations*, 22:3, 630–53.

Sandholtz, Wayne (2008), 'Dynamics of international norm change: Rules against wartime plunder', *European Journal of International Relations*, 14:1, 101–31.

Security Council (1999), 'Resolution 1270', S/RES/1270.

United Nations (2015), 'Report of the High-Level Independent Panel on Peace Operations (HIPPO) on Uniting Our Strengths for Peace: Politics, Partnership and People', A/70/95 – S/2015/446.

United Nations (2016a), 'South Sudan: Ban to put in place measures to improve UN mission's ability to protect civilians', available at: www.un.org/apps/news/story.asp?NewsID=55448#.WCMCkxmumCN (accessed 31 July 2019).

United Nations (2016b), 'Repatriation of commanders, units among steps to tackle sexual exploitation, abuse by peacekeepers, Secretary-General tells Security Council', available at: www.un.org/press/en/2016/sc12274.doc.htm (accessed 31 July 2019).

United Nations Office of Internal Oversight Services (2014), 'Evaluation of the implementation and results of protection of civilians mandates in United Nations peacekeeping operations', A/68/787.

Wiener, Antje (2018), *Contestation and Constitution of Norms in Global International Relation* (Cambridge: Cambridge University Press).

Zarakol, Ayse (2011), *After Defeat: How the East Learned to Live with the West* (Cambridge: Cambridge University Press).

Zimmermann, Lisbeth (2016), 'Same same or different? Norm diffusion between resistance, compliance, and localization in post-conflict states', *International Studies Perspectives*, 17:1, 98–115.

7

Critical security studies

Lucile Maertens

Since the 2000s, concerns about the lack of theoretical developments in the peacekeeping literature have mostly been raised by critical scholars. On the one hand, Paris (2000: 44) denounced the 'cult of policy relevance' that led to neglecting the 'macrotheoretical questions about the nature and significance of these operations for our understanding of international politics'. On the other hand, critical theory assumes that theory is never politically neutral and that scholars should 'be self-consciously theoretical and ask basic questions about what we are looking at and why, and what is excluded when we look at something in a particular way' (Bellamy et al. 2010: 20). A critical approach to UN peacekeeping would then question the values and representations that inform peacekeeping and the political order that peacekeeping interventions shape, promote, or sustain.

Critical security studies (CSS) can be narrowly defined as gathering post-positivist analysis focused on human security and emancipation (Buzan and Hansen 2009: 36). However, in a broader sense, CSS refers to a 'reflexive field' (Salter 2013: 1) that covers a variety of approaches ranging from critical theory to post-structuralism. It encompasses conceptions of security that are contrasting but share the 'assumption that security threats and insecurities are not simply objects to be studied or problems to be solved, but the product of social and political practices' (Aradau et al. 2015: 1). Applied to UN peacekeeping, CSS aims to understand how peacekeeping works in practice and its political and social implications. It questions agency and takes into account non-traditional security issues.

For almost two decades, there has been a growing interest in emerging issues in peacekeeping such as health, gender, or child soldiers. Yet, the process that expands UN peacekeeping practices remains under-theorised within the peacekeeping literature, as well as within CSS. This chapter relies on CSS theoretical and methodological tools to study the specific case of the rise of environmental practices in UN peacekeeping. Since the 2000s, UN peacekeeping missions have been increasingly confronted with environmental challenges, especially as a consequence of their own expansion. This chapter explores the multiple transformations that resulted from growing environmental concerns. Not only does it discuss the impact of peacekeeping activities on the environment as an unintended consequence of the UN intervention but it questions the discourses and power dynamics within the UN system that create the conditions for such an ecological impact. Drawing on the concepts of securitisation and environmentalisation, the chapter shows how peacekeeping has been framed as relevant to environmental policies, while contributing to a broader process of securitisation of the environment.

Critical security studies and International Relations

CSS includes a broad range of approaches that this chapter alone cannot fully cover. Instead, it suggests different directions to address the main themes and questions raised within CSS. From a chronological perspective, critical thinking in security studies is often dated to the 1980s as a reaction to the International Relations (IR) approaches that dominated the Cold War period (Baldwin 1997). Various genealogies of CSS trace the development and evolution of this growing sub-field (Krause and Williams 1997; collective CASE 2006; Buzan and Hansen 2009). In his account of the 'contested concept of security', Smith (2005: 40–2) identifies two main streams in the initial critical writing on security.[1] First, the work by Krause and Williams (1996, 1997) established the distinction between broadening and deepening security and brought a 'theoretically inclusive' approach around 'a shared dissatisfaction with orthodox security studies and a disillusionment with the agenda of mainstream security studies after the end of the cold war' (Smith 2015: 41–2). Second, the Welsh School focused on a more defined approach to CSS with a clear focus on emancipation. Yet these two streams cannot sum up the 'large repertoire of issues and approaches' that CSS incorporates today (Mandelbaum et al. 2016: 133) and that can fit into this definition suggested by Booth in 2005:

> Critical security studies is an issue-area study, developed within the academic discipline of international politics, concerned with the pursuit of critical knowledge about security in world politics. Security is conceived comprehensively, embracing theories and practices at multiple levels of society, from the individual to the whole human species. 'Critical' implies a perspective that seeks to stand outside prevailing structures, processes, ideologies, and orthodoxies while recognizing that all conceptualizations of security derive from particular political/theoretical positions; critical perspectives do not make a claim to objective truth but rather seek to provide deeper understandings of prevailing attitudes and behavior with a view to developing more promising ideas by which to overcome structural and contingent human wrongs. (2005: 15–16)

Classification of the different schools of thought constitutes another way of approaching CSS. Each textbook provides its own typology dividing the diverging approaches thematically or along different ontological, epistemological, and methodological divides (Buzan and Hansen, 2009; Peoples and Vaughan-Williams 2010; Shepherd 2013; Balzacq 2016). For instance, Balzacq (2016) distinguishes four main categories: first, critical theory including the

Frankfurt School and work on human security; second, constructivism with a specific focus on the securitisation theory; third, poststructuralism and Foucauldian approaches revolving around the concepts of genealogy, governmentality, and biopolitics; and fourth, feminism that encompasses diverse theoretical and epistemological approaches. Buzan and Hansen (2009: 37) differentiate perspectives in international security studies along epistemological distinctions (objective, subjective or discursive conception of security) and divergence on the main referent object (states, communities, human beings, etc.), the division between internal and external security, the considered sectors (military and/or non-military) and the view on security politics. These lines of separation lead to eight categories relevant to a broad definition of CSS: critical constructivism, the Copenhagen School, critical security studies, feminist security studies, human security, peace research, postcolonial security studies, and post-structuralist security studies (Buzan and Hansen 2009: 37).

Studies gathered under the CSS umbrella also share a set of specific central research questions. First and foremost, CSS questions the definition of security itself. Throughout the 1980s and 1990s, the widening debate challenged the narrow focus on military threats and national security advocating for an expansion across different sectors (broadening) and different referent objects (deepening) (Huysmans 1998: 227). The Copenhagen School developed the securitisation theory as part of this new security studies agenda (Buzan et al. 1998). For Buzan et al. (1998: 25), '[t]he exact definition and criteria of securitisation is constituted by the intersubjective establishment of an existential threat with a saliency sufficient to have substantial political effects'. This definition refers to security as a social construction based on political elites labelling an issue a threat to survival, through a speech act, and making it recognised as such (Wæver 1995). Despite the success of the securitisation concept and the large body of work inspired by the Copenhagen School, multiple criticisms were raised against the sole focus on discourse (Balzacq 2011) and 'the limitations of securitization theory as a "critical theory"' (Aradau 2015: 303). Huysmans (1998: 226), for instance, shows that the expansion of security studies did not actually question 'the meaning – or more technically, the signifying work – of the noun "security" itself'. He further advocates for a security studies agenda based on a 'thick signifier approach which focuses on the wider order of meaning which "security" articulates' (1998: 226). Hansen also contradicts the Copenhagen School by exposing 'the striking absence of gender' and the 'security as silence' that the speech-act framework cannot capture (2000: 286–7). In a similar vein, McDonald (2008) denounces the securitisation conceptual framework for being too narrow and suggests considering the broader construction of security. Going further, postcolonial security studies, despite disparate perspectives, challenge the Western-centric biases of security studies, including in CSS (Barkawi and Laffey 2006), and denounce 'the inability of CSS to recognize its own particularity and ethnocentrism' (Peoples and Vaughan-Williams 2010: 47).

CSS does not only question the meaning of security but enquires about whose security and who is enacting security. The work of Bigo (2002) and the PARIS School – Political Anthropological Research for International Sociology – on security professionals sheds light on 'the study of everyday (in)securitization processes and practices' (Bigo and McCluskey 2018: 1). CSS encompasses studies that look at security actors, security practices, and security material and visual objects while questioning their political effects on populations (Collective CASE 2006; Balzacq et al. 2010). For instance, critical scholars have extensively explored the 'war on terror' denouncing the *dispositif* of counter-terrorism policies, illiberal practices, and surveillance technologies established in democratic countries (Bigo and Tsoukala 2008). In the case of migration, CSS also points to the process of othering while deconstructing discourse on security threats that allow for discriminatory policies and a 'governmentality of unease' (Bigo 2002). While numerous studies expanded the scope to new security issues such as identity, migration, health, and the environment, CSS sees a continuous development of innovative analytical frameworks that reflect upon the connection between security and other key concepts such as risk, resilience, and exception, to name a few, in constant dialogue with other sub-fields such as Science and Technology Studies or popular culture studies.

In the last ten years, CSS has been concerned with its methodological commitments (Salter and Mutlu 2013; Aradau et al. 2015) and its relations to the political (Mandelbaum et al. 2016; Hagmann et al. 2018). Even though what being critical means has been under much debate recently, Austin et al. (2019: 3) suggest reinvigorating CSS by returning to the everyday of exercising critique. Whilst this chapter provides only a fragmented and limited account of this diverse sub-field, CSS will always gather research with contrasting views on the ontology and epistemology of security, or as Aradau (2015: 300) puts it 'critical approaches to (in)security do not subscribe to a school or a theory but focus on transversal conceptual and methodological work across established disciplinary boundaries'.

Critical security studies and UN peacekeeping

Pugh (2004: 39) opens his 2004 article on peacekeeping and critical theory with the following words: 'Theorists of International Relations have paid little attention to how and why "peacekeeping", "peace support operations" and related "humanitarian" relief missions are significant in sustaining a particular representation of global governance norms'. Drawing on the work of Cox and Duffield, he then deconstructs peace operations that 'can be considered as forms of riot control directed against the unruly parts of the world to uphold the liberal peace' (2004: 41). This critical take on peacekeeping echoes a growing literature in CSS which challenges our understanding of peace operations in world politics. Whilst peacekeeping has not been extensively explored in CSS, scholarship in peace operations increasingly relies on critical approaches to question the world representations that inform and shape UN peacekeeping.

First, some scholars propose a critical assessment of a specific peacekeeping dimension without expressly invoking critical theory. For instance, Tardy (2011) critically discusses the concept of robust peacekeeping, questioning its meaning in the broader context of contemporary peace operations politics. His article does not explicitly draw on critical theory but provides insights on the two main questions that critical theorists examine, as underlined by Bellamy et al. (2010: 28): '1. What theories, values, ideologies, interests and identities shape the way we understand peace operations, and whose theories, values, ideologies, interests and identities are best served through the current practices of peace operations? 2. What theories and practices of peace operations are most likely to advance human emancipation and how might such advances be achieved?' Likewise, the work that explores non-traditional peacekeeping issues draws on the deepening debate in CSS to question the role of UN peacekeepers in the fight against HIV/Aids (Bratt 2002), to advance gender in peacekeeping research (Olsson and Gizelis 2014), or to assess the influence of child soldiers in UN peacekeeping (Bakaki and Hinkkainen 2016). These studies extend the peacekeeping research agenda to much broader questions in contemporary politics while echoing analytical developments in CSS.

Second, several studies challenge mainstream understanding of peace operations through a critical security framework. Among these, two main trends emerge, one engaging the politics of UN peacekeeping; the other one questioning the everyday of peace operations. While traditional studies on UN peace operations have always been interested in the reasons behind member states' engagement, a critical take on this involvement also includes discursive dimensions. In other words, a critical approach intends 'to reflect on the discourse within which theories and practices of peacekeeping, conflict resolution and peacebuilding are formed and reformed' (Fetherston 2000: 191). For instance, drawing on a constructivist approach, Booth Walling (2013) deconstructs narratives and storytelling in the UN Security Council to understand the likelihood of a UN humanitarian intervention. Critical discourse analysis also helps to apprehend the rationale behind a specific country's engagement and the myths that frame peacekeeping narratives. Relying on feminist and critical theorists, Whitworth (2005: 102) questions the Canadian engagement by analysing the discourse around the image of Canada as peacekeeper: she shows that 'an analysis of Canada's reputation as a country committed to the ideals of peacekeeping, and the way in which many features of that reputation were seriously challenged by the murders of Somali citizens by Canadian soldiers, leads us to question the constitution and effects of militarized masculinities'. Member states' engagement also results from the allocation of roles and responsibilities within the peacekeeping system. Revisiting the institutional debate about the UN system, Cunliffe (2009: 324) demonstrates that not only 'political risks are unevenly distributed throughout the UN structure and skewed in favour of wealthier and more powerful states' but 'it is an organizational trait that is reproduced by the political interests it serves'. In other words, the division of labour within the UN peacekeeping system should be critically discussed beyond traditional explanations related to institutional functionalist arrangements and path dependency.

CSS also addresses UN peacekeeping politics by focusing on the political order that peacekeeping operations maintain. Indeed, while Barnett and Finnemore (2004) capture the ideational foundations of peace operations, other studies focus on the political and economic models that peace operations export and sustain. Pugh's (2004: 54) work fits in this category: it questions the role of peacekeeping in the global political economy criticising the ethical discourse justifying the humanitarian intervention. Echoing Duffield's work on humanitarianism, he argues that peace operations intend to promote a neoliberal economic order while being 'value laden in reproducing, or attempting to reproduce, the state system and liberal norms of domestic governance'. Paris and Zanotti further develop this argument by focusing on the role of peace missions in the diffusion of liberal democracy. On the one hand, Paris (2002: 38) contends that international peacebuilding missions 'have attempted to "transplant" the values and institutions of the liberal democratic core into the domestic affairs of peripheral host states', whilst urging students to pay attention to 'the role that peace operations play in the diffusion of norms and institutional models from one part of the international system to another'. On the other hand, Zanotti (2006: 151) relies on a Foucauldian approach to argue that 'international interventions have become an aspect of an international disciplinary regime that took shape in response to the unpredictability of threats'. On the basis of the cases of Haiti and Croatia, she shows how UN peacekeeping imposes democracy through institutional disciplinarity and governmentalisation (Zanotti 2006) and how the importation of political models fosters disorder and dependence (Zanotti 2008). Several postcolonial and feminist theorists also investigate the international system that peacekeeping helps create and/or sustain. For instance, Pratt (2013: 772) challenges the 'particular configuration of gender, race, and sexuality' reproduced in the UN Security Council Resolution 1325 on 'Women, Peace and Security'. She argues that 'rather than challenging or dismantling the dominant practices and discourses of international security, 1325 enables the "international community" to harness women's agency in the reproduction of racial–sexual hierarchies of power that are mobilized in the production of post-9/11 security discourses and practices' (Pratt 2013: 773). By examining the political project that shapes peacekeeping operations, CSS questions taken-for-granted values that justify UN peacekeeping interventions and influence their daily enactment.

A second trend of research within the critical work on peacekeeping precisely looks at the everyday practices of peacekeeping, building on CSS, but also mainstream constructivism, practice theory, international political economy, and critical geography. Considering the broader community of 'international peacebuilders', Autesserre (2014: 54) draws on Bourdieu and the practice turn in IR to study how 'interveners interact with local stakeholders, construct knowledge on their areas of deployment, ensure their safety, and go about their jobs on a daily basis'. Relying on the concepts of practices, habits, and narratives, she shows the significance of daily activities in the reproduction and persistence of specific modes of action and how the values that shape international interventions are concretely 'created, sustained, and reinforced – or challenged – on the ground' (2014: 9). This approach echoes the work on peacekeepers' everyday lives. Drawing on Bourdieu's notion of capital, Henry (2015) explores the ways UN peacekeepers talk about their own experiences of living and working as a peacekeeper. She shows the entanglement between economic dimensions and gendered effects and argues that 'peacekeepers are continually dependent on militarized (especially embodied) resources (or forms of capital), and that this is both a cause and consequence of the everyday contradictions and paradoxes that they experience' (2015: 374). While privileging the everyday experiences, her article also contributes to broader debates within the critical literature on peacekeeping that investigates 'the often invisible effects of socio-spatial and imperial power as it is played out in the form of humanitarian intervention, international aid and peacekeeping' (2015: 374). Drawing on human and critical geography, several scholars have addressed the spatial dimensions of peacekeeping daily practices and performances. Pointing out critical approaches that 'often omit empirical explorations in favour of overarching assertions', Higate and Henry (2010: 33), for instance, intend to provide 'a nuanced insight into how blue-helmet security practices are seen, and in turn how these (usually) taken-for-granted practices contribute towards perceptions of security' by exploring the everyday security through its 'embodied, spatial and performative dimensions'. Drawing on everyday urban geopolitics, Lemay-Hébert (2018) studies the 'securitization of the everyday in Haiti' by analysing the security mapping performed by the UN peacekeeping mission to regulate the everyday of UN expats in Port-au-Prince. He demonstrates how securitisation practices contribute to social segregation between peacekeepers and the local population and thus increase resistance by local actors (Lemay-Hébert 2018). Critical scholars in peacekeeping studies have been particularly concerned with local reactions to UN peacekeeping interventions (Pouligny 2006) and local resistance (Mac Ginty 2011), especially in the face of sex and disease scandals (Lemay-Hébert 2014). Peacekeepers' 'sexual arrangements' have also been critically studied by exploring the gendering of peacekeeping economies (Jennings 2014: 313) that further develops the feminist work on militarised masculinities and peacekeeping (Whitworth 2005). These studies of the everyday practices of UN peacekeeping usually rely on ethnographic field-work, where researcher positionality is often overlooked (Henry et al. 2009). In line with the continuous methodological discussions in CSS, Henry et al. (2009: 469) advocate for a reflexive consideration of the role of the peacekeeping researcher and challenge 'those conducting research to acknowledge that social inquiry is itself a political act'. The following part presents an in-depth case study to highlight the relevance of CSS theoretical and methodological tools in the study of peacekeeping.

UN peacekeeping and the environment

The cholera outbreak brought to Haiti in 2010 as a consequence of wastewater mismanagement in one of the UN peacekeeping mission's camps drew attention to the material footprint of UN peace operations. It raised questions about peacekeepers' pre-deployment health checks and their waste management practices, even though the environmental policy-setting guidelines and standards, which were supposed to prevent environmental mis-management, were already adopted in 2009. Since the 2000s, multiple transformations resulted from growing environmental concerns in UN peacekeeping. Yet, the literature on emerging issues in peace missions has rarely paid attention to the role of environmental issues in peacekeeping. On the basis of data generated through content analysis of UN publications, interviews[2] and participant observation,[3] I explore how environmental concerns are integrated in UN peacekeeping operations. While engaging with the debate on broadening security studies, I draw on CSS to study heterogeneous emerging elements – standards, practices, expertise, equipment management, etc. – which expand peacekeeping activities to a new field of action. I examine the integration of environmental concerns in UN peacekeeping practices through the concept of environmentalisation and argue not only that peacekeeping is slowly framed as part of the environmental realm but that environmentalisation also contributes to the securitisation of the environment.[4]

UN peacekeeping as an environmental concern

Despite growing interest in emerging issues in peace operations, the process that broadens and widens UN peacekeeping practices remains under-theorised within the peacekeeping literature, as well as within CSS. The literature encompassed under the notion of 'environmental peacebuilding' questions both the influence of environmental issues on conflict and the role of environmental co-operation in facilitating peace (Swain and Öjendal 2018), but does not fully address UN peacekeepers' environmental footprint. The environmental impacts of UN peacekeeping have however captured the attention of practitioners and think-tank experts (UNEP 2012; Liljedahl et al. n.d.; Liljedahl and Waleij 2014) who mostly focus on assessing unintended consequences of peacekeeping on the environment. I further explore UN peacekeepers' environmental practices drawing on the concepts of securitisation and environmentalisation.

Securitisation theories have inspired much work on the construction of the environment as a security issue (Trombetta 2008; Floyd 2010; McDonald 2011). First, authors of the Copenhagen School designate the environment as one of the five sectors of security, where they highlight the superposition of two independent agendas: the political and the scientific agendas (Buzan et al. 1998). They conclude that, despite a number of securitising moves, the environment is more politicised than securitised. This conclusion has been challenged by Floyd (2010) and Trombetta (2011), who both demonstrate the success of several securitising moves. In parallel to the literature on the securitisation of the environment in CSS, a concept in sociology can also capture the relation between the environment and security: environmentalisation. Studies have shown that environmental issues can be socially constructed, through a process of 'environmentalisation': 'The term can be used to designate both the adoption of a generic environmental discourse by different social groups, as well as the concrete incorporation of environmental justifications to legitimate institutional, political and scientific practices' (Acselrad 2010: 103). The environmentalisation of security aims to establish security activities as part of the environmental protection norms, policies, and mandates. Security actors also integrate new logics of action inspired from traditional environmental policies, such as preventive actions and non-confrontational responses. Securitisation is therefore not the only concept relevant to question the process that bridges environmental and security fields.[5] Yet, work on the process of environmentalisation has been rather sparse in CSS, which has largely focused on the securitisation of the environment.

Drawing on the concept of environmentalisation is useful to understand the inclusion of environmental concerns and practices in UN peacekeeping. I consider environmentalisation as a slow assembling process that emerges from heterogeneous and mundane elements. In the case of UN peacekeeping, the environment is integrated through emerging practices – standards, expertise, equipment management, etc. – that frame peacekeeping as part of the environmental field. Yet, a sole focus on environmentalisation does not tell the whole story, since environmentalising moves are intrinsically linked with efforts to securitise the environment. The key is then to explore how environmentalisation and securitisation reinforce each other. It means considering not only the power of attraction of the security frame but also reversed processes, where security practices, actors, and discourses are framed in another domain's terms.

A slow transformation from blue to green

The environment came under UN peacekeepers' scrutiny from the 1990s and growingly in the 2000s, with the deployment of new, large-scale operations in Darfur (2004 to present), Haiti (2004–17) and Sudan/South Sudan (2005 to present). From short-term operations with reduced staff numbers, the UN developed into 'very large structures' that are put in place in countries without basic infrastructure, necessary in particular for waste management.[6] As the organisation's image was in jeopardy in the event of poor management of its environmental impacts, the institution has progressively integrated environmental concerns in standards, guidelines, and mandates.

With the mission in Mali in 2013, a UN peacekeeping operation for the first time received a direct mandate to address the environmental consequences of its activities.[7] This mandate followed a general trend: faced with the proliferation of environmental field concerns, the Departments of Peacekeeping Operations (DPO) and of Operational Support (DOS) have taken on a series of measures to mitigate their environmental impact. Whilst the UN Secretary-General prompted all UN organisations to reduce their ecological footprint,[8] in 2009, DPO and DOS, respectively DPKO (Department of Peacekeeping Operations) and DFS (Department of Field Support) at the time, signed the *Environmental Policy for UN Field Missions* (internal document).[9] Concentrating on the practices and behaviours of UN peacekeepers, more so than on technology and equipment, the policy deals with multiple topics: solid and hazardous waste, energy, water and wastewater management, wild animals and plants, and cultural and historic sites. According to the organisation, the policy aims both to reduce environmental impacts and to improve the health and safety of UN staff and local communities. Since 2015, environmental management has become a priority for DFS/DOS. That year, it adopted a Waste Management Policy for UN Field Missions and, at the beginning of 2016, a team dedicated to the environment was created in the executive office of the Under-Secretary-General at the head of the department. An environmental strategy was then developed and officially released in November 2016. It aspires to the following vision: 'responsible missions that achieve maximum efficiency in their use of natural resources and operate at a minimum risk to people, societies and ecosystems; contributing to a positive impact on these whenever possible' (UN DFS 2017a: 1). These heterogeneous elements – official policies, resolutions, technical guidelines, etc. – slowly modify UN peacekeeping. On the one hand, they consider peacekeeping activities as being environmental issues that require 'environmental management' through 'an environmental policy' and 'an environment strategy' – environmentalisation. On the other hand, by bringing the environment on the Security Council's agenda, these heterogeneous elements participate in a broader discourse on the environment as a security issue – securitisation.

The transformation of UN peacekeeping practices is also supported by the development of a specific expertise and of networks of experts. In parallel with the creation of an environmental policy, DFS/DOS has appointed environmental officers, in charge of the environmental footprint of UN peacekeeping operations and of broader awareness-raising on the environment in peacekeeping. Whilst they demonstrate almost symbolically that the UN takes the environmental impact of its operations into consideration, they also facilitate the implementation of environmental projects in the field: they promote environmental activities to be conducted by the missions, oversee environmental assessments, and organise training and awareness-raising campaigns for the field personnel (UN DFS 2017a: 1). With these environmental officers, the traditional boundaries of expertise become blurred: these experts contribute to raising awareness both on the ecological footprint of the missions (environmentalisation) and on the role of the environment in conflicts where peacekeepers intervene (securitisation).

Environmental training activities and material are also slowly emerging. For example, on the basis of its report *Greening the Blue Helmets*, the United Nations Environment Programme (UNEP) developed an online training course on the environment and peacekeeping,[10] which brings together different dimensions: it integrates questions of ecological footprint and issues related to the role of natural resources in conflicts and peacebuilding. Similarly, the lesson dedicated to 'Environment and natural resources' in the 2017 Core Pre-deployment Training Materials (CPTMs), available in the UN Peacekeeping Resource Hub, includes elements on both issues – ecological impact and environmental causes of conflicts (UN DPKO/DFS 2017). The development of environmental training materials relies on heterogeneous actors (member states' ministries of defence, DPKO/DPO and DFS/DOS, individual environmental experts from UNEP) and around multiple devices (formal training session, informal awareness raising seminars, online training, etc.).

DPO and DOS also collect and disseminate 'success stories', 'best practices', and 'lessons learned' on the missions' environmental practices. Whilst a reforestation campaign implemented by the blue helmets was systematically mentioned throughout my investigation, DFS/DOS published a four-page document in November 2017 which lists a series of 'environmental good practices' under each pillar of the environmental strategy: participation in 'clean-up' events, energy efficiency and renewable resources, solid waste reduction, wastewater treatment, etc. (UN DFS 2017b). These 'success stories' show the emergence of environmental practices implemented by peacekeepers which aim both at minimising the risks of environmental damage and at proactively protecting the environment or reducing ongoing degradation. The 'lessons learned' and 'best practices' act both as guides for the action of the organisation and as legitimisation tools for environmental management. However, environmental practices are not systematically disseminated between missions but spread in a more mundane way, through the circulation of UN personnel, discussions in the working groups established by the 2016 environmental strategy, the mainstreaming campaigns organised in missions, the commitment of key individuals and the diffusion of illustrative examples and relevant documents, by UN communication tools and social medias.

When addressing their environmental impacts, military actors first focus on their equipment. In the case of UN peacekeeping missions, issues around equipment and procurement are unevenly addressed because of the heterogeneity of the operations: they are not equipped with the same budget, do not consist of the same troops, and do not take place in similar local circumstances. Yet politics of outsourcing and procurement constitute a major obstacle to more eco-friendly UN peace missions.

The politics of green peacekeeping

The case of the environment engages with two of the questions raised in the critical work on peacekeeping. First, it relates to the relationships with local actors. Second, it illustrates the politics around the governance of UN peacekeeping.

The reasons for the UN peacekeeping operations' interest in their ecological impacts are somewhat different from those of regular armies. Whilst national armies can have long-term prospects, UN peacekeeping operations are primarily clusters of different units and troops from many countries. The main source of concern is the reputation of the organisation and its relationship with local populations. UN peacekeeping operations must deal with criticism from host countries:[11] they are criticised locally either for their waste management or for their use of resources, like water and wood in Darfur.[12] The cholera outbreak in Haiti due to poor wastewater management by MINUSTAH precisely illustrates the way the environmental footprint of the mission influences the relationship between the UN and the local population and, as a result, the implementation of the mandate. In its 2012 report, UNEP (2012: 8) highlights the 'negative perception of UN peacekeeping troops within the local population' which 'led to violent demonstrations against them'. Rather than a specific form of liberal governance, environmental concerns have emerged in relation to criticisms targeting peacekeepers' practices. In a way, the degradation of the environment proceeds as an unintended consequence of the missions' mundane activities. The focus on the ecological footprint of peacekeeping activities therefore responds to a dual need for legitimation in regard to local populations and for security reasons: the environmental degradation affects their reception by host communities *and* can be a source of tensions.

Yet, the environmental case also reveals the power dynamics within the UN system that create the conditions for such an ecological impact. As shown by Cunliffe (2009: 323), there is an uneven distribution of responsibilities between different member states at the expense of those 'least able to bear them'. In the case of the cholera epidemic in Haiti, one could argue that the outbreak resulted not only from wastewater mismanagement but also from the UN system which allowed the sending of peacekeepers – from Nepal – carrying the bacteria. It is both an environmental and a health issue that is a consequence of the uneven distribution of responsibilities between UN member states. These inequalities also concern procurement issues. While troops from developing countries might be unable to purchase more sustainable equipment,[13] some member states, mostly developing countries and Russia, are strongly opposed to environmental standards for contingent-owned equipment, especially under the UN material reimbursement system and the procurement principles for selecting vendors. If contracts incorporate strict environmental standards, the international market may offer more attractive prices and some governments would then protest that their national companies are not competitive enough to meet these standards.[14] For example, Russia refused environmental standards for mission equipment in order to protect its market, being a major supplier for air transport.[15] In that context, the Security Council members could only agree on a press statement rather than on a legally binding resolution when addressing the environmental management of peacekeeping operations in December 2017.[16]

Environmentalisation of peacekeeping and securitisation of the environment

Despite the resistance of some member states, the environmentalisation of peacekeeping activities is a 'work-in-progress' that we should pay attention to. For the UN officials met during my investigation, the environment is perceived at the crossroads between low politics, often related to technical regulations, and high politics, with policies considered of the utmost importance. Therefore, integrating environmental concerns into UN peacekeeping can have underestimated political implications, which go beyond the missions' ecological footprint.

For example, staff from the mission in Darfur were invited to an awareness-raising meeting organised by UNEP. The speaker explained that the bricks used to build the mission camp, bought from the local population in order to promote both the local economy and women's employment, had required cooking over a wood fire, which contributed to deforestation of the area. Starting from the very tangible aspect of the ecological impact of the operation, he then made the link between the deforestation caused by the demand for bricks, desertification, and the conflict in the region.[17] By advising on the operational challenge – environmentalisation of peacekeeping – he communicated on a more comprehensive link between the environment and security – securitisation of the environment. The same strategy was used in the UNEP 2012 report, which is divided into two parts. The first part deals with the ecological footprint of UN peace operations – environmentalisation – whilst the second part discusses natural resources, conflicts and peacekeeping – securitisation.

Two main factors explain this combination. On the one hand, the day-to-day management of peacekeeping bases has concrete consequences for the mission's substantive work, situating the environment at the interface between low and high politics.[18] On the other hand, environmentalisation constitutes a bypass strategy to broadly link the environment to peacekeeping and justify the intervention of environmental actors within the field of peacekeeping while securing governments' approval. Indeed, to publish on the environmental dimensions of conflicts, UNEP had to include the ecological footprint of peacekeeping missions.[19] The lesson dedicated to 'Environment and natural resources' in the 2017 CPTM follows the same assembling strategy: while explaining to peacekeepers that 'the environment affects you, and you affect the environment' and that 'the UN commits to reducing its environmental impact', it also asserts, in the same introduction, that 'the root causes of many conflicts are environment and natural resources' (DPKO/DFS 2017: 1). As a result, the environmentalisation of peacekeeping helped securitise the environment.

Conclusion

After discussing the development of CSS, this chapter draws on a few examples to present the contributions of critical approaches in peacekeeping research. The in-depth case study on the integration of environmental concerns in UN peacekeeping practices then illustrates these contributions. First, it shows how CSS sheds light on activities overlooked in the literature and studies the complex ways through which peacekeeping practices are expanding to new fields of action. It takes seriously the mundanity and the day-to-day role of environmental issues in peacekeepers' activities. Second, while questioning the dominance of CSS in terms of securitisation, this case challenges the security framing by proposing to look at the reversed process. Through the concept of environmentalisation, it shows how security, and in this case peacekeeping practices, can also be shaped by other domains of global politics. By developing an alternative framework to capture the process that connects security to the environment, it applies CSS's commitment to transversality and interdisciplinary dialogue. And third, a critical approach to the integration of environmental practices in UN peacekeeping is politically relevant. Environmental mismanagement in peacekeeping can have dramatic outcomes, as the cholera outbreak in Haiti attests. Like any kind of practices which notoriously affect local populations, environmental conduct in peacekeeping missions deserves our attention, despite its emerging dimension. In sum, CSS helps capture emerging and heterogeneous elements while exposing the power relationships that frame and shape contemporary peacekeeping practices.

Notes

1 In his chapter, Smith relies on a narrow definition of CSS that he distinguishes from feminist security studies, post-structuralist security studies, and human security approaches.
2 Research participants asked to remain anonymous, dates and locations will be indicated.
3 Three months of ethnographic research within the Policy, Evaluation, and Training Division, a shared entity between the Departments of Peacekeeping Operations and of Field Support in charge of developing and disseminating policies, doctrine, standardised training and of evaluating mandate implementation (New York, 17 October 2012 – 1 February 2013).
4 This chapter summarises results published in Maertens 2019; Maertens and Shoshan 2018; Maertens 2016.
5 See also the work of Oels (2012) on the climatisation of security.
6 Interview with an official from DFS, New York, February 2013.
7 UN Security Council Resolution 2100, S/RES/2100.
8 Interview with an official from DFS (Logistics Support Division), New York, February 2013.

9 Participant observation within DPKO and DFS.
10 Participant observation within DPKO and DFS.
11 Interview with an official from DFS (Logistics Support Division), New York, January 2013.
12 Interview with an official from DFS, New York, February 2013.
13 Interview with an official from DFS (Logistics Support Division), New York, January 2013.
14 Interview with an official from DFS (Logistics Support Division), New York, January 2013.
15 Participant observation within DPKO and DFS.
16 UN Security Council, *Press Statement on Environmental Management of Peacekeeping Operations*, 2017.
17 Participant observation within DPKO and DFS.
18 Interview with an official from DFS (Logistics Support Division), New York, February 2013.
19 Participant observation within DPKO and DFS.

References

Acselrad, Henri (2010), 'The "environmentalization of social struggles". The environmental justice movement in Brazil', *Estudos Avançados*, 24:68, 103–19.

Aradau, Claudia (2015), 'From securitization theory to critical approaches to (in)security', *European Journal of International Security*, 3:3, 300–5.

Aradau, Claudia, Jef Huysmans, Andrew Neal, and Nadine Voelkner (2015), *Critical Security Methods: New Frameworks for Analysis* (London: Routledge).

Austin, Jonathan Luke, Rocco Bellanova, and Mareile Kaufmann (2019), 'Doing and mediating critique: An invitation to practice companionship', *Security Dialogue*, 50:1, 3–19.

Autesserre, Séverine (2014), *Peaceland: Conflict Resolution and the Everyday Politics of International Intervention* (Cambridge: Cambridge University Press).

Bakaki, Zorzeta, and Kaisa Hinkkainen (2016), 'Do child soldiers influence UN peacekeeping?', *International Peacekeeping*, 23:4, 540–67.

Baldwin, David A. (1997), 'The concept of security', *Review of International Studies*, 23:1, 5–26.

Balzacq, Thierry (ed.) (2011), *Securitization Theory: How Security Problems Emerge and Dissolve* (New York: Routledge).

Balzacq, Thierry (2016), *Théories de la sécurité. les approches critiques* (Paris: Presses de Sciences Po).

Balzacq, Thierry, Tugba Basara, Didier Bigo, Emmanuel-Pierre Guittet, and Christian Olsson (2010), 'Security practices', in Robert A. Denemark (ed.), *International Studies Encyclopedia Online*, available at: www.oxfordreference.com/view/10.1093/acref/9780191842665.001.0001/acref-9780191842665-e-0337?rskey=2MPdqf&result=385 (accessed 31 July 2019).

Critical security studies

Barkawi, Tarak, and Mark Laffey (2006), 'The postcolonial moment in security studies', *Review of International Studies*, 32:2, 329–52.

Barnett, Michael, and Martha Finnemore (2004), *Rules for the World: International Organizations in Global Politics* (Ithaca, NY: Cornell University Press).

Bellamy, Alex J., Paul D. Williams, and Stuart Griffin (2010), *Understanding Peacekeeping*, 2nd ed. (Cambridge and Malden, MA: Polity).

Bigo, Didier (2002), 'Security and immigration: Toward a critique of the governmentality of unease', *Alternatives*, 27:1: 63–92.

Bigo, Didier, and Anastassia Tsoukala (eds) (2008), *Terror, Insecurity and Liberty: Illiberal Practices of Liberal Regimes after 9/11* (London; New York: Routledge).

Bigo, Didier, and Emma McCluskey (2018), 'What is a PARIS approach to (in)securitization? Political anthropological research for international sociology', in *The Oxford Handbook of International Security*, available at: www.oxfordhandbooks.com/view/10.1093/oxfordhb/9780198777854.001.0001/oxfordhb-9780198777854-e-9 (accessed 31 July 2019).

Booth, Ken (ed.) (2005), *Critical Security Studies and World Politics* (Boulder, CO: Lynne Rienner).

Bratt, Duane (2002), 'Blue condoms: The use of international peacekeepers in the fight against AIDS', *International Peacekeeping*, 9:3, 67–86.

Buzan, Barry, and Lene Hansen (2009), *The Evolution of International Security Studies* (Cambridge: Cambridge University Press).

Buzan, Barry, Ole Wæver, and Jaap de Wilde (1998), *Security: A New Framework for Analysis* (Boulder, CO: Lynne Rienner).

CASE Collective (2006), 'Critical approaches to security in Europe: A networked manifesto', *Security Dialogue*, 37:4, 443–87.

Cunliffe, Philip (2009), 'The politics of global governance in UN peacekeeping', *International Peacekeeping*, 16:3, 323–36.

Fetherston, A.B. (2000), 'Peacekeeping, conflict resolution and peacebuilding: A reconsideration of theoretical frameworks', *International Peacekeeping*, 7:1, 190–218.

Floyd, Rita (2010), *Security and the Environment: Securitisation Theory and US Environmental Security Policy* (Cambridge: Cambridge University Press).

Hagmann, Jonas, Hendrik Hegemann, and Andrew W. Neal (2018), 'The politicisation of security: Controversy, mobilisation, arena shifting. Introduction by the guest editors', *ERIS – European Review of International Studies*, 5:3, 3–29.

Hansen, Lene (2000), 'The little mermaid's silent security dilemma and the absence of gender in the Copenhagen School', *Millennium*, 29:2, 285–306.

Henry, Marsha (2015), 'Parades, parties and pests: Contradictions of everyday life in peacekeeping economies', *Journal of Intervention and Statebuilding*, 9:3, 372–90.

Henry, Marsha, Paul Higate, and Gurchathen Sanghera (2009), 'Positionality and power: The politics of peacekeeping research', *International Peacekeeping*, 16:4, 467–82.

Lucile Maertens

Higate, Paul, and Marsha Henry (2010), 'Space, performance and everyday security in the peacekeeping context', *International Peacekeeping*, 17:1, 32–48.

Huysmans, Jef (1998), 'Security! What do you mean? From concept to thick signifier', *European Journal of International Relations*, 4:2, 226–55.

Jennings, Kathleen M. (2014), 'Service, sex, and security: Gendered peacekeeping economies in Liberia and the Democratic Republic of the Congo', *Security Dialogue*, 45:4, 313–30.

Krause, Keith, and Michael C. Williams (1996), 'Broadening the agenda of security studies: Politics and methods', *Mershon International Studies Review*, 40:2, 229–54.

Krause, Keith, and Michael C. Williams (eds) (1997), *Critical Security Studies: Concepts and Strategies* (London: Routledge).

Lemay-Hébert, Nicolas (2014), 'Resistance in the time of cholera: The limits of stabilization through securitization in Haiti', *International Peacekeeping*, 21:2, 198–213.

Lemay-Hébert, Nicolas (2018), 'Living in the yellow zone: The political geography of intervention in Haiti', *Political Geography*, 67, 88–99.

Liljedahl, Birgitta, and Annica Waleij (2014), *Assessing the Cumulative Environmental Footprint in Crisis and Conflict Situations* (Stockholm: FOI).

Liljedahl, Birgitta, Annica Waleij, Åsa Scott Andersson, Russ Doran, Moha Bhatta, and Svante Olsson (n.d.), 'Environmental Impact Assessment in peacekeeping missions. Challenges and opportunities', available at: https://community.apan.org/cfs-file/__key/docpreview-s/00-00-00-06-49/42 4_2D00_Liljedahl_2D00_Environmental_2D00_Impact_2D00_ Assessment_2D00_in_2D00_peace.pdf (accessed 29 June 2018).

Mac Ginty, Roger (2011), *International Peacebuilding and Local Resistance: Hybrid Forms of Peace* (London: Palgrave Macmillan).

Maertens, Lucile (2016), 'Quand les Casques bleus passent au vert: Environnementalisation des activités de maintien de la paix de l'ONU', *Études Internationales*, 47:1, 57–80.

Maertens, Lucile (2019), 'From blue to green? Environmentalization and securitization in UN peacekeeping practices', *International Peacekeeping*, 26:3, 302–25.

Maertens, Lucile, and Malkit Shoshan (2018), *Greening Peacekeeping: The Environmental Impact of UN Peace Operations* (New York: International Peace Institute).

Mandelbaum, Moran, Anna Maria Friis Kristensen, and Cerelia Athanassiou (2016), 'De/re-constructing the political: How do critical approaches to "security" frame our understanding of the political?', *Critical Studies on Security*, 4:2, 133–6.

McDonald, Matt (2008), 'Securitization and the construction of security', *European Journal of International Relations*, 14:4, 563–87.

McDonald, Matt (2011), *Security, the Environment and Emancipation: Contestation over Environmental Change* (Abingdon: Routledge).

Oels, Angela (2012), 'From "securitization" of climate change to "climatization" of the security field: Comparing three theoretical perspectives', in Jürgen Scheffran, Michael Brzoska, Hans Günter Brauch, Peter Michael Link, and Janpeter Schilling (eds), *Climate Change, Human Security and Violent Conflict* (Berlin and Heidelberg: Springer) 185–205.

Olsson, Louise, and Theodora-Ismene Gizelis (2014), 'Advancing gender and peacekeeping research', *International Peacekeeping*, 21:4, 520–8.

Paris, Roland (2000), 'Broadening the study of peace operations', *International Studies Review*, 2:3, 27–44.

Paris, Roland (2002), 'International peacebuilding and the "mission civilisatrice"', *Review of International Studies*, 28:4, 637–56.

Peoples, Columba, and Nick Vaughan-Williams (2010), *Critical Security Studies: An Introduction* (London: Routledge).

Pouligny, Beatrice (2006), *Peace Operations Seen from Below: UN Missions and Local People* (Bloomfield, CT: Kumarian Press).

Pratt, Nicola (2013), 'Reconceptualizing gender, reinscribing racial–sexual boundaries in international security: The case of UN Security Council resolution 1325 on "Women, Peace and Security"', *International Studies Quarterly*, 57:4, 772–83.

Pugh, Michael (2004), 'Peacekeeping and critical theory', *International Peacekeeping*, 11:1, 39–58.

Salter, Mark B. (2013), 'Introduction', in Mark B. Salter and Can E. Mutlu (eds), *Research Methods in Critical Security Studies: An Introduction.* (New York: Routledge), 1–14.

Salter, Mark B., and Can E. Mutlu (eds) (2013), *Research Methods in Critical Security Studies: An Introduction* (New York: Routledge).

Shepherd, Laura J. (2013), *Critical Approaches to Security: An Introduction to Theories and Methods* (London: Routledge).

Smith, Steve (2015), 'The contested concept of security', in Ken Booth (ed.), *Critical Security Studies and World Politics* (Boulder: Lynne Rienner), 27–62.

Swain, Ashok, and Joakim Öjendal (eds) (2018), *Routledge Handbook of Environmental Conflict and Peacebuilding* (London and New York: Routledge).

Tardy, Thierry (2011), 'A critique of robust peacekeeping in contemporary peace operations', *International Peacekeeping*, 18:2, 152–67.

Trombetta, Maria Julia (2008), 'Environmental security and climate change: Analysing the discourse', *Cambridge Review of International Affairs*, 21:4, 585–602.

Trombetta, Maria Julia (2011), 'Rethinking the securitisation of the environment: Old beliefs, new insights', in Thierry Balzacq (ed.), *Securitization Theory: How Security Problems Emerge and Dissolve* (New York: Routledge), 135–49.

United Nations Department of Field Support (UN DFS) (2017a), *DFS Environment Strategy. Executive Summary* (New York: United Nations).

United Nations Department of Field Support (UN DFS) (2017b), *Environmental Good Practice: 2017 Implementation of the DFS Environment Strategy in Field Missions* (New York: United Nations).

United Nations Department of Peacekeeping Operations / Department of Field Support (UN DPKO/DFS) (2017), 'Lesson 3.5: Environment and natural resources', available at: http://repository.un.org/bitstream/handle/11176/400656/Lesson%203.5%20Environment%20and%20Natural%20Resources.pdf?sequence=5&isAllowed=y (accessed 31 July 2019).

United Nations Environment Programme (UNEP) (2012), *Greening the Blue Helmets: Environment, Natural Resources and UN Peacekeeping Operations* (Nairobi: UNEP).

Waever, Ole (1995), 'Securitisation and desecuritisation', in Ronnie Lipschutz (ed.), *On Security* (New York: Columbia University Press), 46–86.

Walling, Carrie Booth (2013), *All Necessary Measures: The United Nations and Humanitarian Intervention* (Philadelphia: University of Pennsylvania Press).

Whitworth, Sandra (2005), 'Militarized masculinities and the politics of peacekeeping', in Ken Booth (ed.), *Critical Security Studies and World Politics* (Boulder, CO: Lynne Rienner), 89–106.

Zanotti, Laura (2006), 'Taming chaos: A Foucauldian view of UN peacekeeping, democracy and normalization', *International Peacekeeping*, 13:2, 150–67.

Zanotti, Laura (2008), 'Imagining democracy, building unsustainable institutions: The UN peacekeeping operation in Haiti', *Security Dialogue*, 39:5, 539–61.

8

Feminist institutionalism

Georgina Holmes

Feminist institutionalism (FI) aims to understand and explain how power is distributed within institutions. Emphasising gender as a primary unit of analysis, FI's political project seeks to disrupt existing power settlements within institutions and facilitate change by identifying and challenging institutional barriers that maintain gender inequalities and other forms of discrimination. In peacekeeping contexts, these institutional barriers produce gender biases that prevent women from taking up leadership roles and stalls the creation and design of gender-just peace operations. Pillar One of UN Security Council Resolution 1325 (Women, Peace and Security) calls for the participation of women at all decision-making levels, including in international, regional, and national security institutions and in preventing, managing, and resolving conflict. Women's meaningful participation cannot be achieved without institutional change, often facilitated by equality and diversity initiatives and gender-sensitive Security Sector Reform programmes within the institutions engaged in peacekeeping, and within peacekeeping missions themselves. However, little is known about how gendered institutional barriers are sustained over time; the intended and unintended gendered effects of organisational change in peacekeeping institutions; and what change mechanisms are most effective.

This chapter explores how FI contributes to explaining how peacekeeping is a gendered enterprise in the context of the global racialised and classed power relations that underscore contemporary international peacekeeping. The chapter discusses the key assumptions of feminist institutionalism and considers how the theory can help explain why contemporary peace operations take the shape that they do. Applying an FI approach to the study of institutional change and institutional reproduction, the chapter then examines how the implementation of gender-equality initiatives in the Ghana Armed Forces (GAF) impact on the way in which female military peacekeepers from Ghana are deployed to UN peace operations. Drawing on field research conducted in Ghana in 2017, the illustrative case study considers how incremental change processes take effect and examines the frictions that exist when internal 'institutional enforcers' attempt to reproduce the GAF's existing gender order, often by resisting change imposed by external and internal 'feminist activists'. Two institutional barriers that are known to prevent women's meaningful participation in peace operations are examined: recruitment processes and deployment criteria (Ghittoni et al. 2018).

Feminist institutionalism

FI is a body of theory that seeks to understand and explain how power is distributed within and across institutions. The theory-building project of FI began in the mid-2000s, when feminist political scientists examined how seemingly bureaucratically neutral structures, rules, norms, and practices that constitute institutions are gendered and produce gendered effects (Chappell 2006; Kenny 2007). FI builds on new institutionalism, which traces how institutional continuity and change occurs, but argues for the importance of incorporating gender into institutional-level analyses.

FI therefore shares many of the theoretical assumptions of the different strands of new institutionalism, and FI scholars have created dialogues between the two types of theory and identified synergies to demonstrate how a gendered approach can add value to the study of institutions (Lowndes 2009: 92; Mackay et al. 2010). Like new institutionalism, FI reflects the critical turn's rejection of the positivist theoretical approaches applied to earlier analyses of institutions (Lowndes 2009). Feminist institutionalists foreground institutions as a primary explanatory variable in political analysis and gendered social actors as central to the analysis of the economic, social, and political behaviour of institutions (Mackay et al. 2010: 573). Inspired by agency-structure debates, feminist institutionalists contend that institutions are not atemporal, static, monolithic 'things' but dynamic entities that constrain or enable the behaviour of social actors working inside and outside of them. Since they are dynamic, institutions evolve and may be altered by social actors (Chappell 2006: 224).

An FI approach helps to explain how institutions function and elucidates on context-specific relationships between institutions and gendered social actors (Chappell 2006: 223). Formal and informal rules, norms, and practices 'prescribe' and 'proscribe "acceptable" masculine and feminine forms of behaviour' for men and women within institutions and 'produce outcomes which help to … re/ produce broader social and political gender expectations' (Chappell 2006: 225). Formal (codified) rules, norms, and practices as well as 'bureaucratic neutrality' establish the institution's 'gendered logic of appropriateness' which regulates social actors (Chappell 2006: 225). This gender logic is enforced by informal routines, norms, and practices and subtle forms of violence targeting social actors that threaten the stability of the institution. Feminists are also interested in tracing how change occurs within institutions and how different types of change process – such as small incremental changes over time or large exogenous shocks – can result in different intended and unintended gendered outcomes. Examining the relationship between continuity and change, FI scholars identify several types of social actor, including 'reformers' and internal or external 'feminist activists' who seek to re-engineer or transform institutions, and 'institutional enforcers' such as powerful male elites that benefit the most from the established gendered logic of appropriateness, and in whose best interests it is to retain the institution's status quo (Mackay 2014).

As a political project, FI acknowledges that women 'continue to suffer discrimination and lower levels of representation because of their sex' and feminist institutionalist scholars pay particular attention to women's inclusion within and exclusion from institutions, their experience and engagement in institutional dynamics, and how effectively gender-equality reforms facilitate the redistribution of power within institutions (Chappell 2006: 222; Chappell and Waylen 2013). This focus has been enabled by the evolution in thinking about gender within feminist discourse more broadly, and the emergence of more complex understandings of gender as socially constructed, fluid, and continually negotiated (Krook and Mackay 2011: 4). Identifying gender as a process, FI scholars seek to expose and explain how gender relations underscore the seemingly neutral structures of institutions (Chappell 2006: 224). The emphasis on gender as socially constructed has led to the development of intersectional analyses that examine how institutions constrain or enable the behaviour of a diversity of social actors categorised according to prescribed social divisions such as class, race, gender, sex, sexuality, age, ableism, and religion. This has opened up the study of institutions to examine how women and men of colour and other(ed) minority women and men may be enabled or constrained and discriminated against across time and place within a given institution (Kenny 2007; Ahmed 2012). By drawing on feminist theories and a diversity of feminist methodologies, feminist institutionalists have contributed to understanding how boundaries between political institutions and the private lives of social actors become demarcated (Krook and Mackay 2011: 5) – for example, when institutional dynamics shape the policies that impact on the daily lives of those social actors. The aim of this theorising is to help feminist activists and their supporters disrupt existing institutional gender logics and gender biases and facilitate change to create gender-just institutions (Lowndes 2015: 689).

Though feminist institutionalism has significantly enhanced understandings of how institutions operate, and how social actors interact with institutions, much of the research and theorising has concentrated on the study of domestic-level political institutions of governments in the global north and global south, rather than international and regional institutions. Scholars of feminist IR have only recently begun to apply FI approaches to examine how international and regional security institutions such as the UN, NATO, the European Union, and the African Union are gendered and produce gendered effects for social actors that interact inside and outside of them (Holmes et al. 2019). Here, emphasis is placed on how effectively international institutions are implementing UN Security Council Resolution 1325 (Women, Peace and Security) and its related resolutions, though it is recognised that there are many other policy areas that demand attention (see Basu 2010; Wright 2016; Hurley 2018; Bastick and Duncanson 2018; Kronsell 2015; Guerrina et al. 2016).

These scholars draw on theorising about gendered international institutions that predates FI, but apply the conceptual tools developed and employed by feminist institutionalists. Nevertheless, a feminist IR approach has much to offer the FI project and there is still significant potential to develop this body of theorising further. A feminist IR approach can be used to analyse the transnational and transregional workings of international security institutions and adds a global perspective to analyses of formal institutions, as well as the informal within institutions (Holmes et al. 2019). Feminist IR has also tended to engage more extensively with postcolonial theories, which have the potential to facilitate the development of innovative methodological tools and approaches that can be used to overcome access challenges such as uncovering informal rules within institutions – as FI scholars have called for (Kenny 2007: 95; Krook and Mackay 2011; Lowndes 2015). Adopting postcolonial theories may help feminists investigate how competitions and partnerships between patriarchal regimes emerge within international institutions; examine why the bodies of some social actors are regarded as the 'accepted norm' in some institutions and not others (Holmes et al. 2019); uncover why and when social actors choose to comply or challenge an institution's gendered logic of appropriateness; and expose the gendered, classed and racialised power relations within and between national, regional, and international institutions operating within the international system.

Feminist institutionalism and peacekeeping

Unsurprisingly, due to the original focus on national political institutions and the limited engagement with the theory in the field of IR, FI has not been applied to UN peacekeeping, despite synergies between the intentions of scholars researching peacekeeping as a gendered enterprise and the political project of FI. This is most notable in the shared ambition to redistribute power within institutions involved in peacekeeping; to facilitate gender equality reforms; to overcome the institutional barriers that prevent women's meaningful participation in peacekeeping; to redesign and restructure peacekeeping workforces so that women are engaged in decision-making at the tactical, operational, and strategic levels in peacekeeping; to respond to the gender-specific needs and concerns of the host population (the social actors that interact with peacekeeping institutions) (DeGroot 2001; Bridges and Horsfall 2009; Beardsley and Karim 2013; Karim and Beardsley 2017; Heathcote and Otto 2014; Heinecken 2015; Jennings 2011; Pruitt 2016; Rupesinghe et al. 2018), including preventing peacekeeper violence such as sexual exploitation and abuse and child abuse; and to ensure that a gender approach is incorporated at all stages of a peacekeeping mission – from design to drawdown and withdrawal, as recommended in the UN's global study on the implementation of UNSCR 1325 (2015) (United Nations 2015). Feminist institutionalism has informed important research in the field of critical military studies where scholars have examined how national military and police institutions constrain and enable female security actors, and assessed how effectively gender equality reform programmes have been implemented by individual militaries and police forces, but much of this research observes state-level institutional barriers in isolation to the broader institutional structures of international peacekeeping (see Carreiras 2006; Sion 2008; Duncanson 2009; Egnell et al. 2014; Wilén and Heinecken 2018).

So how might an FI approach to the study of peacekeeping research enhance understandings of why and how contemporary peacekeeping operations take the shape that they do? An FI approach would suggest that peacekeeping missions are not stable, monolithic institutions and are instead formed out of constellations of gendered institutions that interact with one another. Whilst contemporary peacekeeping missions are designed prior to mission start-up, they are temporal and dynamic in nature, with mission success dependent on many variables including the political will of the host nation, availability of UN financing, resources offered by UN member states, and deployment constraints. How peace operations experience continuity and change is therefore determined by the interests of a vast network of social actors who operate within or interact with peacekeeping institutions. Collectively, these institutions constitute the peacekeeping institutional matrix.

Contemporary peace operations are formed out of gendered formal and informal rules, norms, and practices that are intended to regulate (govern) peacekeeping institutions and peacekeepers (Holmes 2019). Peacekeeping institutions including troop-contributing countries (TCCs), TCC militaries and police forces, civilian peacekeeping institutions (international NGOs), external contractors, UN organs and agencies (for example, UN Security Council, DPO/DOS, UN Women), and the social actors who work within these institutions must co-operate effectively to deliver mission objectives. Co-operation in international peacekeeping is also shaped by global racialised power inequalities, often described as the 'global colour-line' (Razack 2004: 9; see also Henry 2015) in peacekeeping. Cold-Ravnkilde et al. show how structural inequalities in the UN Multidimensional Integrated Stabilization Mission in Mali (MINUSMA) reinforce cultural differences between (predominantly male) African and European military peacekeepers which in turn determine how dangerous roles and functions, as well as mission supplies, are allocated (Cold-Ravnkilde et al. 2017). African soldiers deployed in their national battalions and companies disproportionately suffered and experienced higher death tolls than European peacekeepers, who tended to work in the more protected UN compounds and in strategic roles within the mission head office. These kinds of racialised structural inequalities, evidenced in the informal rules, norms and practices of MINUSMA, led to intra-mission frictions which slowed down the mission and prevented peacekeepers from effectively delivering mission objectives (Cold-Ravnkilde et al. 2017: 35). In this instance, racial hierarchies informed the logic of appropriateness of MINUSMA.

A feminist institutionalist approach would take this analysis one step further to explore how MINUSMA's logic of appropriateness is informed by gendered and classed inequalities, in addition to racialised structural inequalities. Rather than conceptualise the mission area as primarily a geographical space, as has been the case in many ground-breaking studies to date (see Higate and Henry 2009; Autesserre 2014; Smirl 2015), emphasis is placed on how intersecting global structural inequalities manifest in the formal (visible) laws, standards, and protocols and informal (hidden) rules, norms and practices within and between peacekeeping institutions that operate within and outside of the mission area. Complementing existing studies, a feminist institutionalist approach therefore enables the researcher to 'grasp systems of interaction across formal [and informal] barriers' (Bogason in Lowndes 2009: 94), but adds greater nuance by examining how a diversity of gendered peacekeeping actors are constrained and enabled or are subjected to racialised and gendered effects in different institutional contexts, and how these influence political behaviours and decision-making in international peacekeeping.

An FI approach can help to identify how the behaviour of different peacekeeping institutions, acting both individually and in partnership with other institutions in the context of decentralised governance arrangements results in intended and unintended gendered effects for the recipients of peacekeeping and peacebuilding tasks in the host nation including preventing sexual exploitation and abuse (SEA), helping survivors of conflict related sexual violence (CRSV) and implementing liberal peacebuilding initiatives, for instance educating and empowering women. Undertaking comparative analyses while adopting an FI approach can also expose and explain the institutional conditions under which exogenous and endogenous change processes are successful in delivering the UN's Women, Peace, and Security agenda, and the conditions under which change processes and initiatives are stalled. In doing so, feminist activists may become better equipped with the knowledge and vocabulary required to disrupt existing power settlements in international peacekeeping.

Integrating female military peacekeepers from Ghana

Examining how the UN's directive to integrate more female military peacekeepers is implemented by GAF, the following case study illustrates how a feminist institutionalist approach contributes towards explaining how peace operations take the gendered shape that they do. The case study examines gendered institutional dynamics and the frictions that occur when exogenous feminist activists from the UN's DPO and internal male GAF feminist activists attempt to improve deployment opportunities for Ghanaian female peacekeepers working in UN peace operations. The case study is informed by 45 depth-interviews with senior leaders, trainers, and male and female military personnel of mixed ranks conducted during field research in Accra, Ghana, in January and February 2017. Analysis of GAF policies and procedures was undertaken to gather formal rules and regulations around recruitment and deployment of peacekeepers. Informal gendered rules, norms, and practices were gathered during depth-interviews, wherein research participants shared personal stories about their experiences working in the GAF and in UN peace operations. Through conducting a discourse analysis of these narratives, an understanding of how GAF gender equality initiatives were implemented is constructed. Research participants consented to the interviews and are referred to by rank and role to ensure anonymity.

Incremental change processes within the Ghana Armed Forces

When UNSCR 1325 was unanimously adopted in 2000, Pillar One called for fundamental change to the gendered structure and composition of all security institutions engaged in peacekeeping. Yet feminist scholars and policy-makers have been critical of the resolution's failure to serve as a catalyst for large-scale, rapid change, noting that gender balancing and women's meaningful participation in peacekeeping follows a much slower pace, with small, incremental change processes appearing to be most effective (Heathecote and Otto 2014). DPO in New York decides the number of female military peacekeepers required of TCCs for each peacekeeping mission, though it is the responsibility of individual TCCs to source and recruit female peacekeepers with the appropriate skills and experience from their ranks. Since most peacekeeping troops on the ground are recruited from countries of the Global South, African, Asian, South American, and Middle Eastern militaries are under more pressure to implement gender-mainstreaming initiatives than militaries in the Global North and at a much faster pace. This expectation has placed increased pressure on women from the Global South to carry the burden of security by delivering on gender-sensitive UN mission targets (Henry 2012).

In line with global trends, GAF has been increasing its female contributions since the introduction of UNSCR 1325 in 2000.[1] Rather than design and implement a gender-sensitive security sector reform programme to transform the masculine-dominated culture of the armed forces, facilitate the integration of women into the military, and increase acceptance of female military personnel's skills and abilities at all decision-making levels, GAF senior leaders introduced new gender-sensitive policies incrementally to quickly accommodate women and to mitigate gender issues as and when they arose. This was achieved through the mobilisation of a mechanism called institutional layering, whereby 'new elements' (in this case women and the gendered functions they deliver such as assisting female survivors of CRSV in peace operations) are 'attached to [the] existing institution' (Van der Heijden 2011: 1). Although the aim is to 'gradually change [the institution's] status and structure', institutional layering does not require replacing existing policies, norms, and practices and therefore does not necessarily threaten the status quo of the institution (Van der Heijden 2011: 1). Gender issues that senior leadership addressed tended to be the ones that were perceived to destabilise the existing institutional masculine core of the GAF and were therefore a concern for elite military men. For example, fearing that women's integration into peace operations would result in the decline in discipline among the troops, commanding officers introduced an informal policy preventing men and women from socialising in the Ghanaian base camp after 7 pm.[2] Yet, the gendered consequences of this informal policy – for instance, those related to the social isolation that female peacekeepers experience in the mission – were not formerly addressed by GAF senior leadership.

Institutional layering was evident in the narrative about GAF recruitment policies and processes articulated by a male Lieutenant Colonel. Operating as an 'institutional enforcer' in his capacity as head of an administrative directorate, the Lieutenant Colonel classified the integration of women as part of the process of 'restructuring' the GAF. When further probed what he meant by restructuring, the director changed his phrasing to claim that women's integration constituted 'the expansion [of the GAF] and then adding more rules'. He continued:

> We are required to create specific areas in job descriptions where we have to incorporate women to assist as part of the job. I don't think [the institutional structure is] anything different ... As I said, it's just an expansion of whatever we have. When I look at the expansion of the medical units, where we need more female nurses, or in the communications outfit, the IT areas, we need [women there] as well, and even in the infantry units, where we might require some of the women in clerical roles to support the units.[3]

Although GAF senior leaders always ensured they had enough women to meet UN quotas,[4] their focus on numbers recruited rather than on women in leadership and the lack of equal opportunities for women across all trades and units meant that those women deployed often did not have the skill sets required by the UN. At the time of the field research, the GAF had not developed equal-opportunity recruitment campaigns to encourage women to join conventionally 'masculine' trades such as engineering, critical military functions, and combat units, nor established a talent pipeline to fast-track female military personnel for promotion into leadership positions. Instead, most women were slotted into traditional feminised trades such as administration, cooking, nursing, and accountancy where female officers held management positions. Indeed the most senior woman, who was a brigadier general, worked in finance. The director interpreted women's entry into these trades as evidence of positive discrimination, arguing that all recruitment criteria including age, physical fitness, and academic ability were the same for men and women. He remarked:

> The other thing that maybe favours the females is the trade. So, for example, you have more clerical staff, catering staff, nurses – these ancillary activities. You have more of them going to the females.

And then the hardcore work of the military – that is the infantry and the weapons – they go to the males. It doesn't mean that you don't find females in those units.[5]

Yet, as in many African countries, high unemployment in Ghana and a large pool of educated, young potential workers meant that competition to join the GAF was fierce for both men and women. Several of the women interviewed indicated that they joined the military because it was the only option available to them to pursue a career in the trade that they had trained in. One female lieutenant who was a head nurse stated that she had joined the military during the 'special medical intake' recruitment period, but previously had had no desire to be a soldier.[6] As another male senior leader explained, women tended to apply to join the military because they knew they had the qualifications required to be accepted into feminised trades. Other female soldiers interviewed who signed up as soldiers and who believed they were capable of succeeding in more senior and challenging positions expressed their frustration at being prevented from competing with men for combatant roles and spoke of being segregated throughout their military career and when deployed to UN peace operations.[7] Nevertheless, those women who joined the military for job security alone and did not wish to engage in kinetic activity inadvertently lent credence to the argument proposed by institutional enforcers within the GAF that men and women should deploy to UN peace operations in their 'natural' gender roles. This meant men should work on the front line and women should work in service roles – either in the more protected Ghanaian base camp or in UN headquarters – and should partake in front-line activities only when women were required, for example when liaising with local populations in IDP camps, where they are expected to use 'feminised' skills in com-munication and care.[8] These recruitment processes directly impacted on how GAF could meet the UN's requirement to redress the gender balance in peacekeeping workforces.

Feminist activist work

In a challenge to institutional resistance, external feminist activists and internal GAF feminist activists have used alternative incremental change processes with the intention of replacing discriminatory policies, norms, and practices and with the longer-term view to disrupt and rebalance existing gender power relations in the GAF. To an extent, these incremental change processes were made possible by the ad-hoc approach to gender mainstreaming adopted by GAF senior leaders. For example, DPO staff focused on nurturing a Ghanaian male feminist activist when, in 2012, a male Lieutenant Colonel seconded to DPO in New York for three years was asked to develop gender awareness pre-deployment training materials which would be distributed globally to military peacekeepers. At the time, the trainer did not self-identify as gender-aware, but, after having developed the training package, he began to operate as a feminist activist within the GAF on his return to Ghana. He explained:

> That's how I became involved in these gender matters ... It was good. It was revealing to me because, as a West African, we have these stereotypes about the superiority of men over women and all that stuff, especially in the military. I had to do a lot of research to develop the [training] materials. I had to look back on my own experiences – peacekeeping experiences. It was good. From there, at least that gender awareness came to me. [When I returned to Ghana] I *had* to change the [pre-deployment] training curriculum. I brought in gender and started a crusade – a gender crusade in the military. Whenever we have a meeting, I try to bring up this issue.[9]

Identifying what he called 'subcultures' within the GAF (wherein the dominant culture perpetuated the discriminatory norm that women were not full members of the military institution), the feminist activist claimed that Ghanaian peacekeepers took the stereotypes about Ghanaian women 'to the field' (peace operations) and that 'We [the military] don't want to send the women to the front line in any capacity', whether it be 'in a combatant role or as a nurse or a radio operator'. While deployed as an assistant operations officer in Sierra Leone, this feminist activist tried to end women's occupational and physical segregation in the mission area and improve GAF women's deployment opportunities when he was responsible for placing Ghanaian peacekeepers on duty. However, his efforts backfired when more senior institutional enforcers used subtle, coercive tactics to prevent him from changing conventional practice resulting in a friction that slowed down efforts to meaningfully integrate and effectively utilise skilled women in peace operations. He explained:

> There was this medical lady that I put on duty and the duty was overnight. You go and stay in the office, you stay overnight like a watchkeeper. They [his senior colleagues] were like, 'No, no, no, no. You know you don't have to put the woman on duty.' I said, 'No.' I insisted that she must go, she's also an officer, right? So, she must also go on duty. That day [I had] a barrage of calls. Even my boss called me and said, 'No. You see this one? She's a woman and you know it's only men there.' Then I insisted that day she did the duty. My boss said, 'Okay, put her at risk.' But he didn't accept it. He insisted. So, I didn't put her on duty again. For that night she did the duty. From there, I didn't put her on duty again.[10]

In contrast, a more senior feminist activist who had more power and a stronger voice within the institution was successful in challenging his colleagues' gender biases while deployed to Lebanon, demonstrating how his perseverance significantly improved women's opportunities in the mission during his time and during future rotations. He observed:

> Initially, the females were segregated into a warehouse and in one headquarters, even though we had different locations. But I said, 'No. I think it's wrong. We're not giving the ladies or the females that initiative. We are not integrating them well by putting them in one position at the headquarters and in one building.' So, what I

said was that we will distribute these females to the various positions...
This was the first time we were going to do it. So, when my commander said they [the women] don't have washrooms. I said no
way. The females can use the same washroom as me. It doesn't
matter. They're the same human beings. Or if you insist for cultural
reasons that we should get washrooms, I can get them for you. And
I insisted, and we distributed them [the women]. That was the very
first time it happened in Lebanon. And I did it.[11]

Despite instances where incremental change had been successful,
both external and internal GAF feminist activists were limited in
their ability to facilitate change because they were able to disrupt
discriminatory norms and practices only at the operational and
tactical levels within the military. Without disrupting the power
settlement at the strategic level, the feminist activists were not able
to disrupt the GAF's status quo and the masculine institutional
core remained intact.

Conclusion

Feminist institutionalism, with its emphasis on explaining and
understanding gendered power relations and continuity and change
within institutions provides valuable theoretical and methodological
tools for analysing international peacekeeping, which in this chapter
is conceptualised as a changeable and evolving institutional matrix.
Given the vast range of international, regional, and national
institutions engaged in peacekeeping, a feminist institutionalist
approach has much to offer studies examining why contemporary
peace operations take the gendered shape that they do. Adding a
feminist IR perspective to the study of peacekeeping institutions,
this chapter calls for analyses that consider how global gendered,
racialised, and classed power relations inform institutional change
processes and initiatives, as well as political behaviours and decision-
making in international peacekeeping. As the Ghana case study

illustrated, international pressure to rapidly recruit and deploy female peacekeepers from militaries in the Global South led to an organic, unplanned approach to gender mainstreaming, whereupon strategic-level institutional enforcers used institutional layering – an incremental change process that involves adding formal and informal policies and practices to existing policies and practices – to quickly accommodate a larger number of women into the military without disrupting the institutional status quo. The case study also examined the frictions that exist between institutional enforcers and feminist activists who, often operating covertly, attempt to evolve the military institution by introducing alternative policies and practices incrementally – in this case with the intent of improving GAF women's deployment opportunities. It was argued that these frictions slowed down the DPO's efforts to deploy more gender-balanced peacekeeping workforces to UN peace operations, and to make better use of women's skills and experiences once deployed. In this respect, a feminist institutionalist approach provides a more nuanced understanding of how change management mechanisms sustain or challenge discriminatory rules, norms, and practices in peacekeeping institutions and can be applied to TCC security institutions located in both the Global South and Global North to ascertain the context-specific institutional barriers that hinder the democratisation of contemporary peacekeeping workforces.

Notes

1 Male GAF officer 1, interview with the author, Accra, Ghana, 2 February 2017.
2 Male GAF officer 1.
3 Male GAF officer 2, interview with the author, Accra, Ghana, 1 February 2017.
4 Male GAF officer 2.
5 Male GAF officer.
6 Female peacekeeper 1, interview with the author, Accra, Ghana, 31 January 2017.

7　Female major, focus group with author, Accra, Ghana, 3 February 2017.
8　Male GAF officer 3, interview with the author, Accra, Ghana, 2 February 2017. See Holmes 2019 for an analysis of how women are trained to undertake feminised roles once deployed.
9　Male GAF officer 3.
10　Male GAF officer 3.
11　Male GAF officer 1.

References

Ahmed, Sara (2012), *On Being Included: Racism and Diversity in Institutional Life* (Durham, NC: Duke University Press).

Autesserre, Séverine (2014), *Peaceland: Conflict Resolution and the Everyday Politics of International Intervention* (Cambridge: Cambridge University Press).

Bastick, Megan, and Claire Duncanson (2018), 'Agents of change? Gender advisors in NATO militaries', *International Peacekeeping*, 25:4, 554–77.

Basu, Soumita (2010), 'The UN Security Council and the political economy of the WPS resolutions', *Politics and Gender*, 13:4, 721–7.

Beardsley, Kyle, and Sabrina Karim (2013), 'Female peacekeepers and gender balancing: Token gestures or informed policymaking?', *International Interactions*, 39:4, 461–88.

Bridges, Donna, and Debbie Horsfall (2009), 'Increasing operational effectiveness in UN peacekeeping: Toward a gender-balanced force', *Armed Forces and Society*, 36:1, 120–30.

Carreiras, Helena (2006), *Gender and the Military: Women in the Armed Forces of Western Democracies* (London: Routledge).

Chappell, Louise (2006), 'Moving to a comparative politics of gender?', *Critical Perspectives on Gender and Politics*, 2, 221–63.

Chappell, Louise, and Georgina Waylen (2013), 'Gender and the hidden life of institutions', *Public Institution*, 91:3, 599–615.

Cold-Ravnkilde, Signe, Peter Albrecht, and Rikke Haugegaard (2017), 'Friction and inequality among peacekeepers in Mali', *The RUSI Journal*, 162:2, 34–42.

DeGroot, Gerard Jan (2001) 'A few good women: Gender stereotypes, the military and peacekeeping', *International Peacekeeping*, 8:2, 23–38.

Duncanson, Claire (2009), 'Forces for good? Narratives of military masculinity in peacekeeping operations', *International Feminist Journal of Politics*, 11:1, 63–80.

Engell, Robert, Petter Hojem, and Hannes Berts (2014), *Gender, Military Effectiveness, and Organizational Change: The Swedish Model* (London: Palgrave Macmillan).

Ghittoni, Marta, Léa Lehouck, and Callum Watson (2018), 'Elsie Initiative for Women in Peace Operations: Baseline study' (DECAF). www.dcaf.ch/

sites/default/files/publications/documents/Elsie_GenderReport_2018_ Final.pdf, accessed 15 October 2018.

Guerrina, Roberta, Laura Chappell, and Katharine A.M. Wright (2016), 'Transforming CSDP? Feminist triangles and gender regimes', *Journal of Common Market Studies*, 56:5, 1036–52.

Heathcote, Gina, and Diane Otto (2014), *Rethinking Peacekeeping, Gender Equality and Collective Security* (London: Palgrave Macmillan).

Heinecken, Lindy (2015), 'Are women "really" making a unique contribution to peacekeeping?', *Journal of International Peacekeeping*, 19:3–4, 227–48.

Henry, Marsha (2012), 'Peacexploitation: Interrogating labor hierarchies and global sisterhood among Indian and Uruguayan female peacekeepers', *Globalizations*, 9:1, 5–33.

Henry, Marsha (2015), 'Parades, parties and pests: Contradictions of everyday life in peacekeeping economies', *Journal of Intervention and Statebuilding*, 9:3, 372–90.

Higate, Paul, and Marsha Henry (2009), *Insecure Spaces: Peacekeeping, Power and Performance in Haiti, Kosovo and Liberia* (London and New York: Zed Books).

Holmes, Georgina (2019), 'Situating agency, embodied practices and norm implementation in peacekeeping training', *International Peacekeeping*, 26:1, 55–84.

Holmes, Georgina, Katharine Wright, Soumita Basu, Matthew Hurley, Maria Martin de Almagro, Roberta Guerrina, and Christine Cheng (2019), 'Feminist experiences of "studying up": Encounters with international institutions', *Millennium: Journal of International Studies*, 47:2, 210–30.

Hurley, Matthew (2018), 'The "genderman": (Re)negotiating militarised masculinities when "doing gender" at NATO', *Critical Military Studies*, 4:1, 72–91.

Jennings, Kathleen (2011), 'Women's participation in UN peacekeeping operations: Agents of change or stranded symbols?', NOREF report, available at: www.files.ethz.ch/isn/137505/Women%E2%80%99s%20participation%20 in%20UN%20peacekeeping.pdf.

Karim, Sabrina, and Kyle Beardsley (2017), *Equal Opportunity Peacekeeping: Women, Peace and Security in Post-conflict States* (Oxford: Oxford University Press).

Kenny, Meryll (2007), 'Gender, institutions and power: A critical review', *Politics*, 27:2, 91–100.

Kronsell, Annika (2015), 'Sexed bodies and military masculinities: Gender path dependence in EU's Common Security and Defense Policy', *Men and Masculinities*, 19:3, 1–26.

Krook, Mona Lena, and Fiona Mackay (2011), *Gender, Politics and Institutions: Towards a Feminist Institutionalism* (London: Palgrave Macmillan).

Lowndes, Vivian (2009), 'New institutionalism and urban politics', in Jonathan S. Davies and David L. Imbroscio (eds), *Theories of Urban Politics* (London: Sage), 91–105.

Lowndes, Vivien (2015), 'How are things done around here? Uncovering institutional rules and their gendered effects', *Politics and Gender*, 10, 685–91.

Mackay, Fiona (2014), 'Nested newness, institutional innovation, and the gendered limits of change', *Politics and Gender*, 10:4, 549–71.

Mackay, Fiona, Meryl Kenny, and Louise Chappell (2010), 'New institutionalism through a gender lens: Towards a feminist institutionalism?', *International Political Science Review*, 31:5, 573–88.

Pruitt, Lesley J. (2016), *The Women in Blue Helmets: Gender, Policing, and the UN's First All-Female Peacekeeping Unit* (Oakland: University of California Press).

Razack, Sherene H. (2004), *Dark Threats and White Knights: The Somalia Affair, Peacekeeping and the New Imperialism* (Toronto: University of Toronto Press).

Rupesinghe, Natasja, John Karlsrud, and Eli Stamnes (2018), 'Women, peace and security and female peacekeeping personnel', in Jacqui True and Sara Davies (eds), *Women, Peace and Security Handbook* (Oxford: Oxford University Press), 206–21.

Sion, Liora (2008), 'Peacekeeping and the gender regime: Dutch female peacekeepers in Bosnia and Kosovo', *Journal of Contemporary Ethnography*, 37:5, 561–85.

Smirl, Lisa (2015), *Spaces of Aid: How Cars, Compounds and Hotels Shape Humanitarianism* (London: Zed Books).

United Nations (2015), 'Preventing conflict, transforming justice, securing the peace: a global study on the implementation of United Nations security council resolution 1325', https://wps.unwomen.org/~/media/files/un%20 women/wps/highlights/unw-global-study-1325-2015.pdf (accessed 16 October 2015).

Van der Heijden, Jeroen (2011), 'Institutional layering: A review of the concept', *Politics*, 31:1, 9–18.

Wilén, Nina, and Lindy Heinecken (2018), 'Regendering the South African army: Inclusion, reversal and displacement', *Gender, Work and Organization*, 25:6, 670–86.

Wright, Katharine (2016), 'NATO's adoption of UNSCR 1325 on Women, Peace and Security: Making the agenda a reality', *International Political Science Review*, 37:3, 350–61.

9

Complexity theory

Charles T. Hunt

Complexity theory is not a theory of international relations. Originally developed in theoretical physics and cybernetics (e.g. Wiener 1948; von Bertalanffy 1968), this theory has only recently been transported into the study of global politics and its subcategories. Its application to UN peacekeeping is only just beginning to occur. Complexity theory is primarily concerned with explaining change processes in complex systems (Johnson 2009; Mitchell 2011). In a complicated system, outcomes are determined and finite and can be predicted; the system is stable and 'knowable' (Allen 2001: 36–9).[1] In comparison, in a complex system the interactions between the constituent parts are dynamic and non-linear. Interrelations transform over time, dictating that change does not follow simple cause-and-effect logic making outcomes undetermined, unpredictable, and often unexpected (Coveney and Highfield 1996: 5–10). Examples include ant colonies, the human nervous system, language, financial markets, and political community. The contention of complexity theory is therefore that fixed linear paradigms are both limited and limiting when we seek to understand the causal mechanisms that lead to emergent outcomes in complex systems.[2]

Applications to UN peacekeeping have been rare. Complexity thinking calls for an acceptance of uncertainty and greater modesty around what external intervention can achieve by design. As a result, constituencies with imperatives to show mastery of apparently chaotic situations and immediate impacts are not particularly receptive to its implications. Nevertheless, there are increasingly attempts to use complexity thinking to understand the production and operation of the international system, the norms, and the conflict systems they are deployed to. Furthermore, as discussed in the volume's introduction, the evolution of the UN peacekeeping system over time has seen it become more like a complex system with multiple interconnected stakeholders that rely on feedback to respond to changing dynamics and achieve coherence.

In this chapter, I provide a brief explanation of complexity theory, reflecting on how it considers global politics and the way in which change occurs. I proceed to discuss the application of complexity theory to peacekeeping, explaining the relative paucity of these efforts due to conceptual and practical considerations but pointing out how this leaves us with an incomplete understanding of both the form and function of peacekeeping. The final section draws on extensive research to illustrate how complexity theory provides important insights into the UN peacekeeping system as whole, including missions, their operating environments, and the enabling architecture. The chapter concludes by arguing that there is much to be gained from applying a complexity lens to peacekeeping and reflects on avenues of particular merit.

What is complexity theory?[3]

Today complexity theory is best understood as a loose constellation of ideas and principles developed and embedded throughout the physical and natural sciences – particularly in biology, mathematics, physics, and chemistry, and sub-fields including chaos theory and fractal geometry. Other related disciplines such as systems thinking have also expounded upon and harnessed similar concepts and illustrative models (e.g. Midgley 2008).

Complexity theory

As described above, complexity theory is fundamentally concerned with how change occurs in complex systems. While complexity scholars do not agree on everything, there is generally consensus that complex systems possess particular defining features and display certain systemic behaviours.[4] The first feature is that complex systems comprise multiple actors that are interconnected in a plethora of ways leading to *intricate interdependency*. The degree of interdependence, often referred to as 'connectivity', influences how change occurs in the system (i.e. they are constituted relationally).[5] The second feature is that complex systems are replete with both positive and negative *feedback processes*. It is these feedback processes that control (i.e. enable and constrain) the system. The first two features combine to generate the third key feature, *emergent outcomes*, referring to the behavioural patterns of the system as a whole. Critically, these behaviours are more contingent on the interactions between, rather than the characteristics of, constituent parts.

These three features combine to have important ramifications for how complex systems change over time. First, they dictate that change occurs in a *non-linear* fashion (Westley et al. 2006). That is, in a complex system, an input to the system may have an uneven impact due to the irregular distribution of system elements and the nature of coupling between them. This makes complex systems intrinsically hard to control or predict with any certainty. Second, due to the nonlinear relationships, complex systems are particularly *sensitive to initial conditions*, meaning that minor adjustments in one component of a system may lead to major and disproportionate changes in outcomes under observation (McGlade and Garnsey 2006: 5).[6] Third, change in complex systems is said to happen when a system moves within and between peculiar 'phase spaces' that frame systemic behaviour. In complexity terms these are known as *attractors* which encapsulate the long-term qualitative behaviour of a system and express the patterns of ordering of the system. This creates the possibility that complex systems may have multiple equilibria; where moments of large upheaval are separated by long periods of global stability (Coveney and Highfield 1996: 232).

When complex systems have the inherent capacity to change, precisely because of the adaptive agency of their constitutive elements – that is their ability to respond consciously and strategically to peers and their environment – they fall into a sub-category known as *Complex Adaptive Systems* (Dooley 1996). This particular type of complex system is characterised by two further behaviours. First, they are *self-organising*, referring to the reorganising and self-regulation of a system in response to a disturbance or external constraint (in complexity terms, a 'perturbation'). Second, they are in a continuous process of *co-evolution*. That is to say, system elements interact intricately with each other and their environment (including its emergent properties) influencing the continuous evolution of each. In summary, a system's complexity is the product of its constituent parts interacting and emerges at the systemic level. As Jervis (1997: 12–13) puts it, subtly but significantly altering a popular idiom, with a complex system 'the whole is *different from*, not *greater than*, the sum of the parts' (original emphasis).

Over the past two decades, social scientists have increasingly drawn on complexity theory to better understand political, social, and economic phenomena – particularly for comprehending how and why change occurs within social systems when interaction within and between social entities is conspicuous but predictability of systemic behaviour is low (Byrne 1998).[7] Yet complexity theory is a relative newcomer to the field of International Relations (IR) theory. While systems thinking has been around the study of international politics for some time (e.g. Kaplan 1957; Young 1968), including Kenneth Waltz's seminal *Theory of International Politics* (Waltz 1979), a more direct importation of concepts derived from complexity theory is a more recent development. The shortcomings of orthodox IR theories – such as (neo-)realism and (neo-)liberalism, predicated on linear paradigms borrowed from Newtonian science and the political thoughts of Hobbes, Descartes, and Locke (Rihani

2002: 3) – in predicting milestone events in global politics such as the end of the Cold War or the 2007 global financial crisis led some scholars to see complexity theory as an alternative framework for understanding key episodes in world affairs.

The first major explication was Jervis's (1997) book, *Systems Effects*, which drew on complexity theory to build a new theory of international politics that could explain how a series of events and their unintended consequences resulted in the First World War and the trajectory of the Cold War. This was followed by a number of efforts that sought to use complexity concepts to explain phenomena in the international arena (Urry 2003; Harrison 2006; Kavalski 2007) including a special issue of the *Cambridge Review of International Affairs* (Bousquet and Geyer 2011). More recently, there have been efforts to explain world affairs and global governance more generally (Clemens Jr 2013; Gadinger and Peters 2016; Orsini and Le Prestre 2019).

Overall, complexity theory does not offer a theory of IR. As with constructivism,[8] it does not claim to designate the most significant actors, nor does it purport to predict future events. On the contrary, it offers an alternative framework for revealing how seemingly *insignificant* players can have disproportionate influence over the course of events in highly *unpredictable* ways. However, there are those who have attempted to move in this grand-theory direction, viewing the international order as a complex system comprised of adaptive agents and that feedback between those system agents ensures that change occurs in non-linear ways as the emergent outcome of their various and competing interests and values. These different contributions cohere around a few key theoretical assumptions that implore those applying a complexity lens to draw attention to the interconnections between actors, expect the unexpected and unintended (i.e. seek out surprise), but never suppose certainty about the shape that collectively constituted outcomes will take. It has most salience where interaction within and between social entities is conspicuous but predictability of systemic behaviour is low. This makes complexity theory ripe for application to UN peacekeeping yet thus far this has not yet materialised in any significant quantity.

Complexity theory and UN peacekeeping

The scholarship and practice of international development has drawn increasing attention in the last decade to investigating the value of complexity concepts for better understanding how social change occurs and how this might impact upon development policy-making and implementation (e.g. Rihani 2002; Ramalingam 2013; Green 2016). Research and policy development relating to peacebuilding have also begun to adopt the concepts and tools of complexity thinking in order to account for the complexity of political systems, tacking with gusts of momentary political opportunities rather than assuming a linear path of change (Brusset et al. 2016). Similar approaches have recently been applied to international policing efforts (Hughes et al. 2013), humanitarian delivery (Ramalingam and Jones 2008), and military operations (Richardson et al. 2009; Wiuff Moe and Muller 2017). However, to date there has been little research on the applicability of complexity theory to conflict prevention, management and resolution[9] and even less so with regard to UN peacekeeping.

There is, nevertheless, a fledgling community of academic and policy-oriented researchers who advocate using principles and perspectives synonymous with complexity theory to theorise and analyse UN peace operations. Complexity theory has been utilised in studies of peacekeeping at a number of different levels. First, a number of studies focused on global governance have drawn on complexity thinking to understand how and why peace operations come into being. For example, in earlier work I applied complexity theory to illustrate that, contrary to the dominant linear models of norm diffusion, certain normative agendas relating to the protection of civilians have evolved in nonlinear ways. This was shown to have influenced decision-making at the Security Council and given rise to particular missions with particular mandates (Hunt 2016a). More recently, as part of a special forum in *International Studies Perspectives*, Malte Brosig (2019: 8–12) has argued that complexity is underutilised in IR theory in general and that it can shed light on peacekeeping-related phenomena with a particular reference to the African security regime complex. Brosig argues that a compromise between the postmodern and more positivist poles in complexity thinking can lead to a form of 'restricted complexity' that helps to explain the emergence of complex security arrangements including peacekeeping missions across Africa.

A second body of literature has employed complexity concepts to assess the impacts of UN peacekeeping at both macro- and meso-levels. For example, in previous studies (Hunt 2015; 2016b), I have argued that complexity theory's demand to acknowledge epistemological uncertainty and accept the implications for methodology can inform more meaningful assessments of peacekeeping effectiveness. The research demonstrated how complexity thinking can inform a more iterative and adaptive approach to monitoring and evaluating the contributions of missions to overall outcomes such as security-sector reform that are more impact-focused, and organisational-learning-oriented.

A third set of studies focused more at the mission level have sought to use insights from complexity theory to better understand how missions operate on the ground. Clement and Smith (2009) have examined the challenges to achieving objectives of multidimensional efforts through a complexity lens. Their work emphasises the limits to what co-ordination can achieve in such settings and calls for expectations on peacekeeping to be aligned accordingly. Campbell (2008) for example, has used complexity ideas to highlight issues of disintegration and incoherence of UN post-conflict interventions. She argues that missions should be redesigned to take account of these and that effectiveness is contingent on peacekeeping better understanding the local context (see also

Campbell 2018). Responding to the concern that this 'local' domain will be instrumentalised by interveners, Millar (2016) has used complexity theory to engage in detailed analysis of friction between international and local accord in the case of Sierra Leone. He argues that complexity helps us reveal the limitations on the capacity of global actors to co-opt the local in this way.

A complexity lens has also been utilised in a final body of work that aims to shed light on the mechanisms through which peace operations can contribute to social change. De Coning (2012, 2016), for instance, has employed key concepts from complexity theory to analyse the theories of change underlying peacebuilding interventions – with particular reference to the relationship between international actors and the local sphere. More recently, de Coning (2018) has extended this research, using the same complexity foundations to propose an alternative way of conceptualising and operationalising peacebuilding missions: 'adaptive peacebuilding', as he labels it, draws on the core features of self-organisation (and to some extend co-evolution) to encourage an outsider role that facilitates local actors to make and sustain peace in context-sensitive ways.

These studies emphasise the importance of having a better grasp on how causality operates and how outcomes emerge in the complex social systems that encompass UN peacekeeping missions. Yet applications of complexity theory to research on peacekeeping is probably least prevalent of all the theories addressed in this volume. The limited engagement to date should not come as a surprise. In terms of its theoretical appeal, as a relative newcomer to the IR canon, the barriers to market entry facing any new theory or paradigm are germane to the arrival of complexity theory.[10] Regarding its applicability and practical value, the implicit demand to embrace epistemological uncertainty, recalibrate expectations, and have greater humility regarding policy interventions makes complexity theory difficult to 'sell' to donors and diplomats who have political imperatives to demonstrate 'quick wins'. As discussed in the Introduction to this volume, it is they who have been the main audience for the problem-solving-oriented body of research on peacekeeping until recently. Notwithstanding this inertia, there is arguably much to be gained from being persistent about the added value of complexity thinking. In the subsequent section, I illustrate how complexity theory can offer important new insights when applied to the systemic context within which UN peacekeeping operations exist and function.

Complexity theory and the UN peacekeeping eco-system

The peacekeeping system exhibits the core characteristics of a complex adaptive system.[11] That is, when understood as an overarching eco-system it is comprised of multiple actors who are interconnected in myriad ways leading to intricate interdependency. Peacekeeping operations and the peace processes they assist in implementing are controlled by numerous positive and negative feedback processes. Finally, they continually produce emergent order as a result of their unique authorisation, composition, and partnerships as well as changeable goals and objectives and iterative political calculations of key stakeholders. Each of these features is explored further below.

The peacekeeping system comprises numerous international-, national-, and local-level stakeholders. Similar to Ramalingam and Jones's (2008: 12) description of international aid interventions, peacekeeping operations happen in 'the context of a dense and globalised web of connections and relationships between individuals, communities, institutions, nations and groups of nations'. At UN headquarters the peacekeeping bureaucracy functions through a distorted hierarchy (Cunliffe 2009) that includes member states and various committees in the Security Council and General Assembly, and managers in the Secretariat and Department of Peace Operations. In the field, missions are composed of senior and middle managers as well as a range of uniformed and civilian peacekeepers on the ground in capitals as well as often rural field sites. The interactions between these actors produce vertical relations between stakeholders at all levels of scale. Furthermore, multidimensional missions are comprised of different sectors, *inter alia* the military, police, and numerous civilian substantive sections, oversight, management, and mission support entities as well as partnership and co-operation with host government and civil society. Consequently, the peacekeeping system is typified by multiple interlinked elements.

In addition, a broad spectrum of tasks and activities are performed by different configurations of those same stakeholders. The military, police, and civilian elements of peace operations conduct programming in security, rule of law, humanitarian, economic, governance, political, developmental, and human rights spheres. The relations within each of these pillars are extensive, but the increasingly comprehensive or integrated nature of programmes – such as protection of civilians (PoC), security sector reform (SSR), disarmament, demobilisation and reintegration (DDR), or arranging and securing elections – has led to a proliferation of linkages and interdependencies across these functional areas. These efforts are often guided or supported through bilateral relations with thematic sections at headquarters. In addition, particularly multidimensional UN peacekeeping operations are invariably part of an overarching stabilisation or peacebuilding architecture tasked with co-operatively managing change in conflict-affected environments. This adds another layer or dimension of interconnections. For example, it is now commonplace for UN peacekeeping missions to be deployed alongside parallel forces such as the *G5-Sahel* in Mali or French *Sangaris* in Central African Republic. Similarly, the institutional capacity-building synonymous with modern missions implicates strong interdependencies between the mission and the host government and community. This means that the peacekeeping system contains a plethora of horizontal relationships between and across clusters of implementing agents as well as those with the host state and society.

Complexity theory

This is a straightforward and uncontroversial account of how the peacekeeping system is replete with interconnections and interactions across agents and dimensions of social, economic, and political order. This array of vertical and horizontal relations means that these settings display high connectivity and intricate interdependence between elements and dimensions of which specific peacekeeping missions are only one. This is the archetypal quality of a complex social system. It is hardly new to highlight the multidimensionality of intervention and how it relates to conflict-affected societies. However, complexity theory implies that acknowledging this reality and revealing the degree of connectivity between actors and programmes is a necessary precondition for understanding the intensity of feedback processes that 'control' emergent outcomes in the systemic environment; such as progress towards transformative reform and the prospects for peace but also why peacekeeping manifests as it does.

In human systems, *feedback* relates to influence over action and behaviour, albeit dependent on the degree of connectivity between agents (Mitleton-Kelly 2003: 16). Given the notoriously ad hoc nature of peacekeeping, missions are perennially reacting to both positive and negative events and changing 'on the fly'. This happens in a number of different ways: however, each of the avenues relies upon *feedback* processes to propagate or inhibit the alterations in a mission's conduct in relation to its systemic context. Positive feedback can have a large effect (i.e. amplification) at the headquarters level where strategic decisions that influence the content of mission mandates are made. For example, the practice since 1999 of mandating missions to protect civilians substantively changed the nature of peace operations from the top down – a positive feedback process. However, the unprecedented nature of much activity in peacekeeping means that positive feedback can also emanate from the field when a particular mission pioneers new initiatives that prove successful. For example, the innovation of public information components in the missions in Sierra Leone and Liberia were instrumental in changing the way in which these elements have operated since (Hunt 2006). Negative feedback processes are also prevalent at both the strategic and field levels. For example, the predilections of some members of the Security Council to adhere to a particular conception of peacekeeping based on consent, impartiality, and minimum use of force acts as a control for what peacekeeping can and cannot be designed to do with ramifications for expectations once deployed. In the field, negative feedback processes are omnipresent owing to the prevalence of stringent policies, doctrinal frameworks, and standard operating procedures that govern how mandates are implemented and the conduct of peacekeepers themselves.

Feedback processes in the peacekeeping system are therefore both negative (i.e. they dampen the magnitude of deviation from current systemic behaviour) and positive (i.e. they amplify, and often substantively change, behaviour of the system). Moreover, the feedback processes are multidirectional. That is, they can be instigated from the bottom up, as well as from the top down. Consequently, these feedback processes common to all mission contexts are important to the way in which the actions and behaviours of peacekeeping operations emerge. Feedback in the systemic context is essential to the way a mission progresses over time and how it, in turn, impacts upon its environment. Complexity theory brings a focus on these feedback processes as well as an explanatory framework for understanding the direction and magnitude of their effects: in other words, enabling and disabling *emergent* behaviours through positive and/or negative feedback processes.

The system-level structures and behavioural patterns of peacekeeping operations are difficult to predict on the basis of simple knowledge of the individual traits and preferences of the agents and inputs involved.[12] For example, peacekeeping operations are mandated to accomplish certain core objectives such as DDR. It is straightforward to identify the overarching goals of a DDR programme; disarm ex-combatants, demobilise them from their chain of command, and provide opportunities for them to reintegrate into civilian society. It is also likely that generic guidelines based on previous experiences will inform the design and planning for such a process. However, it is the local rules of interaction between the constituent parts of the system that dictate how such processes unfold. Therefore the constitutive relationships between the UN and the international donor community, the mission and the host government, the DDR programme and the ex-combatants will have a significant impact on how a mission interoperates with its systemic environment that is not easy to predict by observing the behaviours of constituent parts of the peacekeeping system.

The uniformed components of missions (i.e. military and police) are made up of multiple national contingents and units. These contributions often possess extremely different backgrounds regarding training and philosophy. However, notwithstanding operational challenges, they work together in ways and towards goals that do not necessarily reflect what they would normally (or indeed, preferably) do in their own country. Similarly, when these peacekeepers are tasked with reform activities, the intended impact – such as improved local police services – is the emergent property of international–national collaboration and may not be a predictable product of those contributing to the process. Systemic outcomes relating to the work of peacekeepers are a product of multiple contributions but different from what might be predicted on the basis of their separate characteristics (e.g. Aoi et al. 2007). Emergence is accentuated further in peacekeeping due to the high turnover and short tenure of personnel in field missions. The frequent influx of new personnel with little familiarity with the job or the context further contributes to the unpredictability of perpetually new emergent order.

Negative (maladaptive) emergence also occurs in peacekeeping. For example, a recurrent criticism of peace operations is their ineffective co-ordination, particularly between military and non-military components. The various civilian, police, and military elements of a mission have distinct organisational cultures and operate under their own procedures. At times this varies within components. For example, specific military contingents often operate with national caveats. This is a way unpredictable order emerges in the peacekeeping system – in this instance, undesirable systemic behaviour stemming from the local rules of individual units, leading to incoherence at the systemic level (Marion 1999: 29–32).

Given the multi-agency character of peacekeeping and the increasingly integrated nature of programming, the form and function of missions are contingent on idiosyncratic organisational cultures, identities, and procedures and the myriad of ways in which they interact. Furthermore, peacekeeping operations are one element of the broader environment and systemic outcomes are contingent on the ways in which missions interoperate with other security and peacebuilding actors, host governments, civil society, and local communities. The resultant emergent systemic identity and behaviour are consequently difficult to predict accurately on the basis solely on knowledge of each in isolation. Whilst the challenges of integration and co-ordination at the systemic level are well known, complexity theory is a useful framework for uncovering and explaining these phenomena. Although these sorts of emergence can and should be expected in the peacekeeping system, its substance is difficult to predict due to the *nonlinearity* of relationships within the system, and therefore hard to achieve by design. Consequently, complexity theory adds weight to the argument that the unique context-specific solutions that emerge in these settings can be understood as leading to new and oftentimes unexpected order and coherence – that is the *emergent property* of the system. Importantly, complexity theory also reminds us that this emergence is not always an objectively 'good' thing.

In summary, the peacekeeping system is multidimensional and has a range of stakeholders with different interests and perspectives whose interrelationships are often nonlinear. The feedback between these actors produces emergent and often unpredictable outcomes. Complexity theory ensures analyses that recognise that the elements of such a system are conscious and creative agents with interests and memory such that history matters to how these system-level outcomes transpire. Societies embroiled in – or emerging from – conflict are dynamical environments (Wils et al. 2006: 35–6; Coleman et al. 2006: 341–3). The impact of conflict on any specified level or unit of analysis will inevitably have consequences for higher- and lower-magnitude purlieus within the same system, in turn influencing change in that domain (Hendrick 2009: 55). This means that the social outcomes of peace processes cannot be predicted from looking at single issues in isolation, but has to attend to the influence of constantly changing context – that is its dynamics. Contrary to dominant approaches that tend to analyse peacekeeping as if they are addressing singular or isolated problems or puzzles, complexity theory offers a framework for engaging with the realities of what are actually 'wicked problems' and the systemic nature of conflict and fractured social orders and the way in which attempts to resolve them and rebuild in their wake unfold.

As mentioned elsewhere in this volume, most peacekeeping research tends to ignore or gloss over the set of assumptions and theories of change that underpin mission logics. Focused on the policies, processes, and practices of peacekeeping, this literature tends to ask whether missions are *doing things right* rather than asking whether missions are *doing the right things*. Complexity theory provides the conceptual and analytical tools first to question and second to interrogate this. In this way, the complexity approach is not about providing 'solutions for problems', but 'approaches to problems' in ways that can provide important insights above and beyond what other theoretical perspectives can offer.

Whilst the foregoing illustrates that some concepts in complexity theory are relevant to understanding the shape and nature of change in the peacekeeping system, this is not to suggest that all of the theory is applicable all of the time or should be applied uncritically. For example, it would be to draw a long bow to suggest that the notion of 'attractors' can be transposed to map conflict phases or spaces. However, the shocks associated with violent conflict can be understood as perturbations capable of 'shunting' societies into new configurations and patterns of behaviour with implications for the trajectory of conflict and possibilities for peace. Similarly, it might be stretching plausibility to say that 'self-organisation' best describes how missions adjust to meet new political and operational challenges. But some argue that this complexity concept could offer a model for how outsiders should understand their role in facilitating peace in conflict-affected societies (de Coning 2018). The concept of 'co-evolution' certainly does hold promise in understanding the peacekeeping system in relation to its broader meta-systemic environment. For example, it usefully explains how peacekeeping fits into an eco-social system where the practice of peacekeeping responds and adapts in relation to changes in the global political arena – whether that be prevailing normative drivers (such as the growing centrality of PoC) or shifting distributions of power in the international system (such as the influence of rising powers) and corollary decision-making by the Security Council.

Conclusion

This chapter has demonstrated that, whilst a newcomer to the study of peacekeeping, complexity theory can offer a useful theoretical frame for both conceptual and applied or policy-relevant research on peacekeeping. Although still in its infancy, the application of complexity theory to the study of peacekeeping offers new insights and perspectives on processes in the peacekeeping system that are simply deemed to be illogical or idiosyncratic when viewed through the prism of traditional social-scientific theory (Lacayo 2007). Complexity theory is promoted here not as a substitute for existing theories of peacekeeping but rather as an augmentation and supplement to extant analytical frameworks to plug the important gaps that they leave.

Complexity theory

In enabling conceptualisation of a UN peacekeeping eco-system, which includes scales both above and below individual missions, complexity theory allows for the web of actors and factors enabling and constraining peacekeeping to be incorporated into a holistic analysis. This holds promise for refining our understanding of why peacekeeping has taken the shape it has but also why, as well as how, it continues to evolve the way that it does. Furthermore, it offers a way to transcend the limited engagement with cause–effect relationships and provide significant insights into how overall outcomes (i.e. transformational change) relate to the behaviour and actions of the different agents in the UN peacekeeping eco-system. In doing so, a complexity lens can also allow for a deeper engagement with (and challenge to) the set of assumptions that underpin the change theories and logics on which UN missions are predicated.

While there are many areas where a complexity lens could shed new light, one of the avenues that warrants further attention is using the insights from complexity theory to 'endogenise' the UN: that is, rather than treat the UN as an exogenous 'outside' intervener, moving towards analytically including the UN and its peacekeeping missions within the system they are sent to address. This will allow for a more finely grained analysis of how the UN's interventions reverberate through conflict-affected societies as well as how the lessons from these engagements lead to adaptations in the peacekeeping system as a whole and influence the shape of future missions. The need to conduct this type of research is only likely to become more important as stabilisation missions with exit strategies contingent on effective states are involved in making intrusive decisions that can 'tip the scales' in favour of one part or another.

It is increasingly recognised that the peacekeeping system is complex in its composition and behaviours. Accordingly, complexity theory holds genuine promise for enhancing the way we theorise and analyse the existence, as well as the impacts, of these endeavours.

Notes

1 For example, the electronics systems in an aeroplane are extremely complicated with myriad components dependent on numerous technologies. Full mastery of this system may be impossible for a single human mind, but enough of the causal relationships between the system's elements are linear, this modality applies at all times and locations, and, as a result, it is possible to understand its functioning.

2 For further explanation of differences between simple, complicated, complex (and chaotic) systems, see Ackoff (1974) and Snowden (2000).

3 This chapter draws on research published in Hunt 2015. Permission has been granted by copyright holder (PLSclear Ref No: 13825).

4 The following features and properties are a synthesised list drawing on numerous attempts across different disciplines to summarise the core characteristics of complex systems. See Hendrick (2009: 6–7); Ramalingam and Jones (2008); Mitleton-Kelly (2003).

5 Connectivity is defined by tight and loose 'coupling' – i.e. the degree of 'epistatic interaction'.

6 This phenomenon is often depicted by Lorenz's 'butterfly effect' whereby an event, seemingly trivial in size or importance (e.g. a butterfly flapping its wings in Brazil), can lead to a large and significant event (e.g. a hurricane in Japan), through an unpredictable chain of interrelated events. See Lorenz (1972).

7 In development studies, complexity has drawn increasing attention in the last decade by investigating the value of complexity concepts for understanding how social change occurs and how this might impact upon policymaking and implementation (e.g. Cabaj 2009; Rihani 2002). Even in Economics – a discipline synonymous with epistemological rigidity – there are signs that complexity theory is gaining traction in challenging neoclassical orthodoxy and advocating for evolving theory based on complexity concepts to explain economic phenomena such as growth and market failure (e.g. Beinhocker 2007; Ormerod 1998).

8 When the study of complexity is applied to human systems, it is often assumed to imply constructivist perspectives. This confusion is easy to understand because both complexity and constructivism share some basic principles, including emergence, high levels of interdependence in a system, unreliable causality and continuing transformation over time. Indeed, these common principles result in overlapping practices between the two perspectives (see Laurence and Paddon Rhoads, Chapter 5 above).

9 Notable exceptions all emanating in the past two decades include Clemens Jr (2011), Körppen et al. (2011), Jones (2003), Coleman (2006), Coleman et al. (2006), Eoyang and Yellowthunder (2008); Hendrick (2009).

Complexity theory

10 Debates endure around the pros and cons of applying a theory forged in the hard sciences to the social world and doing so partially or as metaphor. See Hunt (2015: chapter 3) for elaboration on various views here.

11 Also discussed as complex evolving systems. See Mitleton-Kelly (2003).

12 Others have discussed this uncertainty in terms of 'peacekeeping ambiguity'. See, for example, Lipson (2010).

References

Ackoff, Russel L. (1974), *Redesigning the Future: A Systems Approach to Societal Problems* (New York: John Wiley and Sons).

Allen, Peter (2001), 'What is complexity science? Knowledge of the limits of knowledge', *Emergence: Complexity and Organization*, 3:1, 24–42.

Aoi, Chiyuki, Cedric de Coning, and Ramesh Thakur (eds) (2007), *Unintended Consequences of Peacekeeping Operations* (Tokyo: United Nations University Press).

Beinhocker, Erik (2007), *The Origin of Wealth: Evolution, Complexity and the Radical Remaking of Economics* (Cambridge, MA: Harvard Business School Press).

von Bertalanffy, Ludwig (1968), *General System Theory: Foundations, Development, Applications* (New York: George Braziller).

Bousquet, Antoine, and Robert Geyer (2011), 'Special issue: Complexity and the international arena', *Cambridge Review of International Affairs*, 24:1, 1–80.

Brosig, Malte (2019), 'Restricted complexity: A middle path between postmodern complexity theory and positivist mainstream IR', in Amandine Orsini and Philippe Le Prestre (eds), 'Forum: Complex systems and international governance', *International Studies Review*, https://doi.org/10.1093/isr/viz005.

Brusset, Emery, Cedric de Coning, and Bryn Hughes (eds) (2016), *Complexity Thinking for Peacebuilding Practice and Evaluation* (Basingstoke: Palgrave Macmillan).

Byrne, David (1998), *Complexity Theory and the Social Sciences: An Introduction* (London: Routledge).

Cabaj, Mark (2009), *Understanding Poverty as a Complex Issue and Why That Matters* (Ottawa, Ontario: Caledon Institute for Social Policy).

Campbell, Susanna (2008), '(Dis)Integration, incoherence and complexity in UN post-conflict interventions', *International Peacekeeping*, 15:4, 556–69.

Campbell, Susanna (2018), *Global Governance and Local Peace: Accountability and Performance in International Peacebuilding* (Cambridge: Cambridge University Press).

Clemens, Walter C. Jr (2011), 'Complexity theory as a tool for understanding and coping with ethnic conflict and development issues in post-soviet Eurasia', *International Journal of Peace Studies*, 6:2, 1–15.

Clemens, Walter C. Jr (2013), *Complexity Science and World Affairs* (Albany: SUNY Press).

Clement, Caty, and Adam C. Smith (2009), *Managing Complexity: Political and Managerial Challenges in United Nations Peace Operations* (New York: International Peace Institute).

Coleman, Peter T. (2006), 'Conflict, complexity, and change: A meta-framework for addressing protracted, intractable conflict – III', *Journal of Peace Psychology*, 12:4, 325–48.

Coleman, P.T., L. Bui-Wrzosinska, R. Vallacher, and A. Nowak (2006), 'Protracted conflicts as dynamical systems: Guidelines and methods for intervention', in A. Schneider and C. Honeyman (eds), *The Negotiator's Fieldbook* (Chicago: American Bar Association).

de Coning, C.H. (2012), 'Complexity, Peacebuilding & Coherence: Implications of Complexity for the Peacebuilding Coherence Dilemma'. PhD dissertation, Applied Ethics, Department of Philosophy, Stellenbosch: University of Stellenbosch. http://scholar.sun.ac.za/handle/10019.1/71891.

de Coning, Cedric (2016), 'From peacebuilding to sustaining peace: Implications of complexity for resilience and sustainability', *Resilience*, 4:3, 166–81.

de Coning, Cedric (2018), 'Adaptive peacebuilding', *International Affairs*, 94:2, 301–17.

Coveney, Peter, and Roger Highfield (1996), *Frontiers of Complexity: The Search for Order in a Chaotic World* (London: Faber and Faber), 5–10.

Cunliffe, Philip (2009), 'The politics of global governance in UN peacekeeping', *International Peacekeeping*, 16:3, 323–36.

Dooley, Kevin J. (1996), 'A nominal definition of complex adaptive systems', *The Chaos Network*, 8:1, 2–3.

Eoyang, Glenda, and Lois Yellowthunder (2008), 'Complexity models and conflict: A case study from Kosovo', paper presented at the Conference on Conflict and Complexity, Conflict Research Society and Conflict Analysis Research Centre, University of Kent, Canterbury, 2–3 September.

Gadinger, Frank, and Dirk Peters (2016), 'Feedback loops in a world of complexity: A cybernetic approach at the interface of foreign policy analysis and International Relations theory', *Cambridge Review of International Affairs*, 29:1, 251–69.

Green, Duncan (2016), *How Change Happens* (Oxford: Oxford University Press).

Harrison, Neil E. (ed) (2006), *Complexity in World Politics, Concepts and Methods of a New Paradigm* (Albany: SUNY).

Hendrick, Diane (2009), 'Complexity theory and conflict transformation: An exploration of potential and implications', working paper (Bradford: Department of Peace Studies, University of Bradford).

Hughes, Bryn, Charles T. Hunt, and Jodie Curth-Bibb (2013), *Forging New Conventional Wisdom Beyond International Policing: Learning from Complex, Political Realities* (Boston: Martinus-Nijhoff).

Hunt, Charles T. (2006), *Public Information as a Mission Critical Component of West African Peace Operations* (Accra: Kofi Annan International Peacekeeping Training Centre).

Hunt, Charles T. (2015), *UN Peace Operations and International Policing: Negotiating Complexity, Assessing Impact and Learning to Learn* (London: Routledge).

Hunt, Charles T. (2016a), 'Emerging powers and the responsibility to protect: Non-linear norm dynamics in complex international society', *Cambridge Review of International Affairs*, 3, 870–90.

Hunt, Charles T. (2016b), 'Avoiding perplexity: Complexity-oriented monitoring and evaluation for UN peace operations', in Emery Brusset, Cedric de Coning, and Bryn Hughes (eds), *Complexity Thinking for Peacebuilding Practice and Evaluation* (Basingstoke: Palgrave Macmillan), 79–109.

Jervis, Robert (1997), *System Effects: Complexity in Political and Social Science* (Princeton, NJ: Princeton University Press).

Johnson, Neil (2009), *Simply Complexity: A Clear Guide to Complexity Theory* (London: Oneworld).

Jones, Wendell (2003), 'Complexity, conflict resolution, and how the mind works', *Conflict Resolution Quarterly*, 20:4, 485–94.

Kaplan, Morton (1957), *System and Process in International Relations* (New York: Wiley).

Kavalski, Emilian (2007), 'The fifth debate and the emergence of complex international relations theory: notes on the application of complexity theory to the study of international life', *Cambridge Review of International Affairs*, 20:3, 435–54.

Körppen, Daniel, Norbert Ropers, and Hans J. Gießmann (eds) (2011), *The Non-linearity of Peace Processes: Theory and Practice of Systemic Conflict Transformation* (Opladen and Farmington Hills: Barbara Budrich).

Lacayo, Virginia (2007), 'What complexity science teaches us about social change', *MAZI Articles*, 10 (South Orange, NJ: Communication for Social Change Consortium).

Lipson, Michael (2010), 'Performance under ambiguity: International organization performance in UN peacekeeping', *Review of International Organizations*, 5:3, 249–84.

Lorenz, Edward N. (1972), 'Predictability: Does the flap of a butterfly's wings in Brazil set off a tornado in Texas?'. Presented before the American Association for the Advancement of Science, 139th Meeting, 29 December. https://static.gymportalen.dk/sites/lru.dk/files/lru/132_kap6_lorenz_artikel_the_butterfly_effect.pdf.

Marion, Russ (1999), *The Edge of Organization: Chaos and Complexity Theories of Formal Social Systems* (Thousand Oaks: Sage).

McGlade, James, and Elizabeth Garnsey (2006), 'The nature of complexity', in Elizabeth Garnsey and James McGlade (eds), *Complexity and Co-evolution: Continuity and Change in Socio-economic Systems* (Cheltenham: Edward Elgar), 1–21.

Midgley, Gerald (2008), 'Systems thinking, complexity and the philosophy of science', *Emergence, Complexity and Organization*, 10:4, 55–73.

Millar, Gearoid (2016), 'Respecting complexity: Compound friction and unpredictability in peacebuilding', in Kristine Höglund, Annika Björkdahl, Gearoid Millar, Jair Vanderlijn, Willemijn Verkoren (eds), *Peacebuilding and Friction: Global and Local Encounters in Post Conflict Societies* (Abingdon: Routledge), 32–47.

Mitchell, Melanie (2011), *Complexity: A Guided Tour* (Oxford: Oxford University Press).

Mitleton-Kelly, Eve (2003), 'Ten principles of complexity and enabling infrastructures', in Eve Mitleton-Kelly (ed.), *Complex Systems and Evolutionary Perspectives on Organisations: The Application of Complexity Theory to Organisations* (Oxford: Elsevier), 23–51.

Ormerod, Paul (1998), *Butterfly Economics: A New General Theory of Social and Economic Behaviour* (London: Faber and Faber).

Orsini, Amandine, and Philippe Le Prestre (eds) (2019), 'Forum: Complex systems and international governance', *International Studies Review*, https://doi.org/10.1093/isr/viz005 (accessed 30 January 2020).

Ramalingam, Ben (2013), *Aid on the Edge of Chaos: Rethinking International Cooperation in a Complex World* (New York: Oxford University Press).

Ramalingam, Ben, and Harry Jones (2008), *Exploring the Science of Complexity Ideas and Implications for Development and Humanitarian Efforts* (London: Overseas Development Institute).

Richardson, Kurt A., Graham Mathieson, and Paul Cilliers (2009), 'Complexity thinking and military operational analysis', in Kurt A. Richardson (ed.) *Knots, Lace and Tartan: Making Sense of Complex Human Systems in Military Operations Research* (Litchfield Park, AZ: ISE Publishing), 27–69.

Rihani, Samir (2002), *Complex Systems Theory and Development Practice* (London: Zed Books).

Snowden, Dave J. (2000), 'Cynefin: a sense of time and place, the social ecology of knowledge management', in Charles Despres and Daniele Chauvel (eds), *Knowledge Horizons: The Present and the Promise of Knowledge Management* (Oxford: Butterworth-Heinemann), 237–66.

Urry, John (2003), *Global Complexity* (Cambridge: Polity Press).

Waltz, Kenneth N. (1979), *Theory of International Politics* (New York: McGraw-Hill).

Westley, Frances, Brenda Zimmerman, and Michael Quin Patton (2006), *Getting to Maybe: How the World Is Changed?* (Toronto: Random House).

Wiener, Norbert (1948), *Cybernetics* (Cambridge, MA: MIT Press).

Wils, Oliver, Ulrike Hopp, Norbert Ropers, Luxshi Vimalarajah, and Wolfram Zunzer (2006), *The Systemic Approach to Conflict Transformation Concept and Fields of Application* (Berlin: Berghof Foundation for Peace Support).

Wiuff Moe, Louise, and Markus-Michael Muller (2017), *Reconfiguring Intervention: Complexity, Resilience and the 'Local Turn' in Counterinsurgent Warfare* (London: Palgrave Macmillan).

Young, Oran R. (1968) *A Systemic Approach to International Politics* (Princeton, NJ: Princeton University Press).

Concluding reflections: International Relations theory and the study of UN peace operations

Mats Berdal

International Relations as a crossroads

In a short but typically incisive survey of the field, written at a time when the so-called 'inter-paradigm debate' (Banks 1985) in International Relations (IR) was still generating as much heat as light, Philip Windsor insisted that 'far too much scholarly time [had] been wasted in disputes about what actually *is* the field of International Relations' (Windsor 2002: 18). Indeed, the absence of an agreed intellectual base or a unifying method led him to question whether IR could usefully be 'spoken of as an academic discipline at all'. He did not, however, view this as a source of weakness or, as others were inclined to suggest, evidence of immaturity in the development of a comparatively young discipline. Instead, he maintained that IR was best understood as a 'crossroads which takes into account various forms of human thought which may range from psychology to law, from anthropology to nuclear strategy, and which at the same time helps us to relate questions arising from those subjects to each other in a way which the traditional demarcation disputes in universities in the past have not enabled us to do' (Windsor 1993: 62). Thus conceived, diversity in methodological approach and multiplicity of theoretical perspectives were, potentially, sources of strength to be welcomed. IR scholars,

Windsor insisted, should be viewed, and should see themselves, as engaged in a discourse, not in the fruitless search for 'paradigm shifts or paradigmatic unity'.

This embrace of methodological pluralism and of IR as a discourse is also how the role of IR theory should be viewed in this book - a book whose central aim is 'to understand UN peacekeeping through different theoretical lenses', and to apply these in ways that cast new light on how and why UN peacekeeping 'as an international institution, has evolved in a particular direction and functions the way it does' (Oksamytna and Karlsrud, Introduction, above). The notion of incommensurability of competing paradigms at the heart of Thomas Kuhn's influential idea of the paradigm was one reason why Windsor found its utility limited when it came to the study of IR, and this may also explain why none of the authors in the present volume use the term. Instead, they see themselves as drawing on broad 'theoretical traditions' and 'programmes' that do not necessarily form coherent bodies of thought, and within which there are often several strands, but which can nonetheless generate critical questions and help illuminate under-studied and neglected dimensions of the UN's rich and multilayered peacekeeping experience. Thus, as Marion Laurence and Emily Paddon Rhoads persuasively demonstrate, the 'constructivist toolkit is well-suited to answering questions about how UN peace operations interact with the communities that host them' (Laurence and Paddon Rhoads, Chapter 5 above). Similarly, Charles Hunt cogently draws on 'a loose constellation of ideas and principles' from the field of complexity theory to bring out how 'complexity thinking calls for an acceptance of uncertainty and greater modesty around what external intervention can achieve by design' (Hunt, Chapter 9 above).

Now, the conception of IR as a crossroads, where forms of human thought meet and scholars engage in a discourse, raises a further consideration when it comes to the study of UN peacekeeping *within* the field of IR. Specifically, it suggests that the charge (alluded to by the editors at the outset of this volume) that writings on peacekeeping have been 'largely atheoretical' or 'theory-averse', concerned largely with questions of 'effectiveness', requires qualification. While the charge, arguably, carries some weight in a narrow technical sense, there is in fact a long and important tradition of prominent IR scholars taking a keen interest in UN peacekeeping as an institution, bringing their own theoretical interests and perspectives to bear on the subject, even though, as Oksamytna and Karlsrud perceptively note, their 'application has often been implicit rather than explicit'. In terms of understanding the evolution and functions of UN peacekeeping, and its place in international politics and international society, the writings of Inis L. Claude Jr, Adam Roberts, and Alan James, to mention three of the most important IR scholars who have taken a sustained interest in the subject, remain indispensable (Claude Jr 1961; James 1990; Roberts 1994). Critically, their work is of continuing relevance, deriving its strength, in part, from the insistence, whether explicit or implicit, that the character and evolution of UN peacekeeping is inseparable, and therefore cannot meaningfully be studied and understood apart, from international politics itself. In the case of Alan James, an influential member of the English School of IR, his writings on peacekeeping – often combining detailed studies of individual operations with larger questions raised by those operations – are especially notable, and certainly cannot be said to emanate from a 'theory-free zone'.

Beyond the fraternity of IR scholars, one might add, are other writers whose reflections have also shed an incisive light on UN peacekeeping, even if their arguments have been advanced in 'idiosyncratic' (Bures 2007) fashion and the theoretical implications of their writings have been more implicit than explicit. Noteworthy among these is Conor Cruise O'Brien who, while certainly no IR scholar in the strict sense, advanced the compelling and memorable thesis, drawing upon his own experience of peacekeeping in Congo, that the UN is best 'seen as a *theatre* in which people improvise versions of contemporary history, posture before the world, let off steam, and occasionally devise rituals that can save the peace' (O'Brien 1994: 86). To O'Brien (O'Brien and Topolski 1968: 298), 'myth and ritual' were absolutely central to the workings of the UN and its activities, including peacekeeping. It was an insight which, in interesting ways, foreshadowed many of the arguments and perspectives highlighted by 'theoretical lenses' applied in this volume.

UN peace operations and International Relations: Sources of continuity and change

UN peace operations may be defined broadly as the deployment of military and police contingents, drawn from member states and authorised by the Security Council, in a third-party capacity to mitigate, contain, and help create the conditions for overcoming violent conflict within the international system. As such, they have been undertaken in a wide variety of historical, political, and geographical settings. Over time, UN peace operations have also come to include a seemingly ever-expanding range of mandated tasks, from the monitoring of ceasefires and buffer-zones at one end to disarmament, demobilisation and reintegration, the administration of war-torn territories and the protection of civilians at the other (de Coning and Peter 2019). Historically, UN peace operations have also witnessed a marked shift in the balance of deployments away from interposition in conflicts between states to operations in intra-state or civil-war-like settings, frequently of a violent or, to borrow the jargon, 'semi-permissive' kind.

Whether viewed as an institution or as set of activities, it is clear from this brief distillation of the range, scope, and evolving character of UN peace operations that they raise large and important questions in IR terms. Indeed, since their inception, UN operations have touched on core issues and concepts at the heart of the study of international relations: conflict and co-operation; sovereignty and intervention; norms and norm diffusion; the use and utility of

Concluding reflections

military force; and the changing character of armed conflict. There is a real sense, in other words, that to study UN peacekeeping is also to study international politics and, by extension, to engage in debates about the bases for international order and prospects for international society.[1] Thus, when UN peacekeeping first emerged in the 1950s, it represented a functional adaptation of the UN to the realities of the Cold War: a distinctive form of third-party intervention involving the deployment of lightly equipped troops aimed at stabilising local conflicts in order to avoid their escalation to major war between rival power blocs. With the passing of the Cold War, as normative boundaries shifted and the state seized to be the sole referent object of security, the scope and transformative ambition of UN peacekeeping expanded accordingly. Although the peacekeeping disasters of the early 1990s – in Angola, Somalia, Bosnia, and Rwanda – were followed by a temporary retrenchment in the pace of deployments, from the 1999 onwards UN operations witnessed renewed growth, now with a more explicit focus on the protection of civilians as a core mandate of peacekeepers.

Now, it is evident from the above and, indeed, from the many excellent contributions to this volume, that the scope, scale, and focus of UN peace operations have evolved over time. And yet, while attention has rightly been devoted to the theme of change in much recent scholarship, there are still good reasons why approaches to the study of UN field operations need to factor in not just discontinuities but also key elements of continuity in the history and practice of UN peacekeeping. Four such elements merit special attention when the vistas of future research are explored.

First, in critical respects, the defining characteristics of the UN organisation itself – specifically, its intergovernmental, deeply political and functionally fragmented character – remain fundamentally unchanged. Given the UN's central role in authorising, mounting, and sustaining field operations, this reality matters greatly. Whilst commentary on the UN's role in world politics easily slips into the language of 'the UN did this' or 'the UN failed to do that', its *actual workings* as an organisation must always take account of the fact that it is a *membership* organisation, not a supranational body or world government-in-waiting. The implications for UN peacekeeping are many. Accounting for and understanding the behaviour of troop-contributing countries – including why unity of command and coherence of strategic effort on the part of UN peacekeepers have frequently proved so elusive – is only one area, albeit an obvious one, where politics and intergovernmentalism are key to explaining outcomes.

Second, elements of continuity are also evident when it comes to the questions around the role and function – and the discussion of these both among member states and within the Secretariat – of the defining principles of UN peacekeeping; that is, the requirement of consent of the parties, impartiality as the determinant of operational activity, and minimum use of force except in self-defence. Although it is undeniably the case that consent has frequently proved partial and incomplete in contemporary mission settings, and also that the UN has been applying force more 'robustly' than in the past (Karlsrud 2018), member states and the Security Council have been reluctant – for an admixture of principled and pragmatic reasons – to jettison the underlying commitment to UN peacekeeping as an *essentially* consent-based activity in favour of enforcement or war-fighting. The offensive mandate given to the Force Intervention Brigade in the Democratic Republic of Congo has proved an exception rather than a harbinger of a new era. Applying the core principles has proved especially challenging in volatile settings where the threat to civilians has been high, leading the 2015 High Level Independent Panel on Peace Operations (HIPPO) to call for their 'flexible and progressive interpretation' (UN 2015: 32). The role of force in peace operations, especially as it bears on the implementation of protection of civilians mandates, remains a major challenge and is certain to spawn further academic work and reflection. Yet, there continues to be a recognition, including by the HIPPO, that the core principles sketched above will always play a key function

Concluding reflections

as long as UN peacekeepers are engaged in activities of a 'secondary' rather than 'primary' kind, that is, as long as their activities are 'dependent, in respect of both [their] origins and success, on the wishes and policies of others' (James 1990: 1).

Third, the actual experience of the UN peacekeepers during the era of so-called 'classical' or 'first-generation' peacekeeping is richer and more varied than is often recognised. The Congo mission from 1960 to 1964 is of particular interest, highlighting, as it quickly came to do, the inherent difficulties of inserting and operating an outside military force in a third-party capacity in the midst of an ongoing civil war.[2] Other operations, too, notably in Cyprus and Lebanon, brought the challenges of peacekeeping and humanitarian assistance in the context of internal conflict into sharp relief. None of these operations can be said to have been exhausted in research terms.

Finally, UN peacekeeping must be understood and analysed against the background of significant continuities in the nature of international politics and the sources of state conduct. Specifically, considerations of interest, power, and prestige continue to matter greatly to states. As Cunliffe (Chapter 1 above) usefully reminds us in his exploration of realist theorising in this volume, UN peacekeeping simply cannot be divorced from an appreciation of power politics.

The value and future of theorising

The present volume admirably brings out the value of applying different theoretical lenses and methodological tools to enhance our understanding of the 'changing character of peacekeeping and the emergence of new concerns, models, and tasks' (Oksamytna and Karlsrud, Introduction, above). Some of the perspectives presented cast a new and more searching light on what has long been understood about the essence of peacekeeping, to wit that it is 'a deeply political activity rather than [merely] a technical policy instrument' (Bode, Chapter 6 above).[3] Other contributions, including the exploration of gendered power relations within institutions engaged in peacekeeping, promise important new perspectives on the subject (Holmes, Chapter 8 above). Similarly, Sarah von Bill-erbeck (Chapter 4 above) shows how a sociological approach and ethnographic research into UN field operations can offer potentially penetrating insights into 'the practices, policy choices, and failures of UN peacekeeping'.

As these and other contributions make clear, theorising is necessarily an iterative process, and the value of different theoretical lenses to our understanding of peacekeeping depends, in the end, on the extent to which they draw upon, and are tested and refined in light of rigorous empirical investigations of actual operations, whether contemporary or historical.[4] Without this, debates around theoretical perspectives and approaches always run the risk of becoming self-referential or, worse, self-indulgent. Fortunately, the increased availability of new primary source material,[5] the growing number of illuminating accounts by practitioners (e.g. Goulding 2002; Gharekhan 2006; Guéhenno 2015; Doss 2020), the recognition among scholars (evident in this book) that theorising cannot be separated from the detailed study of actual operations, and, not least, the very fact that UN operations themselves continue to be in demand; all of these ensure that the UN peace operations will remain a most fertile territory for theorists and practitioners alike for many years to come.

Notes

1 Hence the connection drawn, often explicitly, in several studies of UN 'interventionism' in the 1990s to the larger IR debate about whether or not the post-Cold War international order was moving in a solidarist, as distinct from a pluralist, direction. See, in particular, Mayall (1997).

2 The experience of Congo, quite apart from nearly breaking the back of the organisation, also generated a significant body of high-quality literature on UN peacekeeping. See, for example, Claude (1961), Bloomfield (1963), Bowett (1964), Norwegian Institute for International Affairs (1964), and Higgins (1969).

Concluding reflections

3 For a thoughtful discussion of the 'intrinsic political aspect' of UN peacekeeping, see James (1996).

4 On a lighter note, the reference to different 'generations' of peacekeeping made at the outset of the present volume (Oksamytna and Karlsrud, Introduction) brought to mind a call I made upon Cedric Thornberry, then Head of Civil Affairs for UN Protection Force (UNPROFOR) headquartered in Zagreb, in the spring of 1993. It had been a bad day for UNPROFOR and, although Thornberry had agreed to meet with me, he was plainly sceptical of much of the writings on peacekeeping then in vogue. When I mumbled something about 'second-generation peacekeeping', he quickly cut me off with: 'yes, and fifth generation removed from reality'.

5 See, for example, valuable material relating to Rwanda and former Yugoslavia, collected, declassified, and made available by the National Security Archive, https://nsarchive.gwu.edu/project/genocide-documentation-project.

References

Banks, Michael (1985), 'The inter-paradigm debate', in Margot Light and A.J.R. Groom (eds), *International Relations: A Handbook of Current Theory* (London: Pinter), 7–26.

Bloomfield, Lincoln (ed.) (1963), 'International force – a symposium', *International Organization*, 17:2.

Bowett, D.K. (1964), *UN Forces – A Legal Study* (London: Stevens).

Bures, Oldrich (2007), 'A mid-range theory of international peacekeeping', *International Studies Review*, 9:3, 407–36.

Claude, Inis L., Jr (1961), 'The United Nations and the use of force', *International Conciliation*, 532, 346–55.

de Coning, Cedric, and Mateja Peter (eds), *United Nations Peace Operations in a Changing Global Order* (London: Palgrave Macmillan, 2019, Open Access Publication).

Doss, Alan (2020), *A Peacekeeper in Africa – Learning from UN Interventions in Other People's Wars* (Boulder, CO: Lynne Rienner).

Gharekhan, Chinmaya R. (2006), *The Horseshoe Table – An Inside View of the UN Security Council* (New Delhi: Longman).

Goulding, Marrack (2002), *Peacemonger* (London: I.B. Taurus).

Guéhenno, Jean-Marie (2015), *The Fog of Peace* (Washington, DC: Brookings).

Higgins, Rosalyn (1969), *UN Peacekeeping, 1946-67: Documents and Commentary* (London: Oxford University Press).

James, Alan (1990), *Peacekeeping in International Politics* (London: Macmillan).

James, Alan (1996), 'The dual nature of UN peacekeeping', in Dimitris Bourantonis and Marios L. Evriviades (eds), *A United Nations for the Twenty-first Century* (The Hague: Kluwer), 171–86.

Karlsrud, John (2018), *The UN at War – Peace Operations in a New Era* (London: Palgrave Macmillan).

Mayall, James (ed.) (1997), *The New Interventionism, 1991–1994: United Nations Experience in Cambodia, Former Yugoslavia and Somalia* (Cambridge: Cambridge University Press).

Norwegian Institute for International Affairs (1964), *The Oslo Papers* (Oslo: The Norwegian Institute for International Affairs).

O'Brien, Conor Cruise (1994), *On the Eve of the Millennium* (New York: Free Press).

O'Brien, Conor Cruise, and Feliks Topolski (1968), *The United Nations – Sacred Drama* (New York: Simon and Schuster).

Roberts, Adam (1994), 'The crisis in UN peacekeeping', *Survival*, 36:3, 93–120.

United Nations (2015), 'Report of the High-Level Independent Panel on Peace Operations (HIPPO) on uniting our strengths for peace: politics, partnership and people', A/70/95 – S/2015/446.

Windsor, Philip (1993), 'The evolution of the concept of security in International Relations', in Michael Clark (ed.), *New Perspectives on Security* (London: Brassey's).

Windsor, Philip (2002), 'International Relations – the state of the art', in Mats Berdal (ed.), *Studies in International Relations – Essays by Philip Windsor* (Brighton: Sussex Academic Press).

Index

Index

Index

Index

Index

Index

Index

Index

Index

EU authorised representative for GPSR:
Easy Access System Europe, Mustamäe tee 50,
10621 Tallinn, Estonia
gpsr.requests@easproject.com

www.ingramcontent.com/pod-product-compliance
Lightning Source LLC
Chambersburg PA
CBHW052001270326
41929CB00015B/2738